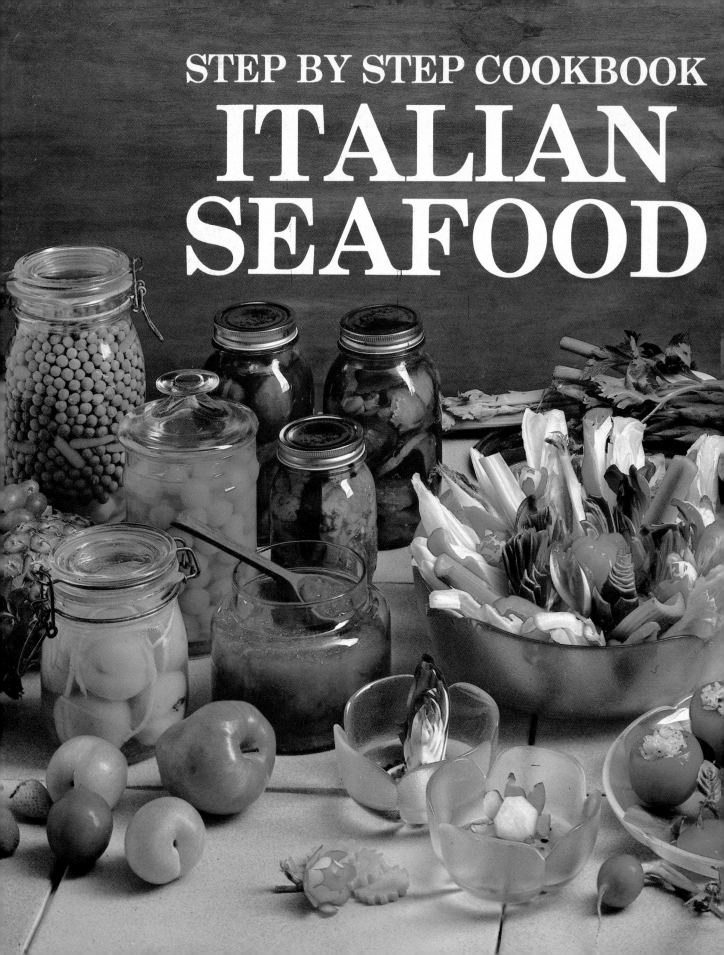

STEP BY STEP COOKBOOK
ITALIAN SEAFOOD

& SALAD

AND MORE...

CHARTWELL
BOOKS, INC.

**CHARTWELL
BOOKS, INC.**

General Editor:
Stephen Schmidt

Consulants:
Nicoletta Grill
Anna Maria Mascheroni
Kerry Milis

Production Services:
Studio Asterisco, Milan

Adapted from CUCINARE OGGI by Simonetta Lupi Vada

Summary

Baked Fish, Fried Fish and Fish Soups *from page 7*

Cooking Fish
Fish Soups and Stews
Baking and Frying

Seafood *from page 69*

Crustaceans
Mollusks

Stuffed Vegetables *from page 131*

Hot Stuffed Vegetables
Cold Stuffed Vegetables

Salads and Decorative Garnishes *from page 193*

Salads
Decorative Garnishes

Sformati, Soufflés and Croquettes *from page 255*

Sformati and Tortini
Soufflés and Timbales
Croquettes

Preserving Fruit and Vegetables *from page 317*

Preserving Fruit
Preserving Vegetables

BAKED FISH, FRIED FISH AND FISH SOUPS

Cooking Fish

In many countries which have long coastlines and are rich in rivers and beautiful lakes, fish should have pride of place at the dining table. But this is not how it is, for a variety of reasons. There are two major ones. First, pollution is now lamentably widespread, though people in various parts of the world are at last trying to remedy it. Second, just as with meat, the more common and thus more readily available types of fish have been neglected for some time now in favor of more sought-after species, which are often in short supply on the home market, and so have to be imported from abroad.

In ancient times, fish were the main source of food for all the different peoples living around the Mediterranean. During the Middle Ages and later in the Renaissance period, fish would invariably feature as important main courses at banquets.

Nowadays we should all be aware of the fact that fish will become all the more important as an alternative to meat, because of its high protein content. Fish is slightly lower in protein than meat, but it is equally nutritious because most of its proteins are rich in essential amino acids. The human body is not capable of making these proteins on its own, and they are vital for the formation and regeneration of our tissues. The fat content which, as in meat, is variable, is on the whole fairly low, and the caloric value is generally slightly lower than that of meat. Fish, especially those from the sea, are also an irreplaceable source of mineral salts, mainly iodine, but also iron, calcium, phosphorus and sulphur. Fish are furthermore an important source of vitamins, such as vitamins A and D, which are contained in the liver.

In conclusion, we can safely say that fish, which is more tender and digestible than the meat of animals, constitutes a rich, light, and delicately flavored source of nourishment, and one that is particularly good for children, the elderly, and the sick. But everyone should eat fish at least twice a week. Nowadays it is relatively easy to lay one's hands on fish of some sort in most countries. If it is not available fresh, then it will usually be available in one of those countless deep-frozen preparations that are stocked in stores all over the world. However, if you decide to eat fresh fish, you must be absolutely sure that it is fresh. This means checking that the flesh is firm, the eyes are clear and bright, the scales shiny and close to the body, the gills a handsome scarlet color, and the smell distinctive, but not unpleasant. Bear in mind as well that freshwater fish deteriorate much more quickly than saltwater fish, so it is advisable to try and buy the former still live, or even better, catch it yourself.

The necessary equipment

When poaching fish, the first thing you will need is a fish poacher. This is usually oval in shape and made of aluminum, stainless steel, or copper. It has a rack with handles at the side, so that the fish can be lifted out of the stock, and it comes with a lid. Because fish poachers are usually rather long, the best solution is to have an oval-shaped burner, designed for this type of pan. But if you do not have such a thing, it is best to buy a cast-iron plate which will cover the flame and spread the heat evenly.

The essential equipment for baking fish in the oven is the ceramic dish—oval for whole fish and round for fish pieces.

There are many different kinds of ceramic dishes and some are attractive enough to grace the dinner table.

For grilling fish over charcoal, the best solution is the two-piece grill. This is very practical because it enables you to turn the fish simply by flipping it over, without breaking it. But for cooking fish on the stove you should have a heavy cast-iron griddle, preferably rectangular, and a broad spatula with a slightly curved tip for turning the fish as it cooks.

The best solution for frying fish is an electric fryer fitted with an adjustable thermostat and a removable basket for draining the fish. If you do not have an electric fryer, use an ordinary high-sided iron frying pan, fitted with a basket, so that once cooked, all the fish can be drained together.

Various smaller utensils help to streamline and simplify the job of preparing and cleaning fish. First and foremost there is the scaler, which is similar to a grater and which speeds up the operation considerably and prevents the scales from flying all over the kitchen. When it comes to serving your fish dishes, a wide, flat fish server, oval platters (preferably of stainless steel) for whole fish, and decorative china or ceramic tureens with accompanying smaller bowls for soups and fish stews, make attractive serving implements.

Cleaning fish

Cleaning fish is certainly not a pleasant task, and everyone would prefer it to be done by the fish seller. But because this is not always possible, let us try to explain how it can be done as quickly and as easily as possible.

First make sure you have a newspaper or piece of heavy paper ready to gather up the scales and innards, so they can be thrown away immediately. Then start the job of scaling the fish, using a knife or a special scaler, which resembles a grater and which you can find in a hardware store. Take the fish by the tail and work the scaler or knife along the body towards the head, against the grain, as it were. Try not to press too hard, because this might break the skin beneath (1). If the fish is fresh the scales will come away very easily. With a pair of kitchen shears, or something similar, make a cut about halfway along the abdomen (2) and remove the innards by scraping them out and then cutting them away (3). Also remove any dark parts clinging to the abdominal cavity. Rub the fish with fine salt, and wash repeatedly under running water. Now lay the fish on its back on the chopping board and cut away the gills. If the head is to be removed, do so by making a circular incision beneath the gills. Trim the tail and fins, and if you want to stuff the fish, also remove the central bone. After cleaning and gutting the fish, wash it again inside and out in cold running water to give the abdominal cavity a thorough rinse and to remove all the scales.

Let the fish drain for a few minutes, then wrap it in a kitchen towel before cooking to keep it moist. All these hints apply to large fish. Very small fish are usually not cleaned, just washed. But if you do want to gut them, squeeze the belly between your thumb and forefinger to force the innards out. Anchovies and sardines are easy to clean, on the other hand, because when you cut off the head, the innards also come free. But if you are going to fry or stuff them, open them half way up the belly and proceed as for all other fish.

1 Scale the fish from the tail to the head.

2 With a pair of shears make a cut halfway along the abdomen...

3 ...then remove all the innards, cutting them free with a pair of kitchen scissors.

How to fillet porgy or other round fish

Many recipes require you to cook fillets instead of the whole fish. In this case, after cleaning the fish, you must separate the fillets of meat from the backbone and all the other bones.

This operation varies depending on whether the fish in question is round, yielding two fillets (porgy, red bream, sheepshead, and so on), or flat, giving four fillets (like sole, flounder, turbot, etc.).

Let us now see how to fillet a porgy and other similar fish. First of all, in addition to the various small utensils already mentioned, you must have ready a pair of kitchen shears and a long, pointed knife. After removing the scales, tail to head, cut the ventral and dorsal fins away with the shears (these may be quite hard and tough) (1). Then, with the knife, cut all the way along the underside of the fish (2) and take out the innards and dark parts

1 After scaling the fish, use the shears to cut away the often hard, tough dorsal fins.

2 Cut along the whole length of the underside and remove the innards.

3 Make a deep cut in the middle of the back, following the line of the dorsal fins.

4 Keeping the knife close to the backbone, remove one complete fillet.

inside the abdominal cavity. Now, with the point of the knife, cut quite deeply into the middle of the back, following the line of the dorsal fins (3) and then run the knife along the line of the central fin, head to tail, gradually deepening the cut until one half of the fish comes completely away from the backbone in a single piece (4). Now turn the porgy over and remove the other fillet from the backbone in exactly the same way. At the end of the operation the two fillets will be completely detached not only from the backbone, but from each other as well, although they will still be attached to the head and tail.

With the point of the knife make a diagonal cut around the gills (5), thus separating the fillet from the head, and do the same at the tail end (6). To free the sec-

ond fillet, lift up the backbone with your fingers (7) and then make the same diagonal cut at the lower gills, thus enabling you to remove the backbone with the head still attached to it. Now trim away any smaller bones, especially at the edges of the fillets (8), and then cook the two fillets as required.

Fish fillets are particularly suitable for children, because there is no risk of the child swallowing any bones. Porgy fillets, which are lean and firm, are almost always either grilled or baked. Fillets of delicate fish, such as hake or perch, are best stewed or fried. Fish fillets make an excellent main dish when served with rice pilaf, french fries or a risotto on the side. One delicious combination is perch or redfish fillets browned in butter and served with a tasty risotto.

5 After detaching both fillets, make a diagonal cut near the gills...

6 ...then make a similar smaller cut by the tail, to remove the whole fillet.

7 To remove the second fillet, raise the backbone and make a cut by the gills.

8 With both fillets removed, trim away any other bones remaining, especially at the edges.

How to fillet sole or other flat fish

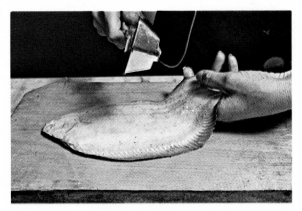

1 First, scale the sole on both sides...

2 ...then make a small cut near the tail, raise the skin a little, hold it tight...

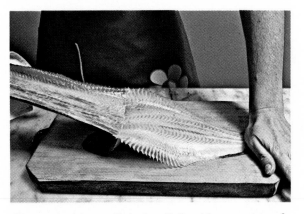

3 ...and with a swift jerk pull the skin away towards the head.

This flat-bodied fish has a slimy skin with small scales. It is dark on one side and white on the other. The dark skin must always be removed. In small fish the white skin may be left on, as long as its small scales are removed, but in larger specimens it is best taken off. Begin by scaling your sole (1). Then, to remove the dark skin, make a small cut near the tail, raise the skin a little to give you something to grip (2) and then, with a swift jerk, pull the skin up towards the head and wrench it away (3). If the skin slips in your fingers and you cannot tear it off cleanly, use a cloth to help you. At this point, cut through the dark skin near the head (4) and next, if you have not already done so, carefully open the sole on the side from which you have removed the skin and take out the innards. Now, using a small knife with a thin, very sharp blade, make a straight cut through the middle of the side of the fish facing you, head to tail or vice versa; detach the upper fillet from the backbone and from the fillet beneath as well, scraping the knife against the backbone (5). Next, cut the fillet cleanly at the gills and remove it (6). After so doing, lay the sole with its tail to your right and do the same thing to free the lower fillet (7). Then turn the fish over and in exactly the same way detach the other two fillets (8). You will now have four fillets. With the fillets removed you will be left with the carcass, including the head, the backbone, and the ring of smaller bones (9). These are excellent for making soup, which should be strained through a colander. Before cooking the fillets, rinse well and then, with the blade of a large knife or with a meat mallet, flatten them very gently so as not to break the fibers. Fillets of sole can be cooked flat, folded in two, or rolled up. Classic cooking methods include *à la menunière,* which we shall describe later, or frying in a light covering of bread crumbs.

4 Remove the dark skin by cutting it away at the head.

5 Cut along the middle of the sole, head to tail, and detach the upper fillet from the backbone.

6 At the head make a clean cut by the gills.

7 Do exactly the same with the lower fillet, after turning the fish so that the tail is to your right.

8 Turn the fish over and detach the other two fillets in the same way.

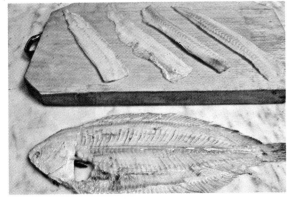

9 After removing all four fillets, you will be left with the head, the backbone, and the ring of bones around the edge of the body.

How to fillet trout

Trout is the best known of all the freshwater fish and the easiest to find fresh in the shops, its abundance partially the result of modern trout-farming techniques. If you want to fillet your trout to avoid the risk of swallowing any bones, or because your recipe so requires, you must first scale it, using the same technique as for other fish, and then cut off the dorsal fins with kitchen shears.

With a sharp knife, cut along the underside of the trout, remove the innards, and start carefully separating the upward facing fillet from the backbone (1) in such a way as to completely open up the body of the fish. Similarly, detach the downward facing fillet, then lift up the backbone (2), leaving the two fillets joined together. Because a trout can be opened easily without separating into two halves, it is ideal for stuffing. Now cut off the trout's tail (3) and head (4). After rinsing and drying the fillet, flatten it carefully. Fillets of trout may be stuffed or prepared like fillets of sole.

1 With a pointed knife carefully detach the upward facing fillet from the backbone...

2 ...then similarly remove the downward facing fillet from the bone.

3 Now remove the tail, making a clean cut with your knife.

4 Make another cut below the head and remove it; you should be left with just one large fillet.

Freezing fish

Even those of you who are suspicious of frozen products will probably at some stage buy some kind of frozen fish.

Generally speaking, frozen fish is processed as soon as it has been landed in fishing boats specially equipped for this purpose, so there is a reasonable guarantee that it is fresh. And frozen fish is almost invariably cleaned, and is thus a practical proposition for the cook. But as with all frozen products, make sure that the fish you buy has been continually frozen.

To do this, check that there are no ice crystals around the fish or surrounding individual packages. If there are, the product has been thawed at some stage, even if only for a short time, and the fish will be ruined. Those of you who have easy access to fresh fish — and it must be good and fresh — can also freeze it at home; just remember that fish with lean meat can be frozen for a longer period than fish with fatty meat. The former will last for three months approximately, the latter for just two.

Here's how to proceed: clean and scale the fish, remove the fins (1), and if the fish is large, cut off the head and tail to save room in the freezer. Then wash it carefully, let it drain head down, dry, and put into a plastic bag. Put one or more fish in each bag depending on their size, but just enough for one meal.

Fish steaks or fillets must be frozen with each piece separated so they do not form a single solid block. You can also freeze various types of fish soups and stews. Suck out any air from the bag with a straw (2) and close it tightly, using a plastic tie or a small sealing machine (3). Label the bag with the type of fish, the date and the expiration date and put it in the freezer. Before use, thaw the fish if necessary. If it is to be poached and you do not defrost it, the cooking time will be longer. The best method of defrosting is to put the fish in the refrigerator overnight.

1 When freezing fish at home, first scale them and clean as already described.

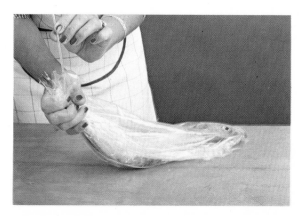

2 After putting the fish into a plastic bag, suck out any air with a straw...

3 ...and seal tightly with a string.

Conserving fish in salt

Use this method for carefully cleaned and boned anchovies and sardines. Wash the fish and lay out on a clean cloth to dry, with another cloth laid on top. In the meantime, have ready a deep, wide-mouthed glass or earthenware jar with a lid. Making sure the jar is very clean and dry, spread a layer of rock salt on the bottom (1), about ½ inch deep. Lay the fish in a close layer, in a pattern resembling the spokes of a wheel (2). Sprinkle plenty of salt over this layer, add another layer, cover with salt, and continue in this manner, adding a bay leaf every now and then (3), until you reach the top of the jar. Cover with a layer of salt (4). Cover the jar (5) with a lid of glass, china, or slate and hold down with a weight or stone (6). Tie wax paper around the top and let the jar stand for about a month, but check now and then to make sure that the topmost layer of fish is always moist. Add a little salted water if it appears to be drying out.

1 Spread a layer of rock salt on the bottom of a tall glass or earthenware jar.

2 On the salt, arrange a layer of fish close together in a pattern like the spokes of a wheel.

3 Fill the jar with alternate layers of salt and fish, adding a bay leaf every so often.

4 Before covering the jar, add a generous layer of salt on top.

5 Cover with a lid (glass, china, or slate)…

6 …and last of all, put a weight (or a couple of stones) on top of the lid.

Sardines in salt

Ways of cooking fish

Poaching — Poaching is the best way of cooking large whole fish. The quickest, though least orthodox, method involves putting the cleaned fish into a fish poacher, covering with cold water, adding half a cup of white vinegar or the juice of two lemons, a carrot, a sliced onion, celery stalks, a clove of garlic, peppercorns, and salt, bringing it to a boil and cooking for the time required at a slow simmer.

However, the fish will be tastier if you cook it in a court bouillon or fish stock. Simmer all the ingredients for the court bouillon or stock for about twenty minutes, strain, and pour over the fish. Then proceed to cook. The ingredients of your court bouillon will vary depending on the type of fish. You can use white wine instead of vinegar if you are cooking freshwater fish such as trout or pike, and red wine with eel or perch. Although this is a less common method, you can use milk instead of vinegar. This keeps the meat of the fish white. Do not use lemon juice in the court bouillon if the meat of the fish is pink, like that of salmon or sea trout; it will make the color fade. Whole fish must be put in cold water to stop the skin from cracking and breaking. To help prevent this from happening, you can also rub the skin before cooking with half a lemon.

If the fish is in slices or fillets, you may use the stewing method. This involves putting the slices or fillets in a buttered baking dish, adding herbs, and pouring a stock made with fish trimmings over them. Then cover the baking dish with buttered aluminum foil and put it in the oven. Baste the fish every now and then with the juices. Poached fish is done when the eyes look like two small white balls in their sockets. The fish should be very carefully removed from the kettle and laid on a platter if it is to be served hot; it should be left to cool in the stock if it is to be served cold. After being boned, poached fish should be served with oil and lemon or with a sauce such as a simple vinaigrette with lemon and herbs or a classic sauce for fish, like mayonnaise or aïoli.

Stewing — This is the ideal cooking method for fatty fish. First, clean and wash the fish and remove the head (which you will use with the other leftovers to make stock). Butter the pan and cover with thin slices of onion, carrot, and celery, plus herbs to taste. Lay in the fish, either whole or in slices, and pour in enough dry white or red wine mixed with water or fish stock to cover the fish completely. Add salt and pepper, cover and simmer until the fish is cooked. At this point, if you want to serve a really sophisticated dish, drain the fish, fillet it, put the fillets aside, and return the bones to the stock. Bring this to a boil, reduce slightly, and strain. Thicken with half a tablespoon of cornstarch mixed with a little brandy. Cover the fish fillets with the sauce and brown in the oven for a few minutes.

Grilling — After carefully cleaning the fish, put it in a marinade made with a little oil, salt, pepper, and herbs such as parsley, thyme, and bay leaf. Then get the grill or griddle red hot and arrange the fish crosswise on the grid, basting now and then with the marinade. Turn and cook in a similar fashion. If the fish is large, you can slice it before grilling or else just brown the outside on the grill and finish it in a moderate oven.

Baking — The best fish for baking are large or medium in size, with firm meat. After carefully cleaning the fish, cut along the backbone and insert pieces of garlic, season with salt, pepper, and chopped herbs, and if you wish, put whole sprigs of rosemary or thyme in the belly. Then put the fish into an oiled dish, sprinkle again with herbs, and moisten with melted butter. Cook for the time required in a moderately hot oven, basting frequently with the pan juices or a few tablespoons of water or dry white wine.

Cooking in foil — All small fish are ideal for this method of cooking. Lay each fish on a sheet of buttered aluminum foil, fold the foil over the fish and pinch the ends to seal. If you like, you can smear the top of the fish with a tablespoon of tomato sauce flavored with mushrooms, oregano, or other ingredients such as anchovies, ham, bacon, shellfish or even caviar. Put in a moderate oven.

Frying — There are various ways of frying fish. The most common one involves dipping the fish, either whole or in fillets or steaks, in lightly salted beer or milk, draining and then dusting with flour until the pieces are thoroughly coated. Shake to dislodge excess flour and fry a few at a time in hot oil until golden. Fish can also be fried after being dipped in a batter made with or without eggs and perhaps flavored with grappa or brandy. Remove from the batter with a large spoon and then fry in plenty of hot oil. If you decide to use bread crumbs, dredge the fish in flour, shake, and roll in beaten egg and then in the bread crumbs, patting firmly with the palm of the hand before plunging into hot oil. Finally, the method known as *à la meunière* is ideal for trout, sole, and all the more delicate fish. After sprinkling the fish with salt and pepper, sauté in a little oil and then drain on absorbent paper. In a separate pan, brown plenty of butter flavored with small sage leaves. When it starts to froth, pour it over the fish, arranged in a ceramic dish, adding a few drops of lemon juice and chopped parsley. Place in a hot oven for a few minutes before serving at table.

Boiled trout

Marinating fish

Fish that has been fried can be preserved for several weeks by putting it in a marinade. The marinade is prepared with ingredients such as vinegar, lemon juice, and white wine, all of which are acidic and will conserve and "cook" food. As a rule the marinade is made with the same oil in which the fish was fried. Fry the fish in oil, then remove it and lightly sauté sliced onion until golden. Pour in the vinegar or a mixture of half vinegar and half wine, and let boil. In a bowl arrange a layer of fish, a layer of onion, and cover with the marinade. Cover tightly and let stand for at least three days.

There is an infinite variety of marinades. You can add various other vegetables and herbs to taste and even raisins and pine nuts to the onion. Lastly there are "raw" marinades prepared simply with lemon juice or vinegar mixed with herbs, salt, and pepper. These are used to marinate small raw fish, which are then served as hors d'oeuvres.

Marinated sardines

Fish Soups
and Stews

There can be little doubt that fish soups are the result of the sound common sense that enables humble folk to turn the lowliest of ingredients into a dish that is nothing less than a masterpiece. In fact, it was the wives of fishermen who would use the fish that remained unsold at the end of the day to make a bracing soup for supper. These haphazard dishes have gradually given rise to recipes that are familiar to people all over the world, like the renowned French *bouillabaisse,* in which fish, leeks, and tomatoes are cooked together and sometimes flavored with saffron. In Italy you will find some of the spiciest of fish soups. These vary in style from place to place, some having a marked foreign flavor, such as the Sardinian *mazzamorru,* a soup with a base of stale bread that was once the staple diet of the galley slaves in the Spanish fleet. Further north you will find the famous *kalakeitto* of Finland, a simple and homely fish soup, and the equally well known *muhennettu made,* a tasty burbot stew. In Sweden, there are *makrillsoppa,* or mackerel soup, as well as the specialty of Falkenber, cod stew. And let's not forget the famous chowders of both Canada and the United States. It is a small step from the fish soup to fish stew. Both are very often served as a main dish. Soups contain a wide range of ingredients and are often accompanied by bread that has been lightly fried with garlic to make croutons; the croutons may be laid on the bottom of each person's soup bowl. Stews are invariably accompanied by vegetables, pilaf, boiled rice, or polenta. One good example is the famous cod stew called *baccalà,* a specialty of the Vicenza region of Italy, which is traditionally served with a dish of piping hot polenta.

Fish soup

Cacciucco

- ■ **Yield: 4 servings**
- ■ **Time needed: 2 hours**
- ■ **Difficulty: ***

Ingredients: 4¹/₂ lb assorted fish and shellfish (choose among whiting, hake, mullet, octopus, shrimp, crayfish, etc.), 1 lb clams, 1 large onion, 2 cloves garlic, 1 small piece hot red pepper, 1 handful parsley, 4-5 ripe tomatoes, 1 bay leaf, 1¹/₂ cups dry white wine, 4-8 slices toasted bread, 1 cup olive oil, freshly ground pepper, salt.

Clean the whole fish, removing the innards but leaving the fins, bones, and heads attached. Cut large fish in thick slices but leave small fish whole; wash well. Wash the shellfish (such as shrimp, or small crayfish) and leave them whole in their shells. If you are using octopus, remove the eyes and beak, wash well and dry, separate the body from the tentacles, remove the skin, and cut into pieces. Scrub the clams with a brush, wash, open over a flame in a pan, and strain the clam liquor (1). Sprinkle the shellfish with a little white wine, add the strained clam juice, and reduce the sauce over a fairly hot flame.

In about half a cup of oil, cook the chopped onion and a whole clove of crushed garlic until soft (2). Add the pepper, chopped parsley (3), bay leaf, peeled tomatoes, seeded and cubed (4), drained clam liquor (5), and enough water to make plenty of broth. To the broth, first add the larger whole fish with the firmest meat (6); then add the octopus, the slices of fish, the smaller whole fish, and finally the shrimp and other crustacea. Season with salt and pepper.

When everything is almost cooked, add the clams, still in their shells. During cooking, shake the casserole every so often, but do not actually stir the contents. Rub the slices of bread with the remaining clove of garlic (7), lay in very hot bowls, arrange the fish on top, trying not to break it (8) and cover with piping hot stock (9).

This is a typical regional Italian dish, associated particularly with Tuscany. You may serve it in the same dish in which it was cooked with the garlic bread slices on the side. This is best made in the summer when there is a greater variety of fish to be had in your local markets.

1 Open the clams in a pan over the flame and strain the stock through fine cheesecloth.

2 In a pan, over a low flame, gently sauté the chopped onion and crushed garlic...

3 ...and when softened, add the pepper, chopped parsley...

4 ...bay leaf and peeled tomatoes, seeded and cut in large cubes.

5 Dilute with the reserved clam juice, adding a little water if necessary.

6 In the pan, first cook the larger fish with the firmest meat, then the smaller ones.

7 Rub the toasted slices of bread with the remaining clove of garlic.

8 Put bread in hot bowls, arrange fish on top, dividing different types among each of the bowls.

9 Cover with the piping hot broth, filling the bowls generously.

Cacciucco

Fish soup (1)

- **Yield: 4 servings**
- **Time needed: 2 hours**
- **Difficulty: ***

Ingredients: 4 small red or grey mullet, 4 small freshwater perch or porgy, 8 jumbo shrimp, 2 lb clams, 1 lb ripe tomatoes, 1 small handful parsley, chopped, 1 chopped onion, 1 bunch chopped basil, 1 clove garlic, 1 cup white wine, 12 slices toasted whole-wheat bread, 1/4 cup olive oil, pepper, salt.

Remove the fins from the mullet and perch or porgy, but leave the tails attached; scale, remove the innards, wash, and drain. Carefully wash the shrimp or prawns, but leave in their shells. Scrub the clams with a brush and place in a large pan set over high flame and, as the shells gradually open, remove from the broth with a skimmer and put aside, leaving in the shell. Strain the juice and set this aside too.

If possible, use a fairly large casserole so that the fish can be laid full length on the bottom. In the casserole, lightly brown the chopped onion in oil. Add half the chopped parsley and basil and the chopped garlic; cook a minute or two, then pour in the white wine. Reduce the liquid a little, season with salt and pepper, add the peeled tomatoes, seeded and cubed, and simmer for about 20 minutes. Then arrange in the stock (of which there should be a good quantity) the mullet, porgy, and shrimp or prawns and simmer for about 10 minutes, adding the clam juice too. Last of all, add the clams in their shells and cook for a further five minutes. Before taking the soup off the flame, sprinkle the remaining chopped parsley and basil over it.

Arrange the slices of bread in four bowls (if possible of earthenware), lay the fish on top, and pour plenty of the broth over the top. Serve at once.

Fish soup (2)

- **Yield: 4 servings**
- **Time needed: 2 hours**
- **Difficulty: ***

Ingredients: 3 lb assorted fish (mullet, eel, scrod, sole, etc.), 1 lb squid, cut in rings, 1 lb mussels, 1 sliced onion, 2 leeks, 1 clove crushed garlic, 4-5 anchovies, 2 bay leaves, 2 tbsp chopped parsley, pinch thyme, 1 small hot red pepper, 3 cups dry white wine, 4-8 slices toasted bread, 1 1/2 cups olive oil, pepper, salt.

Clean the fish and wash thoroughly. Set aside. Put all the trimmings — heads, tails, and fins — in a casserole with 2 cups water, 2 cups white wine, the sliced onion, a little pepper and salt. Simmer the broth for about 20 minutes. Set aside.

Heat the carefully washed mussels in a large pan with 3 tablespoons oil till they open, then drain off the liquid, strain it through cheesecloth, and set aside. Heat the remaining oil and add the squid and fish, stirring well. Add the leeks, cut into rounds, thyme, bay leaf, salt, and pepper, and cook over a medium flame for about 45 minutes. Add the remaining cup of wine, the finely chopped anchovies, and the whole fish. Let stand for a few minutes, then add half the finely chopped parsley, cover with the strained fish broth, and simmer for an additional 10 minutes. Last, add the mussels and the reserved juice to the soup. In a separate pan, heat a few tablespoons oil with the clove of crushed garlic and the hot pepper; after removing the garlic, stir this spicy oil into the soup. Lay the bread in the bowls, pour in the soup and the fish, and sprinkle with parsley.

Flounder soup

- **Yield: 4 servings**
- **Time needed: 2 hours**
- **Difficulty: ***

Ingredients: 2 lb flounder, 10 oz tomato purée, 1 tbsp tomato paste, 2 cloves garlic, 1 bunch parsley, 1 cup dry white wine, 1/2 cup wine vinegar, olive oil, freshly ground pepper, salt.

Clean the fish, wash thoroughly, and cut into large pieces. In a large casserole, lightly fry the cloves of garlic in plenty of oil and remove. Add the fish, brown a little, and then add the tomato paste. Finally, sprinkle with the vinegar and white wine, and reduce by half. Then add the tomato purée, gradually pour over enough water to cover, season with salt and pepper, and cook for about an hour. Remove the fish from the sauce, bone and purée the meat, and put it back into the casserole. Sprinkle with chopped parsley and serve. You can accompany this soup with bread or polenta. If you do, reduce the soup until it becomes very thick.

You may use any other type of fish in place of flounder. A particularly good one is mullet.

Fish soup, Venetian style

- **Yield: 4 servings**
- **Time needed: 2 1/2 hours**
- **Difficulty: ***

Ingredients: 4 lb mullet or similar fish, one 8-oz can puréed tomatoes, 1 small onion, 1 stalk celery, 1 carrot, 1 leek, 1 lemon, 1 bunch parsley, chopped, 2 bay leaves, 1/2 tsp thyme, 1 clove garlic, 1 cup dry white wine, 3 tbsp olive oil, 4 slices bread, pepper, salt.

Clean, scale, and wash the fish thoroughly, but leave the heads intact. Put the fish in a large casserole, cover with cold water, add the wine, salt, and pepper, and bring to a simmer. Skim the stock two or three times, then add the onion, carrot, celery, leek, and juice of one lemon. Cook for about 20 minutes. Drain the fish and remove the heads and bones. Return the trimmings to the pot and cook for another hour. Purée the fish in a food mill or food processor and strain the stock through a sieve, discarding the bones and heads.

In a deep casserole brown the garlic and chopped parsley in the oil. Remove the garlic and add the thyme, bay leaves, and tomatoes, and cook for 10 minutes. Before removing from the flame add the reserved stock and puréed fish. Lightly fry the slices of bread in oil, arrange in bowls, and pour on the hot soup. Serve at once as a first course.

Bouillabaisse

- **Yield: 6 servings**
- **Time needed: 2 hours**
- **Difficulty: ***

Ingredients: 3 1/2 lb assorted fish (hake, whiting, eel, red mullet, etc.), 6 large shrimp, 1 lb clams, 1 large onion, 2 cloves garlic, 1 bunch parsley, 3 ripe tomatoes, seeded and cubed, 1/4 tsp fennel seed, 1 bay leaf, 1 chopped small red pepper, 1/4 cup dry white wine, 6-12 slices bread, pinch saffron, crumbled, 1/2 cup olive oil, salt, pepper.

Clean all the fish, but leave the fins, bones, and heads attached. Cut the larger fish into steaks but leave the smaller fish whole. Leave the shrimp in their shells. Clean and wash the clams thoroughly and put in a pan over a high flame to open them. Pour off the juice through a strainer. With the clams still over the flame, sprinkle with white wine, then return the strained juice and add the saffron. Mix well for a few moments and take the pan off the heat. Set aside.

In a large casserole lightly fry the chopped onion and the whole cloves of garlic in half a cup of oil. Add the tomatoes, fennel seed, chopped parsley, bay leaf, and hot pepper, then add first the larger fish, then the smaller ones. Season with salt and pepper and add enough water to cover. Cook over a low flame, adding the shrimp when the fish is nearly done. A few minutes before taking the soup off the heat, add the clams and their juice and stir well.

Toast the bread, put in the bowls, and pour on a little of the broth. Arrange the fish on top and ladle on the remaining broth. If served in large enough helpings, *bouillabaisse* makes a good main dish.

Fish soup with olives

- **Yield: 4 servings**
- **Time needed: 2 hours**
- **Difficulty: ***

Ingredients: 4 1/2 lb fish and shellfish (red mullet, eel, octopus, mussels, clams, etc.), 4 chopped anchovy fillets, 1 1/2 lb ripe tomatoes, peeled and cubed, 2 oz pitted green olives, 1 oz capers, 2 cloves garlic, 1 handful parsley, 1 small red pepper, chopped, 8 slices toasted bread, 1 cup dry white wine, 1 cup olive oil, salt, pepper.

Scrub clams and mussels with a brush and wash well under running water to get rid of all the sand. Put in a large pan over high flame till they open, then strain the resulting broth. Set shellfish and broth aside. Clean all the other fish, removing the scales and the innards. Cut off the heads and tails, and set aside. Cut the larger fish into pieces. Crush the cloves of garlic and put in a casserole with the oil, anchovies, red pepper, half the chopped parsley, the capers, and the pitted olives. Gently sauté all the ingredients, stirring well. Add the fish heads and tails, sprinkle with the white wine and reduce by one-third over moderate heat. Add the tomatoes. Season with salt and pepper, and cook for about 15 minutes. Dilute with about 8 cups of water, cook for an additional 20 minutes, then remove the fish trimmings. Arrange the fish in the stock, cover the casserole, and cook for another 20 minutes. Add the clams and mussels in their shells along with their juice, and cook until warmed through. Before removing from the flame, sprinkle with the remaining parsley. Arrange the bread in the bowls and pour the soup over it.

Dried cod stew-baccalà

- **Yield: 4 servings**
- **Time needed: 1½ hours**
- **Difficulty: ***

Ingredients: 1½ lb dried cod, 1 lb small whole white onions, 1 chopped yellow onion, 1 carrot, chopped, 1 stalk celery, chopped, 1 cup tomato purée, flour, 1 tbsp parsley chopped with 1 clove garlic (optional), ¼ cup fish stock or bottled clam juice, oil for frying plus additional 3 tbsp oil, salt, pepper.

Soak the cod for at least 12 hours in several changes of cold water. Wash the cod, bone, remove the skin, cut into pieces, dry, roll in flour, and brown in plenty of hot oil (1), turning once (2). Put a large pan over moderate flame with 3 tablespoons oil. Add the chopped onion, carrot, and celery and cook until soft (3). Add the whole small onions (4) and brown well, seasoning with salt and pepper. After this add the tomato purée, thinned with hot stock or clam juice (5). Stir well and simmer briskly until the onions are completely tender. If necessary, add a little more stock. Arrange the pieces of cod in the sauce (6) and let them absorb the flavor over low heat, about 5 minutes. Before removing from the flame, sprinkle, if you like, with 1 tablespoon parsley chopped with a clove of garlic.

1 Heat plenty of oil over moderately high flame and brown the floured pieces of dried cod.

2 When cooked on one side, turn with a spatula and cook on the other.

3 Chop up a small onion, a carrot, and stalk of celery and cook lightly.

4 Add the whole onions and brown well on all sides, turning frequently...

5 ...then add the tomato purée, thinned beforehand with a little stock or clam juice.

6 Arrange the pieces of dried cod in the sauce and let them absorb the flavor over a very low flame.

Dried cod stew (Baccalà)

Dried cod, Vicenza style

- **Yield: 4 servings**
- **Time needed: 2 1/2 hours**
- **Difficulty: ***

Ingredients: 1 1/2 lb dried cod or dried salt cod, 2 large onions (about 1/2 lb), 3-4 anchovy fillets, 1 large handful parsley, 1 clove garlic, chopped, flour, 3 cups milk, oil for frying plus additional 1/4 cup oil, salt.

Soak the cod for at least 12 hours in several changes of cold water. Cut into pieces and dry on a dish cloth (1). Remove any bones (2). Heat a few tbsp of oil over the flame, add the sliced onions, and cook until soft but not brown. Arrange the pieces of fish, lightly floured, in the pot and brown lightly (3). Add milk (4). Turn the pieces and cook over very low heat for about 2 hours, gently shaking the pot every so often so that the fish does not stick to the bottom. When three-quarters cooked, add chopped garlic, parsley, anchovy fillets, and 1/4 cup oil, and finish cooking in a 350° oven. Add salt if required and serve.

1 Cut the pre-soaked fish in pieces and dry well in a cloth.

2 Make sure there are no bones.

3 Gently sauté the sliced onions and add the lightly floured pieces of fish.

4 After browning all over, cover the fish using all the milk.

Dried cod, Vicenza style

Mullet, Leghorn style

■ Yield: 4 servings
■ Time needed: 1 hour
■ Difficulty: *

Ingredients: 1½ lb mullet, 1 lb plum tomatoes, peeled and cubed, 1 chopped onion, 1 tbsp chopped parsley, 1 small minced clove garlic, 1 whole clove garlic, flour, 1 crushed bay leaf, ¼ tsp dried thyme, 12 small slices toasted bread, 3 tablespoons olive oil, pepper, salt.

Clean the mullet, wash, and drain. Put a pan on the flame with the oil, arrange in it the lightly floured fish and, turning once, cook for about 5 minutes or until the fish is lightly browned and nearly cooked. Drain and set aside.

In a casserole briefly cook the onion with the minced garlic, then add a whole clove of garlic, thyme, bay leaf, and tomatoes. Add salt and pepper and simmer the sauce for about 15 minutes. Add the mullet and let them absorb the flavor for a few minutes over low heat. Arrange the fish on a deep platter, cover with the boiling sauce, sprinkle with chopped parsley, and serve with toasted bread.

Broiled swordfish

■ Yield: 4 servings
■ Time needed: 1 hour
■ Difficulty: *

Ingredients: 4 swordfish steaks about 8 oz each, 1 lb ripe tomatoes, 5 oz green olives, 1 oz raisins, 1 oz pine nuts, 2 tbsp capers, 2 cloves garlic, 1 bay leaf, 1 small onion, 1 stalk celery, flour, 1 cup olive oil, pepper, salt.

Soften the raisins in warm water, pit the olives, and chop the onion and celery. Peel the tomatoes and break up with a fork. Bone the fish steaks with care. Place a skillet over moderately high flame, add oil, and as soon as the oil starts smoking, lay in the fish steaks, lightly floured and salted. Brown on both sides and drain. Set aside.

Brown the onion and celery in the same pan, add the crushed garlic and tomatoes, season with salt and pepper, and simmer gently for about 15 minutes, stirring every so often. Add to the sauce the raisins, drained, the capers, pine nuts, and olives.

Arrange the fish in a baking dish, cover with the sauce, add a bay leaf, and gradually pour on enough warm water to cover the fish. Put the dish in an oven set at 350° for about 20 minutes. Once the dish is cooked, the juice should have almost evaporated.

If you so wish, serve with toasted or fried bread.

Porgy aux fines herbes

■ Yield: 4 servings
■ Time needed: 1 hour
■ Difficulty: *

Ingredients: 1 porgy weighing about 2 lb, 1 lb ripe tomatoes, peeled, seeded, and chopped, 2 tbsp butter, 1 onion, 1 bunch parsley, 1 bunch basil, ¼ tsp sage, ¼ tsp rosemary, 1 bay leaf, 1 stalk celery, 1 carrot, 1 clove garlic, flour, ½ cup dry white wine, 5 tbsp oil, pepper, salt.

Chop up all the vegetables and herbs.

Clean the fish, wash, and dredge lightly in flour. In a pan heat 3 tbsp oil, lay in the fish, and brown on both sides. Drain on a piece of paper towel. Put an oval casserole on the flame and add the butter, 2 tbsp oil, the onion, celery, carrot, and herbs, and fry briefly. Add the fish, season with salt and pepper, and add the tomatoes. Cook the fish slowly, pouring on a little white wine every so often and basting with the sauce in the pan.

Catfish with olives

■ Yield: 4 servings
■ Time needed: 1 hour
■ Difficulty: *

Ingredients: Two 1-lb catfish, 4 oz green olives, 2 tbsp chopped parsley, 1 clove minced garlic, 1 tbsp tomato paste, 3 tbsp oil, ½ cup dry white wine, salt, pepper.

Briefly sauté the parsley and garlic in the olive oil, then pour in the white wine and reduce by half. Add the tomato paste and two cups hot water, seasoning with salt and pepper. Scald the olives for 5 minutes in boiling water, then add to the sauce. Cook for a further 10 minutes, then put the cleaned and washed catfish in the sauce and simmer for 25 minutes, turning once.

Baking and Frying

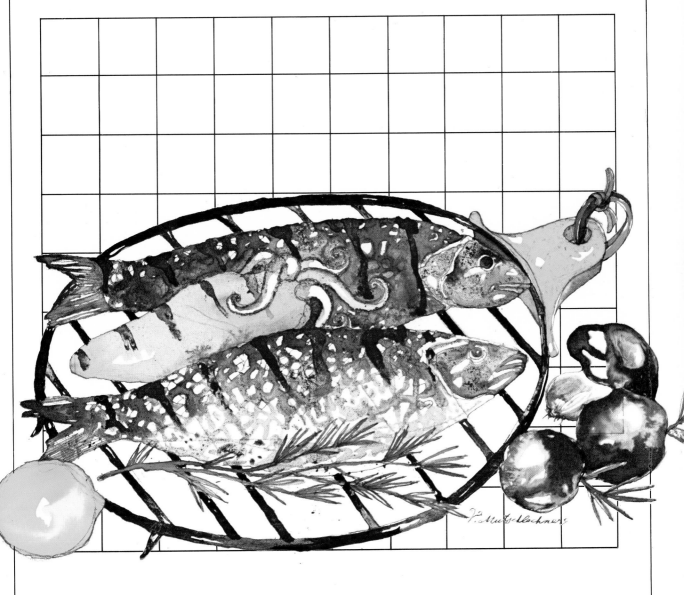

In Genoa there is a saying that goes: "Even shoes are good fried." More than any other, this method brings out the very best taste of even the dullest and humblest of foods. This is evident enough from the countless fish-fry restaurants that have sprung up in many countries around the world, even in towns nowhere near the sea. Here whole familes eat meals or snacks of various types of fried fish, or else take it back home — still wrapped up in newspaper in some parts of Britain.

Small fish are best for frying. Obviously, plenty of oil is required. Since earliest times, the olive has been widely cultivated around the Mediterranean.

It has more recently become an important crop in parts of the United States too. Olive oil was once considered to have divine origins, and it was produced in honor of the gods. Olive oil is the vital ingredient for obtaining a beautiful golden brown crust. It can be heated to a high temperature without burning, and thus, when the fish is plunged in it, a thin outer crust immediately forms, protecting the inside, which stays tender and soft.

The sea of course does not brim just with shoals of anchovy, sardines, and other small fish particularly suitable for frying. It also yields larger prey such as porgy, grouper, and bass which are ideal for barbecuing at the seashore or baking in the oven at home as well.

Grilled hake

Grilled mullet

- ■ **Yield: 4 servings**
- ■ **Time needed: 1 hour**
- ■ **Difficulty: ***

**Ingredients: 4 small mullet each weighing about ¹/₂ lb, 2-3 cloves garlic, ¹/₂ tsp crushed dried rosemary, ¹/₄ tsp dried sage, ¹/₂ cup olive oil, salt, pepper.
Sauce ingredients: 2 lemons, 2-3 cloves garlic, 1 bunch parsley, ¹/₂ tsp crumbled dried mint, ³/₄ cup oil, vinegar, pepper, salt.**

Scale all the fish (1), cut off the fins (2), make a small incision in the belly, and remove the innards (3). Wash the mullet under running water, then dry thoroughly with a dish cloth. Make shallow slashes in five or six places on each side (4). Put the fish into a bowl, adding slivers of garlic, rosemary, and sage (5). Season with salt and pepper, and moisten with ¹/₄ cup olive oil (6).

Marinate while you prepare the sauce. Cut the lemons into very thin slices, and chop the garlic, parsley, and mint finely. Mix all the ingredients in a small bowl or sauceboat.

Beat in ³/₄ cup oil, vinegar to taste, and season with salt and pepper. Set aside.

Heat a griddle until red hot and arrange the mullet (drained of their marinade) on it (7). Cook until they have formed a thin golden crust, then turn, using a small spatula (8). Baste every so often with ¹/₄ cup lightly salted oil (9).

When cooked, arrange the mullet on an oval platter and serve with the sauce on the side. If you like you can accompany the fish with cubed boiled potatoes and garnish with bunches of parsley. Alternatively you can serve with sautéed vegetables or with halved tomatoes that have been sprinkled with bread crumbs, chopped garlic, parsley, thyme, and marjoram, and broiled for about 10 minutes.

1 Scale the fish.

2 With a pair of shears, cut off the fins by the head and on the back.

3 Make a small cut in the belly of each fish and remove the innards.

4 Slash the sides of each mullet, but not too deep.

5 Arrange slivers of garlic, sage, and rosemary over the fish.

6 Salt and pepper the fish and moisten with a little oil. Let fish stand to absorb flavor for a few minutes.

7 Arrange fish on a red-hot griddle and cook until a thin crust has formed on the skin.

8 Turn the fish over, using a small spatula to prevent them from breaking apart.

9 During cooking, baste with a little oil, lightly salted.

Grilled mullet

Porgy en papillote

- Yield: 4 servings
- Time needed: 1 hour
- Difficulty: *

Ingredients: Two 2-lb porgy, 2 tbsp butter, 1 shallot or 3 scallions, 2 bay leaves, 1 bunch parsley, 1 lemon, 4-5 anchovy fillets, 1 tbsp vinegar, $1/2$ cup oil, salt, pepper.

Clean, wash, and dry the porgy. Generously butter sheets of "heavy-duty" foil or parchment paper (1). Chop the anchovies, put in a small bowl, and mix in vinegar and the juice of the lemon (2). Season with salt and pepper, and slowly add about $1/2$ cup oil, beating constantly. Stir in the shallot or scallions, chopped with the parsley (3). Lay fish on foil or paper, make a cut along the back (4), and sprinkle both sides with the sauce (5). Put the bay leaves on top and wrap the foil or paper tightly around the fish (6). Place in a baking dish and bake at 350° for about 20 minutes.

Bring the porgy to the table still wrapped in foil or paper, opening just before serving.

1 Generously butter a sheet of "heavy-duty" foil or parchment paper.

2 Chop the anchovies and mix with vinegar and lemon juice.

3 Add shallot or scallions, chopped very fine with the parsley.

4 After laying the fish on the foil or paper, make a cut along the back with a knife.

5 Sprinkle uniformly both porgy's sides with the sauce.

6 Wrap the fish in the foil or paper, sealing the edges tightly.

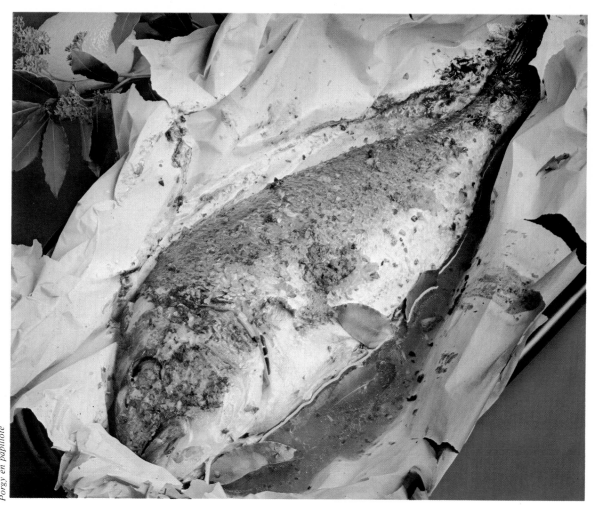

Porgy en papillote

Baked stuffed grouper

- **Yield: 4 servings**
- **Time needed: 1 hour**
- **Difficulty: ****

Ingredients: 1 large grouper (or substitute a striped bass) weighing 3-3 1/2 lb, 2 tbsp butter, 1 oz dried mushrooms, 3 tbsp bread crumbs, 2 tbsp parsley finely chopped with 1 clove garlic, 1 additional clove garlic, 1/2 tsp rosemary, 1 egg, about 1/2 cup dry white wine, oil, salt, pepper.

Soak the dried mushrooms for at least half an hour in warm water, wash, squeeze well, and sauté briefly in butter (1). Before removing from the flame, flavor with half the chopped parsley and garlic (2) and cook about 1 minute.

Pour the mushrooms into a bowl and add the bread crumbs (3), the remaining parsley and garlic, salt and pepper, and the whole egg (4). Set aside.

1 Soak the mushrooms in warm water, squeeze well, and cook briefly in a little butter.

2 Before removing from the flame, add some of the chopped parsley and garlic.

3 When the mushrooms are cooked, put into a bowl and add the bread crumbs...

4 ... the remaining chopped parsley and garlic, salt and pepper, and the whole egg.

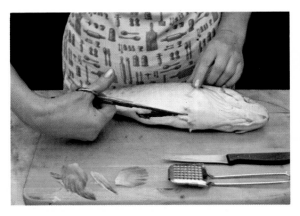

5 Remove the fins and scales from the grouper and make a long cut along the belly...

6 ...then remove the innards, wash under running water, and dry in a cloth.

7 Open the belly wide and fill with the mushroom stuffing....

8 ...then close firmly, making sure all the stuffing is safely inside the fish.

9 Oil a baking dish, lay in the grouper, and moisten with oil.

10 Top with dots of butter, rosemary, and slivers of garlic, and bake.

Remove the fish's fins and scales and make a cut in the belly (5); scoop out the innards, wash, drain, and dry in a dish cloth (6). Fill the cavity with the reserved mushroom stuffing (7), pressing it in as far as possible, then close the flaps, squeezing with your hands to keep the stuffing safely inside (8).

Generously oil an oval baking dish large enough to hold the fish flat, lay the fish in it, moisten with a little oil (9), and cover with dots of butter, rosemary, and thin slivers of garlic (10). Bake at 350° for about 45 minutes. After about 15 minutes pour white wine over the fish; after 25 minutes turn it with a long spatula. Baste every so often with the juices in the dish. Transfer the cooked fish with the spatula to a heated oval platter and surround with mashed or boiled potatoes (sprinkled with chopped parsley) or with broiled tomatoes.

Baked grouper

- **Yield: 4 servings**
- **Time needed: 1 hour**
- **Difficulty: ***

Ingredients: 1 grouper weighing 2 lb, 2 tbsp butter, 1 clove garlic, 1/2 tsp rosemary, 1/2 tsp ground sage, 2 crushed bay leaves, 1/2 cup bread crumbs, 1 cup dry white wine, 1/4 cup oil, salt, pepper.

Clean the fish, wash thoroughly, and drain. Salt and pepper inside and out, and in the belly place half the herbs and the garlic cut in slivers. Lay in an oval baking dish, moisten with half the oil, dot with butter, and put in a 350° oven. After about 15 minutes, pour the wine over and continue cooking for about 30 minutes longer, or until the flesh flakes easily. Ten minutes before removing from the oven, sprinkle the grouper with the bread crumbs mixed together with the remaining rosemary, sage, bay leaf, and oil.

Porgy au gratin

- **Yield: 4 servings**
- **Time needed: 1 hour 20 minutes**
- **Difficulty: ***

Ingredients: 1 porgy weighing about 2 lb, 6 tbsp butter, 1 onion, 1/2 lb fresh mushrooms, 1 clove garlic, 1 bunch parsley, 1/2 cup bread crumbs, grated zest of 1/2 lemon, 3/4 cup dry white wine, salt, pepper.

Finely chop the onion and fry lightly in a pan with half the butter. Meanwhile clean and slice the mushrooms, then add to the fried onion. Season with salt and pepper, add 1/4 cup wine, and simmer over a medium flame until the liquid evaporates. Chop the parsley with the garlic and mix in bread crumbs, lemon zest, and a pinch of salt and pepper.

Clean the porgy, wash, dry, and fill the belly with the bread crumb stuffing. Butter a pyrex dish, cover the bottom with the mushroom mixture, and lay the porgy in the middle. Season with salt and pepper, pour on the remaining wine, and dot with 1 tbsp butter. Cover with aluminum foil and put into a 400° oven for about 20 minutes.

Remove the paper, sprinkle the fish with the remaining bread crumbs, drizzle with the remaining butter, melted, and return the dish to the oven until done, about 10 minutes longer. Remove from the oven when the skin of the fish is a golden brown and serve at once.

Porgy with mushrooms

- **Yield: 4 servings**
- **Time needed: 40 minutes**
- **Difficulty: ***

Ingredients: 1 porgy weighing at least 2 lb, 4 tbsp butter, 1 lb chopped mushrooms, 2 finely crushed bay leaves, pepper, salt.

Clean and wash the porgy, then strip off the skin (to make this easier to do, first plunge the fish quickly into boiling water). Butter a baking dish and lay the porgy in it. Season with salt and pepper, strew the mushrooms and bay leaves on top, and moisten with the remaining butter, melted. Cover with aluminum foil and cook in a 400° oven for 20-25 minutes.

Mullet, island style

- **Yield: 4 servings**
- **Time needed: 1/2 hour (plus 1/2 hour for marinade)**
- **Difficulty: ***

Ingredients: 1 large mullet weighing about 2 lb, 2 bay leaves, juice of 1/2 lemon, 1 clove garlic, 1 cup olive oil, salt, pepper.

Clean the fish, wash carefully, dry, and cut into four pieces. In a large and fairly deep dish, mix the lemon juice with the oil, freshly ground pepper, 2 crushed bay leaves, crushed garlic, and salt to taste. Lay in the slices of mullet and marinate for half an hour. Thread fish on a skewer. Moistening every so often with the marinade, cook over charcoal or broil the fish in your oven.

Grilled sea bass with fennel

- **Yield: 4 servings**
- **Time needed: 1/2 hour**
- **Difficulty: ***

Ingredients: 1 sea bass weigthing 2 lb, stalks of fresh or dried wild fennel, brandy, oil, salt, pepper.

Clean and wash the fish, dry, and make a long cut along the back. Season with salt and pepper, fill the cut with fennel, and moisten with a little oil. Cook on a hot griddle. When cooked, pour a little brandy over the fish, flame, and serve at once.

Stuffed eel

- **Yield: 6 servings**
- **Time needed: 1½ hours**
- **Difficulty: *****

Ingredients: 1 fairly large eel weighing 3-3½ lb, ½ lb ground swordfish, 1 tbsp capers, 1 tbsp parsley chopped with 1 clove garlic, 2 tbsp chopped sour pickles, 2 tbsp butter, 1 egg, 1 small carrot, 1 stalk celery, 1 small onion, 1 bay leaf, pinch thyme, pinch marjoram, 1 cup dry white wine, corn meal, 2 tbsp brandy, 3 tbsp oil, pepper, salt.

Rub the eel vigorously with corn meal to remove the slime. Make a round cut just beneath the head through the skin (1). Using a cloth to help you get a grip, remove the skin by pulling towards the tail (2) as if you were taking off a glove (3). Make a cut the whole length of the eel along the belly (4) and remove the innards. Using a pointed knife, carefully remove the backbone (5) and other bones. Wash and drain the eel, lay out on a surface, and spread it open with your hands.

Now make the stuffing: combine ground swordfish, capers, and pickles in a bowl and add the chopped parsley and garlic, the marjoram, thyme, and the egg. Season with salt and pepper, pour in the brandy, and mix (6). Fill the eel with the stuffing, spreading it evenly (7). Then fold the flaps of the eel over so that all the stuffing is safely held inside (8). Using a large needle and fine string, sew up the eel with close stitches (9). Sprinkle with salt and pepper.

In a large pot, melt the butter and oil, stir in the carrot, onion, and celery, all finely chopped, and add the bay leaf.

Cook over moderate heat for 7 minutes, stirring. Arrange the stuffed eel in a spiral shape on the vegetables and fasten the ends with wooden skewers. Brown lightly, then pour in wine, cover, and cook for about half an hour without stirring.

If needed, add a little more wine. Remove the eel to a serving platter, force the sauce through a food mill, and cover the eel with it. Serve hot.

1 Make a round cut just beneath the head, piercing the skin.

2 Grip the skin with a cloth and pull away from the neck...

3 ...until you reach the tail, rather like taking off a glove.

4 With a small pointed knife make a long cut along the eel's belly.

5 Carefully remove the backbone and other bones.

6 In a bowl, beat together all the ingredients of the stuffing, until the mixture holds together.

7 Stuff the eel evenly with this mixture.

8 Fold in the flaps so that all the stuffing is securely enclosed.

9 Sew up the eel with close stitches, with a needle and fine string.

Stuffed eel

Fried eels in wine vinegar

- ■ **Yield: 4 servings**
- ■ **Time needed:1½ hours**
- ■ **Difficulty: ***

Ingredients: 4 small eels each weighing about 1 lb, 2 sliced carrots, 1 onion, 1 stalk celery, 3 oz olives, zest of 1 lemon, 2 cloves garlic, slivered, 2 bay leaves, flour for dredging, 3 cups white wine vinegar, 2 cups white wine, small piece of red pepper, oil for frying plus 1 additional cup for marinade, salt, pepper.

Rub the eels vigorously with corn meal to remove slime (1). Remove the innards, cut into 3-inch pieces (2), wash and dry (3). Roll pieces of eel in flour (4) and fry slowly in hot oil (5); drain when well cooked (6) and add salt and pepper. In a saucepan mix the vinegar, wine, garlic slivers, green pepper, pepper, bay leaves, 1 cup oil (7), lemon zest, sliced carrots, olives, and salt (8); boil for 5 minutes. Put the eels in an earthenware dish (9), pour the boiling marinade over them (10), and marinate for at least two days before serving.

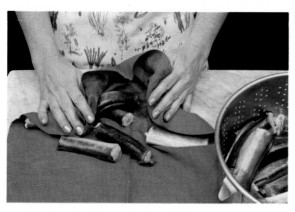

1 Rub the eels vigorously in corn meal to get rid of the slime.

2 Remove the innards, and cut into 3-inch pieces.

3 Wash the pieces under running water and dry well.

4 Put a little flour on a plate and roll the eel in it.

5 Then fry slowly in hot oil until thoroughly cooked.

6 As the pieces are cooked, drain on absorbent paper.

7 Over a flame, mix the vinegar, wine, garlic, pepper, green pepper, bay leaf, and oil...

8 ...then add the lemon zest and other vegetables, cut into pieces.

9 When the pieces of eel are cold, lay them in an earthenware dish...

10 ...then pour in the boiling marinade along with all the vegetables, covering the eel completely.

Fried eels in wine vinegar

Sole Colbert

■ **Yield: 4 servings**
■ **Time needed: 1 hour**
■ **Difficulty: ****

Ingredients: 4 medium-sized sole, 10 tbsp butter, 2 eggs, 1 large handful parsley, chopped, 2 lemons plus a little extra lemon juice, 1/3 cup flour, 1 cup bread crumbs, ¼ cup milk, 2 tbsp oil, pepper, salt.

Clean, wash, and dry the sole. Remove the skin on one side and then the other as described on pages 16-17.

With a sharp, pointed knife, separate the fillets down the middle on one side of the fish, starting at the backbone (1). Then fold back so that each fillet is folded over itself lengthwise (2). With a sharp blow, cut the backbone at both ends, breaking it, but do not remove (3). You will remove it once the sole has been breaded and fried so that the meat in the middle remains uncovered.

Before cooking the sole prepare your *maître d'hôtel* butter. In a bowl beat 8 tablespoons (1 stick) soft butter until creamy (4), add a pinch of salt, pepper, the chopped parsley, and a few drops of lemon juice (5). Cut the lemons in half, making a deep saw-toothed pattern with the knife. Cover the halves with the *maître d'hôtel* butter, level with a knife (6), then put in the refrigerator.

Dip the sole in milk (7), then in flour, then in the eggs beaten with a pinch of salt (8), and last of all in the bread crumbs, pressing with the palms of your hands to make sure they stick to the fish (9).

Heat the oil and the remaining butter over moderate flame and sauté the sole until browned on both sides. Drain on absorbent paper. Starting at the head, gently pull out the backbone, taking care not to break the fish (10). With a small knife pry the hardened butter out of the lemon halves and put each piece of butter on a small lemon slice (11) (you can make the slices from the lemon halves used to shape the butter).

Arrange the fried sole on an oval platter, put a slice of lemon with the butter on top in the middle of each one, and garnish with parsley.

1 Separate the sole fillets on one side of the fish down the middle...

2 ...then fold back the meat so that the fillets are folded in two lengthwise.

3 With a sharp blow break the backbone at both ends, but do not remove it.

4 In a bowl beat a stick of soft butter until creamy...

5 ...then add a pinch of salt and pepper, chopped parsley, and a little lemon juice.

6 Cover saw-toothed lemon halves with the *maître d'hôtel* butter, flattening with a knife.

7 Pour a little milk into a flat dish and dip the fillets in it one by one.

8 After allowing the milk to drain off, dip sole in flour and beaten egg...

9 ...and last of all in bread crumbs, pressing gently with your hands to make sure they stick to the fish.

10 After frying the sole, remove the backbone starting at the head.

11 Remove the hardened butter from the lemon halves and place each piece on a slice of lemon.

Sole Colberi

Sole in red wine

■ **Yield: 4 servings**
■ **Time needed: 50 minutes**
■ **Difficulty: ***

Ingredients: 4 sole, 6 tbsp butter, 1 leek, 1 clove garlic, 1 small onion or 2-3 shallots, 1 bunch chopped parsley, 2 tbsp snipped chives, 1 cup dry red wine, 1 lemon, pepper, salt.

Clean, wash, and carefully dry the sole. As described on pages 16-17, remove the skin on both sides.

Generously butter a baking dish, arrange the sole in it, and sprinkle with salt and pepper. Chop the white part of the leek with the garlic and onion (to make a more refined dish you can use two or three shallots instead of onion). In a small casserole melt 3 tbsp butter, add the chopped leek mixture, and pour over the sole. Add the red wine and sprinkle with the chopped onions. Cover the dish with a sheet of foil, and place in a 350° oven for 20-25 minutes (cooking time varies with the size of the fish). When done, remove the foil, drain the fish, place on a preheated oval platter, and keep warm.

Reduce the pan juices by half over a hot flame and then mix in the remaining 3 tbsp butter cut into small pieces, plus the lemon juice. Pour the hot sauce over the sole. Sprinkle the fish with parsley and chives and serve at once.

Fillets of sole in anchovy sauce

■ **Yield: 4 servings**
■ **Time needed: 1/2 hour**
■ **Difficulty: ***

Ingredients: 8 fillets of sole, 6 tbsp butter, 1 oz capers, 3-6 anchovy fillets, 1 handful parsley, flour for dredging, 3 tbsp oil, pepper, salt.

Chop the anchovy fillets with the capers. In a small pan combine 4 tablespoons of butter, add the chopped capers and anchovies, and gently cook the sauce for a few minutes, stirring with a wooden spoon. Put the remaining butter and oil in a large pan, heat over a low flame, and arrange in it the fish fillets, seasoned with salt and pepper and dredged in flour. Cook them for a few minutes on both sides, remove to a preheated oval platter, spoon on the hot anchovy sauce, and sprinkle with the chopped parsley. Serve at once.

Fillets of sole in sparkling wine

■ **Yield: 4 servings**
■ **Time needed: 1 hour**
■ **Difficulty: ****

Ingredients: 4 fairly good sized sole, 1 cup peeled tomatoes, 3/4 cup heavy cream, 2 tsp mustard, 2 tsp Worcestershire sauce, 1/2 cup good quality dry sparkling wine, 4 tbsp butter, flour for dredging, salt, pepper.

First make the sauce. Sieve the tomatoes, removing peel and seeds, and mix the pulp with the cream, one or two tablespoons mustard (depending how piquant you want the sauce to be), the Worcestershire sauce, freshly ground pepper, and salt. Set aside.

Clean the sole, wash, and fillet as described on pages 16-17. Dry the fillets, dip in flour, then cook in butter until brown. Pour in half a glass of sparkling wine, turn up the flame, and reduce by half. Add the sauce and simmer for a few minutes to the thicken. Remove the sole from the heat and serve at once.

Fillets of sole in cream

■ **Yield: 4 servings**
■ **Time needed: 40 minutes**
■ **Difficulty: ***

Ingredients: 8 sole fillets, 1/2 lb sliced mushrooms, 1 small onion, 2 tbsp butter, 1 cup heavy cream, 1 cup dry white wine, 3 tbsp chopped parsley, 2 tbsp snipped chives, salt, pepper.

Gently sauté the chopped onion in butter until soft in a baking dish. Add the sliced mushrooms, salt, and cook until mushrooms are wilted, stirring now and then. Arrange the sole fillets over the mushrooms, add salt and pepper, moisten with wine, cover the dish with aluminum foil, and put in a 400° oven for about 15 minutes or until cooked. Remove the foil, transfer the fillets with a slotted spatula to a preheated platter, and keep warm. Reduce the juice over a high flame by about half, then add the cream, boil for several minutes to thicken, and remove from the heat. Stir in the parsley and chives and pour over the fish. Serve with mashed potatoes.

Mixed fry

4 small hake or scrod, 4 squid cleaned and cut into rings, 4 prawns or jumbo shrimp, 4 small red mullet or perch, 1 lb whitebait, 10 oz fresh sardines, flour for dredging, oil for deep-frying, 2 lemons, salt.

Clean all the fish, wash, drain, and dry (1). Place the whitebait in a bag with flour and shake to coat evenly (2). Flour the sardines by putting a little flour in a sieve and shaking (3). Dip the other fish in flour and shake off excess. Heat 2-3 inches oil in a deep, heavy casserole with a frying basket; when the oil is hot, a small piece of bread will brown in 1 minute (4). Add the whitebait first and drain when cooked (5). Salt and keep hot. Heat additional oil in a 12-inch skillet and fry all the other fish in small batches (6). Serve all the fish together on a single platter with slices of lemon.

- ■ Yield: 4 servings
- ■ Time needed: 1 hour
- ■ Difficulty: *

Ingredients: Select among the following: 4 small sole,

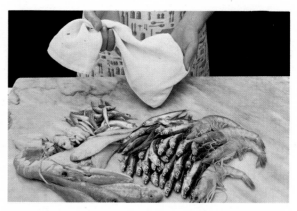

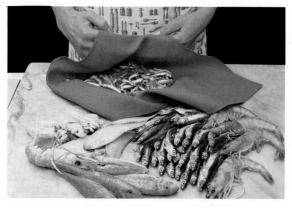

1 Clean all the fish, wash in running water, drain, and dry well.

2 Put the smaller fish in a bag with flour and shake to coat evenly.

3 Also flour the sardines, putting a little flour in a sieve and shaking.

4 Heat oil; when the right temperature is reached, a small piece of bread will brown in a minute.

5 First, fry the smaller fish. When golden brown, drain all together by removing the frying basket.

6 In a large frying pan, heat additional oil and fry the remaining fish in batches.

Mixed fry

Fish croquettes

- **Yield: 4 servings**
- **Time needed: 1 hour**
- **Difficulty: ***

Ingredients: 1 lb swordfish, codfish, or eel, 3 medium sized potatoes, 4 oz chopped mushrooms, 2 oz cooked ham, 4 tbsp butter, 1 clove garlic chopped with 1 tbsp parsley, 3 eggs, ½ onion, 1 bay leaf, ½ cup flour, 1 lemon, 3 tbsp milk, 1-1½ cups bread crumbs, oil for deep-frying, salt, pepper.

Boil the potatoes, mash, add 2 tablespoons butter, a pinch of salt, 3 tablespoons milk (1), and stir the purée over heat until dry. Off the flame, mix in the yolk of one egg and a little of the white (2). Set aside. Blanch the slices of fish for 2 minutes in simmering water flavored with onion, carrot, bay leaf, a slice of lemon, salt, and pepper. Drain (3), cool, chop and combine with the remaining butter, chopped mushrooms (4), chopped ham (5), and chopped parsley and garlic. Mix all this with the potatoes (6), shape into small balls (7), flour (8), dip in the remaining egg, beaten (9), and then roll in bread crumbs (10). Fry in hot oil (11) and drain (12).

1 Boil the potatoes and mash, adding butter and milk; dry over heat.

2 Remove the potato purée from the heat when it has dried out and add one egg yolk and a little white.

3 Drain the slices of fish from the court bouillon and allow to cool.

4 Add the mushrooms, washed and finely chopped, to the fish meat.

5 Let fish and mushroom mixture stand for 1-2 minutes to blend flavors, then add the chopped ham.

6 Add this mixture to the potato purée and mix well.

7 Shape the mixture into small balls with your hands.

8 Roll the fish balls in flour.

9 Then dip them in beaten egg, covering completely.

10 Last of all, roll the croquettes in bread crumbs, making sure they are evenly covered.

11 Heat plenty of oil in a large frying pan and fry the croquettes.

12 Turn the croquettes every so often in the hot oil and drain when golden.

Fish croquettes

Mixed fish and vegetable fry

■ **Yield: 6-8 servings**
■ **Time needed: 2¹/₂ hours**
■ **Difficulty: ***

Ingredients: 1 lb whitebait or fresh sardines, 1 lb sliced fish, 1 small cauliflower, 3 small zucchini, 2 cooked artichoke bottoms, 8 squash flowers (optional), 2 oz grated Parmesan cheese, ¹/₄ cup very thick béchamel sauce, 3-4 eggs, ¹/₃ cup white flour, 1¹/₂-2 cups bread crumbs, 1 bay leaf, 1 carrot, oil for deep-frying, 3 tbsp butter, 1 clove garlic, crushed, salt, pepper.

Lightly brown the slices of fish in the butter, adding the crushed clove of garlic and the bay leaf. Season with salt and pepper, and cook through. Purée the fish and add to the béchamel sauce, along with the grated Parmesan cheese, the yolk of an egg, and a little of the white. Put in the refrigerator to solidify.

Meanwhile, boil the cauliflower and separate into flowerets. Cut the artichoke bottoms into quarters and the zucchini into strips; wash and dry the optional squash flowers. In a bowl beat the remaining eggs with ¹/₄ teaspoon salt. Shape the fish paste into fairly small oval or round croquettes. Dip in flour, then in the beaten egg, and last in the bread crumbs. Dip the vegetables in eggs and bread crumbs.

Heat plenty of oil in a large pan. When hot, fry the vegetables first, then the fish croquettes. Flour the whitebait and fry. After draining, keep all the ingredients warm in the oven. Neatly arrange the fish croquettes, vegetables, and whole fish on a platter and serve at once.

Whitebait in batter

■ **Yield: 4 servings**
■ **Time needed: 1 hour**
■ **Difficulty: ***

Ingredients: 1¹/₂ lb whitebait, 1 cup flour, 2 cups water, 2 egg whites, 2 lemons, 2 tbsp olive oil plus additional oil for frying, salt.

Whitebait are the newly hatched young of sardines and anchovies and are only fished in spring.

Put the flour in a bowl, add two cups of lukewarm water, two tablespoons oil, and a pinch of salt. Blend until smooth and let stand for 30 minutes. Whip the egg whites until stiff but not dry and carefully fold into the batter. Wash the whitebait thoroughly, dry, and dip in the batter. Heat ¹/₂ inch oil in a large cast-iron skillet over moderately high heat. When hot, fry the whitebait in their batter, a small batch at a time. Brown on one side, then turn and brown on the other side. When golden brown and crusty, drain on absorbent paper. Salt, arrange in a mound on a platter and serve hot after garnishing with lemon slices and curly parsley.

Fried stuffed sardines

■ **Yield: 4 servings**
■ **Time needed: 1 hour**
■ **Difficulty: ***

Ingredients: 1¹/₂ lb fairly large fresh sardines, 2 stale rolls or 3 slices bread, ¹/₃ cup milk, 1 tbsp pine nuts, 1 clove garlic, 2 tbsp grated Parmesan or Romano cheese, ¹/₂ tsp dried basil, 3 eggs, 1-1¹/₂ cups bread crumbs, ¹/₃ cup flour, 3 tbsp olive oil plus additional oil for frying, 2 lemons, salt, pepper.

Clean the sardines, slit down the back, and pull off the heads along with the backbones. Wash well and dry. After trimming off the crusts soak rolls or bread in milk. In a pan heat 3 tbsp oil, add 3-4 sardines, and brown. Place sardines in a blender or food processor along with pine nuts, bread (squeezed to remove excess milk), garlic, cheese, and basil. Grind finely, add a pinch each of salt and pepper and a whole egg and mix well.

Spread the stuffing in the remaining sardines and close. Dip sardines first in flour, then in the remaining eggs, beaten, and last of all in the bread crumbs, pressing firmly with the palms of the hand to enclose the stuffing as tightly as possible. Fry the stuffed sardines in hot oil. As soon as they are golden brown on one side, turn and cook on the other side. Remove with a spatula and lay on absorbent paper to drain off excess oil. Serve hot with lemon wedges.

Breaded fried whitebait

■ **Yield: 4 servings**
■ **Time needed: 20 minutes (plus 2-3 hours for marinade)**
■ **Difficulty: ***

Ingredients: 1¹/₂ lb whitebait, 2 beaten eggs, 2 cups milk, ¹/₂ cup flour, 1¹/₂ cups bread crumbs, 2 lemons, oil for frying, salt.

Wash and dry the fish, cover with milk, cover and let stand for 2-3 hours in the refrigerator. Drain, pat dry, and dip in flour, beaten eggs, and bread crumbs. Fry in small batches in ¹/₂ inch of hot oil. When golden brown, drain, sprinkle with salt, and serve hot with lemon slices.

Bass au gratin with olives

- Yield: 4 servings
- Time needed: 50 minutes
- Difficulty: *

Ingredients: 2 lb bass fillets, 1 clove minced garlic, 1 small chopped onion, 2 tbsp tomato purée, 1 large pinch oregano, 1 chopped bunch parsley, ¹/₂ cup bread crumbs, ¹/₄ cup pitted green olives, 6 tbsp oil, salt, pepper.

Rinse the bass, dry, and brown in a pan with 3 tablespoons oil. Drain and lay in a baking dish.

In a small casserole, fry the chopped onion in a tablespoon of oil. Add the tomato purée, a pinch each of salt and pepper, the oregano, and the olives, chopped fine. Simmer until the sauce is reduced and thick enough to mound on a spoon. Salt and pepper the fish, lay atop the sauce, and sprinkle with the bread crumbs, chopped parsley, and garlic, all mixed together. Moisten with the remaining oil and bake in a 400° oven for about 20 minutes, or until the top is browned. Serve at once.

Baked cod

- Yield: 4 servings
- Time needed: 1 hour
- Difficulty: *

Ingredients: 2 lb cod steaks, 2 tbsp butter, 1 small onion, 1 tbsp capers, 2 beaten eggs, 1 tsp ketchup, 2 tbsp grated Parmesan cheese, 1 lemon, 1 cup dry white wine, 2 tbsp oil, salt.

Rinse the fish, pat dry, and sprinkle with lemon juice and salt.

Chop the onion and fry in a pan with the butter and oil. Add the fish steaks, brown on both sides over a hot flame. Add the wine, capers, and ketchup, and simmer over a low flame until the fish is cooked. Transfer the fish to a baking dish. Blend the sauce in the pan with the beaten eggs plus a pinch of salt, and pour over the fish. Last of all sprinkle with the Parmesan and place the dish under a hot broiler for 2-3 minutes or until the top has formed a thin, golden brown crust.

Serve at once with small boiled potatoes.

Baked hake piquant

- Yield: 4 servings
- Time needed: 40 minutes
- Difficulty: *

Ingredients: Four 8-oz hake or scrod, 2 cloves garlic, 1 tbsp capers, 4 anchovy fillets, 3 tbsp pitted green olives, 1 bunch parsley, 1 lemon, ¹/₂ cup dry white wine, 3 tbsp white vinegar, 3 tbsp olive oil, salt, pepper.

Clean, wash, and dry the hake. Finely chop the parsley with the garlic cloves, capers, olives, and anchovy fillets. Fill the hake with half the mixture and place a slice of lemon in each, closing the vents.

Arrange fish in a lightly oiled baking dish. Sprinkle with salt, pepper, and the remaining parsley mixture and pour on the oil and white wine, mixed with the vinegar. Cover the dish with aluminum foil and cook the fish in a 400° oven for about 15 minutes. Arrange cooked fish or an oval platter and serve with the juices in which the fish have cooked.

This dish is excellent served cold with mayonnaise.

Hake en brochette

- Yield: 4 servings
- Time needed: 40 minutes (plus 1 hour for marinade)
- Difficulty: *

Ingredients: Twelve 1-inch cubes of hake or cod (1¹/₂-2 lb), 20 fresh or dried sage leaves, pinch thyme, 1 lemon, ¹/₂ cup oil, salt, pepper.

In a large bowl mix the oil with the juice of the lemon, the thyme, and a few pinches of salt and pepper. Add the cubes of fish to the marinade and leave for an hour, turning every so often.

Thread the fish and sage leaves alternately on

skewers. Brush with some of the marinade and cook over a charcoal grill, turning the skewers frequently to brown all over and brushing from time to time with the marinade. Serve with a tossed green salad, grilled tomatoes, or other vegetables.

Baked sheepshead

■ **Yield: 4 servings**
■ **Time needed: 50 minutes**
■ **Difficulty: ***

Ingredients: 1 sheepshead weighing 3 lb, 1 lemon, 1 bunch parsley, chopped, 1 clove garlic, minced, 1 bay leaf, 3 tbsp bread crumbs, 1/2 cup dry white wine, 1/2 cup olive oil, salt, pepper.

Clean, wash, and dry the sheepshead. In a bowl mix the chopped parsley, garlic, bread crumbs, pepper, salt and oil. Arrange the fish in a baking dish, salt lightly, sprinkle with the prepared sauce, and moisten with the white wine and a few drops of lemon juice. Add the bay leaf and bake in a 400° oven for about 45 minutes, basting frequently with the juices in the dish. Serve directly from the baking dish.

Marinated mackerel fillets

■ **Yield: 4 servings**
■ **Time needed: 40 minutes (plus 4-6 hours for marinade)**
■ **Difficulty: ***

Ingredients: 8 mackerel fillets, 3 oz chopped pitted black olives, 4 lemons, 1 bay leaf, 2 tbsp soft butter, pinch marjoram, 1/4 cup dry white wine, 2 tbsp olive oil, salt, pepper.

In a bowl mix the juice of the four lemons, oil, white wine, bay leaf, and a pinch each of salt and pepper. Arrange the mackerel fillets in a flat dish, cover with the marinade, and leave for 4-6 hours, turning every so often. Next, lay the fillets in a lightly buttered baking dish, pour the marinade over them, and sprinkle with the olives. Cream the butter with the marjoram and the grated zest of half a lemon, then spread over the fish.

Bake the dish in a 400° oven for 20-25 minutes, basting every so often with the juice. Serve hot directly from the dish.

Savory fish rolls

■ **Yield: 4 servings**
■ **Time needed: 1 1/4 hours**
■ **Difficulty: ***

Ingredients: 8 fish fillets (preferably flounder or sole), 6 oz boiled shrimp, 6 tbsp butter, 1/3 cup flour, 3 tbsp bread crumbs, 1/2 clove minced garlic, 1 egg yolk, 1 bunch chopped parsley, 1 cup heavy cream, 2 cups fish stock or 1 cup each white wine and bottled clam juice, 1 lemon, 2 tbsp dry white wine, 1 pinch thyme, pepper, salt.

Pour into a small casserole one third of the fish stock and reduce by half over moderate heat. In a bowl mix the bread crumbs, parsley, garlic, the juice of half the lemon, white wine, egg yolk, and a pinch each of salt and pepper. Stir until you have a smooth paste. Keeping a few whole shrimp to one side, chop the remainder finely and add to the paste. Spread the mixture on one side of the fish fillets, then roll up and secure with a toothpick. Arrange in a buttered baking dish, pour on the reduced fish stock, cover the dish with buttered aluminum foil and bake in a 400° oven for 10-15 minutes.

Meanwhile, prepare the sauce. In a casserole melt 4 tablespoons of butter and mix in the flour, stirring well to remove lumps. Little by little add the remaining 1 1/3 cups boiling stock, stirring all the while. Last of all add the cream, simmer for a few minutes, and remove from the heat. You should end up with a fairly thick sauce; season with a little salt and pepper and a pinch of thyme. Transfer the fish fillets with a slotted spatula to a shallow buttered baking dish. Add the juice from the cooked fish to the sauce, then pour this over the fillets and place under a hot broiler for a few minutes to brown lightly. Before serving, garnish with the reserved whole shrimp.

Swordfish steaks

■ **Yield: 4 servings**
■ **Time needed: 1 1/4 hours**
■ **Difficulty: ***

Ingredients: 4 swordfish steaks each weighing about 6 oz, 3 yellow or green peppers, 1 onion, pinch oregano, flour for dredging, 4 tbsp olive oil, 1/2 cup dry white wine, salt, pepper.

Fried whitebait in batter

Slice the onion thinly and fry gently in 2 tablespoons oil until soft. Add the peppers (cut into pieces) and brown lightly over a hot flame. Add oregano, salt, and pepper. In a separate pan, brown the fish, lightly floured and seasoned with salt and pepper, in 2 tablespoons oil. Pour on the wine and reduce by half. When the peppers are almost cooked, add the fish with its juice and simmer slowly for a few minutes to blend the flavors. Remove from heat and serve each fish steak with a good helping of the peppers.

Fried whitebait in batter

- ■ **Yield: 4 servings**
- ■ **Time needed: ¹/₂ hour**
- ■ **Difficulty: ***

Ingredients: 1½ lb whitebait, 2 lemons, ½-¾ cup flour, oil for frying, salt.

Wash the fish, dry in a cloth, and dip in flour. Shake well to remove any excess flour (a large sieve is handy here). Put a frying pan on high flame and add ½ inch oil. When it is hot, fry the fish in small batches, removing with a slotted spatula and laying on absorbent paper to drain. Arrange the fish on a platter covered with lettuce leaves, the heads facing outwards. This makes an unusual presentation. Garnish with lemon wedges.

Trout baked in foil

- Yield: 4 servings
- Time needed: 1 hour
- Difficulty: *

Ingredients: 4 trout each weighing about ½ lb, 6 oz pitted black olives, 1 lb ripe tomatoes, 1 minced clove garlic, 6 tbsp butter, flour for dredging, 2 tbsp chopped parsley, ½ cup dry white wine, 1 tbsp bread crumbs, 3 tbsp olive oil, salt, pepper.

Scale the trout, remove the innards and fins, wash thoroughly, and drain. Put 1 tbsp oil and 2 tblsp butter in a casserole and briefly fry the chopped parsley with garlic and olives. Take one half of this mixture, add the bread crumbs, and stuff the trout with it. Add tomatoes, peeled and cubed, to the remaining mixture and cook for about half an hour over a low flame.

Flour the trout and brown well in the remaining butter. Pour in the white wine and simmer until almost evaporated. Take four square pieces of foil, lay a trout in the middle of each one, spread the sauce on top, add salt and pepper to taste, and moisten with remaining oil. Close the foil wrappers carefully and put in a 350° oven for about 10 minutes. Open the wrappers at the table.

Grilled trout

- Yield: 4 servings
- Time needed: ½ hour (plus 1 hour for marinade)
- Difficulty:*

Ingredients: 4 trout each weighing about ½ lb, 6 tbsp soft butter, 1 bunch parsley, 1 lemon, ¾ cup olive oil, white pepper, salt.

Clean, wash, and drain the trout. Arrange in a flat dish and cover with oil, lemon juice, salt, and white pepper. Let marinate for about an hour. Heat an oiled griddle or skillet until good and hot and lay the trout on top, cooking on both sides and brushing every so often with the marinade.

Now prepare a *maître d'hôtel* butter. In a bowl mix the softened butter with parsley, finely chopped. Add plenty of white pepper, salt, and a few drops of lemon juice. Mix with a wooden spoon until paste very soft, and put in a sauceboat. Arrange the small trout on a platter and serve with the butter.

Fried fillet of perch

- Yield: 4 servings
- Time needed: 40 minutes
- Difficulty: *

Ingredients: 8 perch fillets (frozen or fresh), 1 cup beer, ⅔ cup flour, 2 tbsp olive oil, 1 egg, separated oil for frying, salt, pepper.

If you are using frozen perch fillets, let them thaw at room temperature. Dry and season with salt and pepper. Sift the flour into a bowl, make a well in the middle, add egg yolk and the olive oil, and mix well, gradually stirring in the beer until you have a fairly thick batter. Last, fold in egg white, beaten until stiff but not dry. Put a frying pan over the flame with ½ inch oil. When the oil is hot, lay in the fillets, completely coated with the batter. Fry until browned on both sides and serve at once.

Salmon steaks with mushrooms

- Yield: 4 servings
- Time needed: 40 minutes
- Difficulty: *

Ingredients: 4 salmon steaks (frozen or fresh) each weighing about ½ lb, 8 tbsp butter, 1 lb mushrooms, 2 cloves garlic, pepper, salt.

Melt the butter in a large frying pan. When hot, brown the salmon steaks on both sides, then remove from the pan and put on a plate. Wash and dry the mushrooms and cut into thin slices. Brown in the pan in which you have cooked the fish, add the garlic, salt, and pepper and cook until done. Five minutes before removing from the heat, add the slices of salmon and continue to cook slowly.

SEAFOOD

Crustaceans

P. Nils Hechner

This group includes the spiny lobster, the Atlantic lobster, the crayfish, all varieties of prawns and shrimp, and the various species of crabs. Crustaceans derive their name from their tough, crust-like, calcareous shells. Because they have two feelers and ten legs, they are also sometimes called decapods. These legs enable them to move about nimbly on the bottom of a sea or river, their natural habitats. Many crustaceans also have two pincers or claws which are used both for catching food and for defense. With the exception of the crabs, crustaceans have a long abdomen ending in a fan-shaped tail.

Crustaceans are so delicate and tasty that throughout the world they have always been sought after by gourmets. However the firm but slightly fibrous meat is not always easy to digest and so is not recommended for people with delicate stomachs. Nutritionally, crustacean meat is low in fat, high in nitrate, and average in mineral content. It also has only 80 to 90 calories per every 4 ounces. Since crustaceans are expensive, it is a good idea to use every morsel of the meat in the chest, legs, claws, and elsewhere.

Preparation and cooking

Crustaceans are usually cooked in their shells. They need only be scrubbed with a brush and washed under running water before being cooked. Crustaceans such as lobster and crab must be cooked live, for once dead their meat deteriorates quickly. The most common way of cooking them is by boiling, either in water or in a court bouillon, which kills these creatures in the swiftest and most humane way possible. They can also be grilled, broiled, baked, or stewed. All that is required is to choose the right crustacean for the method you have selected and then to follow an appropriate recipe.

Spiny or rock lobster—This is a large marine crustacean with long feelers, no claws, and a purplish brown shell which turns scarlet after cooking. The meat is firm and compact, with a very delicate, almost sweet flavor which improves with chilling. When boiling a spiny lobster you can first tie it to a narrow length of wood or a wooden spoon handle to prevent it from curling up while it cooks. Next, plunge the lobster in plenty of boiling water or court bouillon made with water, wine or vinegar, carrot, onion, herbs, salt, and pepper. Once cooked (after some 20 minutes), separate the lobster into two halves with a sharp knife to remove the meat. Throw away the intestines and the gills and then follow the recipe as indicated. Boiled lobster can be served cold in aspic, with mayonnaise, or covered with a sauce and baked. It can also be cut in two lengthwise, brushed with oil or melted butter, sprinkled with salt and pepper, and broiled. Finally, rock lobster can be grilled, oven roasted, or cooked on a spit. For certain dishes you can also use frozen rock lobster tails.

Atlantic lobster—The Atlantic lobster resembles the spiny lobster but has a deep blue shell, a long chest, and two powerful claws filled with extremely delicate flesh. This lobster is ideal for dishes that require the meat to be cut into pieces. The same recipes can be used as for spiny lobster.

Shrimp — These are small saltwater crustaceans with long bodies and lots of small legs. When cooked, the shells turn pink. The meat is lean and tasty, and may be boiled, fried, grilled, or stewed.
There are many varieties, some quite large and others rather small, ranging in color from pink to grey.

Crab — This is a saltwater crustacean with a large thorax, a small abdomen, and no tail. The tough shell is reddish brown and the underbelly is yellowish. Crabs come in all shapes and sizes. The meat is lean and tasty. Crabs can be cooked whole, either boiled or fried. One type that deserves special mention is the renowned and plentiful Atlantic Blue Crab, of which some 200 million are taken from the Chesapeake Bay annually. This crab contains excellent meat both in the claws and body.

Mantis shrimp — These are small, long bodied, and slightly flattened crustaceans with spiny claws and a kind of half-shell, pearl grey in color, which does not protect all of the thorax. The meat is lean, firm, and tasty.
These shrimp can be cooked with or without the shell and can be boiled, baked, or used in soups. They are far too infrequently found in the United States.

Dublin Bay prawn or langoustine — This small saltwater crustacean, which is similar in shape to the lobster, is available only in frozen form in the United States. However, jumbo shrimp can always be substituted in a recipe. The highly prized meat is found mostly in the tail, with a little in the front claws. It can be boiled, fried, cooked in a sauce, or grilled. The result is invariably a tasty dish.

Note: We should also mention that female crustaceans are often found carrying eggs. These are usually red and clustered beneath the belly. They are regarded as a great delicacy by those in the know.

Lobster: cooking and presentation

Tie the live lobster to a narrow wooden board or a wooden spoon handle to stop it from curling (1). Now put it belly down in the fish poacher and cover it completely with boiling court bouillon (2). When it is cooked, remove the twine and lay the lobster on the cutting board belly upwards. Remove the legs, claws, and feelers, cutting them off at the first joint (3). Now separate the top shell of the chest (4) and pull out the gills (5). Scoop out the contents of the shell (6). Lay the lobster belly upwards and cut lengthwise through the thick membrane covering the flesh (7). Remove the meat from the shell (8) and slice (9).

Last of all, using a special cracker, break claws and legs into small pieces so that you can easily remove the meat inside (10).

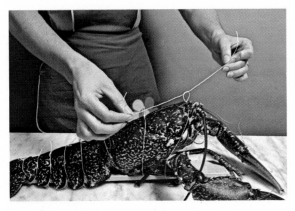

1 Tie the lobster securely to a narrow wooden board with twine.

2 Put the lobster in the fish poacher and cover with court bouillon.

3 Lay the lobster belly upwards and cut off the legs and claws at the first joint.

4 Remove the top shell of the chest...

5 ...then remove the lobster's gills from the shell...

6 ...and empty out the contents with a spoon.

7 With the lobster still belly upwards, cut down the middle of the tail.

8 You will now be able to remove the tail meat.

9 Put the meat on the cutting board and use a sharp knife to slice it into rounds.

10 Using a special cracker, break the claws and legs and remove the meat inside.

The necessary equipment

For crustaceans and mollusks no special utensils are essential, though some can be helpful.

For crustaceans, for example, there are specially designed shears for cutting the shell, and crackers for breaking the claws and legs before removing the meat from them.

For opening clams and oysters, it is a good idea to get a special knife which is shaped like a small dagger and has a molded grip. This knife gives you better leverage for the tightly closed shells. You can also buy a special heavy glove to protect the hand holding the bivalve.

For the presentation of a cold shellfish cocktail, stemmed crystal goblets are extremely elegant. There are also two-piece cocktail servers: in the lower dish you put crushed ice, while the upper one holds the shellfish. For hot dishes, oven-proof ceramic shells are very handsome.

Freezing

Useful hints

Because all crustaceans are expensive and very perishable, freezing is a good way to preseve shellfish bought fresh in your local market. Cool boiled lobster in their cooking broth, drain, then make a small hole at the base of the tail to let all the liquid in the shell drain out as well. Remove the feelers and put the lobsters in individual bags, removing all the air with a straw. Seal the bag, label, and arrange carefully in the freezer so that the lobster will not be crushed. Thaw overnight in the refrigerator and serve cold. To freeze shrimp, first remove the heads, then shell, and place flat in bags so that they will freeze quickly. You can cook shrimp still frozen if you boil them, but thaw first if you fry and grill them. Shrimp can also be boiled before freezing. Drain, cool briefly, shell, and seal in bags as above. Thaw at room temperature before cooking. Do not freeze lobster more than six months; three to four months is maximum for all other crustaceans.

It can't be said too often: Eat only the very freshest crustaceans, and buy all lobsters and crabs live. To check shrimp for freshness, see that they smell pleasant, never "high". Also, when lifted, shrimp should remain curled. Choose lobsters that are heavy in proportion to their size as this is a sure sign that the shell is well filled. Bear in mind that the larger the lobster is, the drier and less tasty its flesh will be; a lobster weighing around 3 1/2 pounds will be ample for four people. Remember too that the shells of crustaceans can be used to make your court bouillon and give flavor and color to your sauce. Scraps of meat from small shrimp or the less-choice meat from lobsters — from the chest, for example — can be used for preparing stuffings, sauces, tasty risottos, and marvelous crepes. The meat of king crabs from Alaska is sold frozen and is ideal for salads. Frozen crab claws are also on the market. In fact, a wide variety of crustaceans can be found either frozen or canned at the supermarket.

Lobster soup

- ■ Yield: 4 servings
- ■ Time needed: 2 hours
- ■ Difficulty: *

Ingredients: One 2-lb spiny or Atlantic lobster (or two smaller ones), 2 tbsp butter, 1½ cups tomato purée, 1 sliced lemon, 1 bay leaf, 2 chopped carrots, 1 stalk celery, chopped, 2 small onions, chopped, 1 tbsp chopped parsley, 1 minced clove garlic, 2 tbsp olive oil, salt, pepper.

Make a court bouillon with the water, half of the carrot, celery, onion, bay leaf, sliced lemon, salt, and pepper (1). Simmer slowly, partially covered for 15 minutes. Tie the lobster to a small board (2), then plunge into the boiling court bouillon (3). Cook about 12 minutes and remove the meat as described on pages 74-75.

Return the shells to the broth and simmer for an hour. Brown remaining finely chopped onion in the butter and oil (4), then the carrot and celery (5). Stir in the parsley and garlic, then add the tomato (6), season with salt, and simmer slowly for 10 minutes. Add 3 cups of the stock flavored with the shells, strained (7) and, off the heat, two-thirds of the lobster meat, shredded (8). Cook for a few minutes, stirring frequently (9). Just before serving, add the remaining meat, cut into thin slices (10).

1 Make a court bouillon with water, the bay leaf, aromatic vegetables, and lemon.

2 Tie the live lobster to a small wooden board...

3 ...and then plunge it into the court bouillon, brought to a boil.

4 Heat the butter and oil in a pan and brown the finely chopped onion...

5 ...then the carrot and celery.

6 Pour the tomato purée into the pan and simmer for ten minutes.

7 Combine the tomato mixture with 3 cups of the stock made with the lobster shells, strained.

8 Remove the pan from heat and add two-thirds of the lobster meat, shredded.

9 Return to the heat and cook for a few minutes, stirring frequently.

10 Pour the soup into a tureen and add the remaining meat cut into thin slices.

Lobster soup

Lobster salad, Sardinian style

■ **Yield: 4 servings**
■ **Time needed: 1 hour**
■ **Difficulty: ***

Ingredients: One 2-lb lobster, 1 sliced carrot, 1 sliced onion, ½ tsp peppercorns, 1 bunch parsley, 1 clove garlic, 2 lemons, ½ cup olive oil, salt, pepper.

Pour 2 quarts water into a fish poacher, add one lemon, sliced, the carrot, onion, peppercorns, and a pinch of salt. Bring to a boil. Tie the live lobster to a small wooden board and plunge into the court bouillon. Cook and remove the meat as described for the lobster on pages 74-75.

Cut the meat into rounds and arrange in a mound on a platter. Chop the parsley finely with the garlic, put in a bowl, and add a pinch of salt, a little pepper, the juice of the remaining lemon, and the oil. Stir well to blend all the ingredients. Pour the sauce over the lobster and refrigerate until serving.

Baked lobster

■ **Yield: 4 servings**
■ **Time needed: 40 minutes**
■ **Difficulty: ***

Ingredients: Two 1-lb lobsters, 6 tbsp melted butter, 4 tbsp bread crumbs, 1 lemon, pinch thyme, 2 bay leaves, salt, pepper.

Kill lobsters by cutting them swiftly and deftly in half lengthwise or by plunging them into salted boiling water for a few minutes after tying them to a wooden board.

Also use frozen lobster tails, but do not tell your guests — they will have a tough time telling the difference. If you have not already done so, cut the lobsters in half lengthwise. Lightly crack the legs and claws with a cracker so that it will be easy to remove the meat later. Put the lobster halves in a baking dish, sprinkle with salt and pepper, and moisten with the melted butter. Sprinkle with the bread crumbs, to which thyme and the grated zest of the lemon have already been added, lay the bay leaves on top, and sprinkle with

the juice of the lemon. Bake at 375° for half an hour or until the meat is thoroughly cooked and golden brown on top.

Lobster in cream

■ **Yield: 4 servings**
■ **Time needed: 2 hours**
■ **Difficulty: ***

Ingredients: One 2-lb lobster, 1 sliced carrot, 1 sliced onion, 1 sliced lemon, ½ tsp peppercorns, 4 tbsp butter, 1 cup heavy cream, ¼ cup brandy, salt, pepper.

Cook lobster as described for Lobster salad, Sardinian style, above, and cut the tail meat into slices.

In a frying pan heat the butter until it colors very lightly.

Add all the lobster meat from the tails, legs, and claws, season with salt, and cook for a few minutes over a hot flame. Add brandy, and cook rapidly until brandy has nearly evaporated. Last of all, pour the cream over the top, add plenty of pepper, and simmer for 10-15 minutes or until thickened. Serve over rice.

Grilled lobster

■ **Yield: 4 servings**
■ **Time needed: 40 minutes**
■ **Difficulty: ***

Ingredients: Two 1½-lb lobsters, ½ cup olive oil, salt, pepper.

Cut the lobsters in half lengthwise, as described for Baked Lobster, above. Gently crack the claws and legs so that the meat can be easily removed later. Brush lobster halves with ¼ cup of the oil and lay them, shell side down, on a charcoal grill. Cook for about 20 minutes, basting frequently with oil and turning lobsters when half cooked.

Serve with béarnaise sauce or melted butter.

Shrimp cocktail

- **Yield: 4 servings**
- **Time needed: 45 minutes**
- **Difficulty: ***

Ingredients: 24 large shrimp or prawn tails, 1 stalk celery, 1 carrot, 1 small onion, 1 celery heart, 1 head Boston lettuce, 2 egg yolks, 1 lemon, 1 cup dry white wine, 2 tbsp brandy, 1 tbsp ketchup, few drops Worcestershire sauce, 1 1/4 cups olive oil, pepper, salt.

In a small bowl beat the egg yolks until thick with a pinch each of salt and pepper and a few drops of lemon juice. Drop by drop add 3 tablespoons olive oil, whipping constantly until the mixture begins to thicken. Gradually add remaining oil (1), whisking all the while and every so often sprinkling on a few drops of lemon juice. Last of all, add brandy (2), season with a few drops of Worcestershire sauce (3), and stir in ketchup.

In a small casserole heat the wine with the celery, carrot, and onion, all finely chopped (4). Simmer for a few minutes, stirring (5), then add the shrimp or prawn tails, carefully washed, but still in their shells (6). Simmer for about ten minutes. Let cool a little, then shuck by opening their shells with your fingers along the belly (7) and carefully removing the meat (8). Reduce the sauce to just 1/4 cup over a high flame, then strain it through cheesecloth into a bowl (9). Squeeze the cheesecloth to wring out the last drops of juice (10). Add the juice to the mayonnaise (11). Set aside 10 or so whole shrimp and 4 tablespoons of the sauce. Cut the remaining shrimp into small pieces and add them to the remaining sauce (12). Two-piece cocktail servers are ideal for this dish. If you do not have these, you can use ordinary small bowls inside larger ones. Fill lower dish with crushed ice, place the upper dish on top, and lay on a bed of slivered celery hearts (13). Fill each goblet with the shrimp mayonnaise, cover with the reserved mayonnaise (14), and garnish with lettucce leaves (15) and the whole shrimp. Serve at once.

1 Make a mayonnaise by whisking olive oil into the egg yolks, sprinkling on lemon juice now and then.

2 When the sauce is ready, add a small glass of brandy, whisking well...

3 ...then flavor with a few drops of Worcestershire sauce.

4 Heat the white wine in a small casserole with the celery, carrot, and onion, all finely chopped.

5 Bring to the boil and simmer for a few minutes, stirring.

6 Add the shrimp or prawn tails carefully washed but still in their shells.

7 When cooked, shuck by opening the shells at the belly...

8 ...and then carefully removing the meat in one piece.

9 Strain the broth through cheesecloth into a bowl...

10 ...and then wring the cheesecloth to extract the last drops of the juice.

11 Last of all, add the broth to the mayonnaise, whisking well.

12 Set aside several whole shrimp; cut the remainder into thin slices and add them to the larger bowl of mayonnaise.

13 In the upper dish lay thin slivers of celery heart.

14 Fill the dishes with the shrimp mayonnaise and spoon the reserved mayonnaise on top.

15 Garnish each serving with lettuce leaves.

Shrimp cocktail

Shrimp on the skewer

- ■ **Yield: 4 servings**
- ■ **Time needed: 40 minutes**
- ■ **Difficulty: ***

Ingredients: 24 large shrimp (preferably with the heads still attached) 6 tbsp butter, 1 lemon, 1 tsp dry mustard, 1 clove garlic, handful parsley, few drops Worcestershire sauce, about 30 bay leaves or sage leaves, ¼ cup olive oil, salt, pepper.

Finely chop the parsley and garlic. Put the butter, slightly softened, in a bowl and beat with a wooden spoon until creamy. Then add the mustard (1), a few drops of Worcestershire sauce (2), the chopped garlic and parsley, and a few drops of lemon juice. Set aside.

Wash the shrimp very carefully, but keep in the shell; dry in a dish cloth (3). Thread shrimp on long metal skewers, with a bay leaf or sage leaf between each one (4). Brush lightly with oil and put on a hot griddle or beneath a preheated broiler (5). When a dark crust has formed on one side, turn (6) and continue to cook until done, about 5 minutes altogether. Season with salt and pepper, and serve in a platter with the mustard.

1 Cream the softened butter, add the mustard powder...

2 ...and flavor with drops of Worcestershire sauce and finely chopped parsley and garlic.

3 Wash the shrimp carefully but leave in the shell; dry in a dish cloth.

4 Thread the shrimp on skewers, with a bay leaf be tween each one.

5 Arrange the skewers side by side on a hot griddle or beneath a preheated broiler.

6 When a dark crust has formed on one side, turn and cook until done.

Shrimp on the skewer

Mantis shrimp in parsley sauce

- Yield: 4 servings
- Time needed: 40 minutes
- Difficulty: *

Ingredients: 2 lb mantis shrimp or ordinary large shrimp, 1 clove garlic, large handful parsley, ½ onion, 1 bay leaf, ½ lemon, ¼ tsp thyme, 1 cup dry white wine, ⅔ cup olive oil, ½ tsp peppercorns, salt.

Finely chop the parsley and garlic, put in a bowl, and add a pinch each of salt and pepper, ½ cup of the olive oil (1), plus the juice from the half lemon (2). You should have a medium-thick sauce. Set aside.

Wash the shrimp. In a large frying pan, brown the chopped onion in remaining olive oil. Add the shrimp and cook over a high flame, stirring with a wooden spoon. Add wine (3), one cup water, thyme, bay leaf, peppercorns (4), a pinch of salt, and bring to a boil. Cover and simmer slowly 10 minutes. Transfer the shrimp to a deep platter with a skimmer (5), sprinkle with the parsley sauce (6), and serve.

1 Add olive oil to the finely chopped parsley and garlic to make a medium-thick sauce.

2 Add to the sauce the juice of half a lemon, stirring with a wooden spoon until smooth.

3 After sautéing the shrimp with onions, pour in white wine...

4 ...and water, then add thyme, bay leaf, and peppercorns.

5 Once cooked, transfer the shrimp to a deep platter...

6 ...and sprinkle with the prepared parsley sauce.

Mantis shrimp in parsley sauce

Shrimp with curried rice

- **Yield: 4 servings**
- **Time needed: 1¼ hours**
- **Difficulty: ***

Ingredients: 1 lb large shrimp or prawn tails, 6 oz mushrooms, 1½ cups rice, 8 tbsp butter, 1 cup heavy cream, 6 shallots, 6 cups chicken stock, 1 cup dry white wine, about 2 tsp curry powder, 3 tbsp brandy, salt, pepper.

If you are using prawns, remove the heads (1), then gently squeeze the tail shells to release the meat in one piece (2). Pull out vein running through the tail, wash thoroughly, and dry. If you are using shrimp, simply shell and devein.

Wipe the mushrooms clean, using a damp cloth if necessary, and cut into thin slices. In a frying pan melt half the butter and lightly brown 2 finely chopped shallots (3). Add the mushrooms and sauté until golden (4). Add the shrimp (5), sprinkle with the brandy (6), salt, and pepper, simmer for several minutes, then pour on the cream (7). Simmer gently for several minutes to reduce the sauce a little. Set aside.

Now prepare the curried rice. In a casserole sauté remaining shallots in remaining butter. When the shallots are soft but not brown, add the rice (8), and stir with a wooden spoon until the butter is absorbed and the rice is translucent and beginning to brown. Add the curry to taste (9), then pour in the wine (10) and simmer until nearly evaporated. Add the boiling stock (11) and bring rice to a boil. Cover the pan (12) and place in an oven preheated to 350° (13). Cook the rice (without stirring) for 18 minutes, then remove from the oven and fluff with a fork (14). Arrange the rice in a deep platter and put the shrimp and sauce in the center (15). Serve at once.

1 If you are using prawns, detach the heads...

2 ...and gently squeeze the tail shells to remove the meat in one piece.

3 In a frying pan lightly brown two finely chopped shallots in 4 tablespoons butter....

4 ...add the mushrooms, and mix well with a wooden spoon.

5 After a minute or two add the shrimp or prawn tails.

6 Sprinkle a small glass of brandy over the shrimp and let it partly evaporate.

7 When the shrimp are almost cooked, add the cream and reduce until thickened.

8 Gently sauté chopped shallots in remaining butter, add the rice...

9 ...stir until the butter is absorbed, and then add the curry powder.

10 Pour in a glass of white wine and simmer until nearly evaporated, stirring all the while...

11 ...then add the boiling stock.

12 Bring to a boil over high flame, cover...

13 ...and bake in an oven preheated to 350° without stirring at all.

14 After about 18 minutes remove the rice from the oven and fluff with a fork.

15 Arrange the rice on a platter and put the shrimp in the center.

Shrimp with curried rice

Shrimp in paprika and brandy

- **Yield: 4 servings**
- **Time needed: 25 minutes (plus 1 hour for marinade)**
- **Difficulty: ***

Ingredients: 1 1/2 lb shrimp, 1 clove garlic, handful parsley, 1 tbsp tomato sauce, 2 tsp stock or water, 1/2 tsp paprika, 3 tbsp oil, 1/2 cup brandy, pepper, salt.

Shell and devein the shrimp, then thoroughly wash and dry. Place them in a bowl, add brandy, cover, and let marinate in a cool place for about an hour.

Finely chop the parsley and the garlic and fry briefly in a pan with the oil. Add the shrimp, drained, and cook over a high flame, stirring constantly with a wooden spoon. Season with salt and pepper and sprinkle with the paprika. Remove from heat. In a small pan, warm the brandy used as the marinade, pour it over the shrimp, and ignite it. When the flames have gone out, mix in the tomato sauce diluted with water or stock and simmer the sauce for a few minutes to reduce. Serve with boiled potatoes if you wish.

Fried shrimp

- **Yield: 4 servings**
- **Time needed: 1/2 hour**
- **Difficulty: ***

Ingredients: 1 1/2 lb large shrimp, 2 eggs, 1/2 cup flour, 3 tbsp beer, 1 lemon, oil for frying, salt.

Peel and devein the shrimp, then wash and dry thoroughly. In a bowl, beat the eggs with the beer and a pinch of salt. Roll the shrimp in flour, shaking off the excess, and then dip in the egg and beer batter. Deep fry in 2-3 inches hot oil until golden, then drain. Serve at once with lemon wedges.

Shrimp in herbs

- **Yield: 4 servings**
- **Time needed: 1/2 hour**
- **Difficulty: ***

Ingredients: 1 1/2 lb shrimp, 3-4 tbsp mixed finely minced fresh herbs (basil, tarragon, parsley, etc.), 1 clove garlic, 1/2 cup dry white wine, 1 cup olive oil, pinch paprika, pepper, salt.

Peel and devein the shrimp, then thoroughly wash and dry. In a large frying pan brown the crushed garlic in the oil, then discard the garlic. Add the shrimp and cook for a few minutes, stirring. Add salt and pepper, the paprika, and all the herbs, pour in the white wine, and simmer gently for 2-3 minutes. Remove from the heat and serve at once.

Baked stuffed jumbo shrimp

- **Yield: 4 servings**
- **Time needed: 40 minutes**
- **Difficulty: ***

Ingredients: 12 jumbo shrimp, 2/3 cup toasted bread crumbs, 1 egg yolk, handful parsley, 1 minced clove garlic, 1 lemon, 4 tbsp olive oil, pepper, salt.

Wash the shrimp thoroughly and dry. With a sharp knife, make a lengthwise cut along the belly of each one, being careful not to cut through the shell on the other side and thus detach the two halves.

Place bread crumbs in a bowl and add half the oil, the egg yolk, the parsley, finely chopped, garlic, and a pinch each of salt and pepper. Fill shrimp with stuffing, arrange in an oiled baking dish, add salt, and moisten with remaining 2 tablespoons oil. Bake in a 350° oven for about 20 minutes. Before serving, sprinkle with lemon juice.

Crab fritters

- **Yield: 4 servings**
- **Time needed: 1/2 hour**
- **Difficulty: ***

Ingredients: 1 lb canned crabmeat, 2 beaten eggs, 1 tsp flour, 2 tbsp bread crumbs, 2 tbsp finely chopped parsley, 1/2 clove minced garlic, 1 lemon, oil for frying, salt, pepper.

Drain the crabmeat and shred. Put crabmeat in a bowl and add bread crumbs, beaten eggs, flour, parsley, garlic, and a pinch each salt and pepper. If the mixture is runny, add a few more bread crumbs. Heat 2-3 inches oil and drop the mixture into the oil by spoonfuls. Fry 2-3 minutes or until golden. Drain on absorbent paper and sprinkle with a little lemon juice. Serve at once with a tossed salad.

Mollusks

T he term "mollusk" describes creatures that have soft boneless bodies. Mollusks can be divided into two types: those that have a sac-like body from which the head and tentacles emerge, and those that are enclosed in a shell.

The former, called cephalopods, are divided into two groups: the octopods, having eight tentacles (the octopus); and the decapods, having ten tentacles, two of which are longer than the rest (the various squid). Both groups have large eyes and suckers on their tentacles. Squid also have a calcareous bone inside the body and a sac containing a blackish liquid or ink, that is expelled in moments of danger to camouflage the animal.

The shelled mollusks can also be divided into two types: the univalve mollusks and the bivalves. The univalves have a single shell, generally spiral in shape, as in the case of the snail. The bivalves, on the other hand, have two shells joined at a hinge; the bottom shell is larger and convex and holds the organism, while the upper shell is smaller and flat and acts as a lid. The head of the bivalve is not separate from the body, and they are not truly locomotive. To make up for this they have powerful muscles in the hinge of their shells so that they can shut tightly in the event of danger. The commonest bivalve mollusks are the oysters, the mussels, the scallops, and the various clams. By the way, the sea urchin is also considered a mollusk, although it does not have a proper shell but rather a tough casing covered with sharp spines all too familiar to swimmers.

Mollusks are fairly low in calories and contain very few carbohydrates, proteins, or fats, but they are extremely high in minerals (particularly phosphorus) and vitamins such as A. If improperly cooked, mollusks can be tough and hard to digest.

Preparation and cooking

Mollusks with shells — The most important thing to remember about all mollusks bought in the shell is that they must be alive when purchased. The shells should either be tightly closed or they should close at once if touched. The shells should not be too light in weight for this is a sign that the mollusk may be dead. It is worth being particularly careful when choosing seafood that is to be eaten raw. Buy only from a reliable fishmonger whose shellfish are harvested from inspected state beds that are unpolluted.

Cleaning shellfish can be a time-consuming business requiring considerable patience because it is important to remove vegetation, grit, and clinging barnacles on the shells.

First, wash each shell individually under running water and scrub it clean with a wire brush and, if it should be necessary, scrape off deposits with a short-bladed knife.

Then soak the mollusks in salt water for up to 12 hours so that they will expel both impurities and sand. Considerable skill is required to open some shellfish. One example is the oyster, which is often eaten raw and should be opened shortly before it is eaten. A special oyster knife with a strong triangular blade is almost a necessity. Alternatively, oysters and other mollusks can be placed very briefly in a 500° oven until they open just a crack. Any shells that do not open should be discarded.

Clams and scallops, as well as oysters, can be eaten raw with lemon juice.

All shellfish can be used to make very excellent sauces, soups, sautés, mixed grills, deep-fried fritters, or kabobs.

Squid and octopus — When you buy squid or octopus be sure that the body is firm, the color bright, and the tentacles curled. The cleaning operation starts with the removal of the thin film of skin. Next remove the eyes and mouth (or horny beak), the insides, and the inner bone in squid, and turn the sac inside out and wash it thoroughly. The small sacs containing the black and yellow liquid can be used in certain dishes. It is a good idea to pound the octopus with a mallet to soften the fibers and make the meat more tender and digestible. Sometimes this is done by the fishmonger beforehand. It is wise to parboil all species of octopus before cooking. Either simmer briefly in salted water mixed with a light court bouillon, or else hold by a tentacle and dip briefly into boiling water two or three times. Then put in a pan and simmer until cooked.

Squid are excellent when cut into small pieces, rolled in flour or batter, and fried. They are best served piping hot with plenty of lemon juice. Stewing is another good way of cooking squid. Smaller squid are cooked whole, while larger ones are cut into pieces or rings. Place in a pan, preferably earthenware, with oil, garlic, and onion, white or red wine, and herbs; tomato purée may also be added.

Squid can be cooked on the grill. Reserving the tentacles for other dishes, cut bodies into three or four pieces, and marinate in oil, lemon juice, salt, and pepper. Place on the grill and baste every so often with the marinade. Squid can also be stuffed with a mixture of chopped tentacles and a variety of other ingredients such as bread crumbs, grated cheese, parsley, eggs, and so on. They can then be stewed or baked in a tasty sauce of herbs and tomatoes.

Freezing

All mollusks can be satisfactorily frozen, but octopus and squid take particularly well to freezing. Squid that is to be frozen must be as fresh as possible. Thoroughly clean, wash, and dry, then place in a small plastic bag in a quantity sufficient for one meal (1). Press with your hands to flatten into a single layer and prevent from forming a single block (2). Squeeze all the air out of the bag, sucking the air out with a straw if necessary (3). Seal (4) and lay flat in the freezer. If you have frozen several bags of squid or octopus, put all the bags into a single rigid box to protect them and to allow you to find them quickly and easily. They cannot be kept frozen longer than 3 to 4 months. Thaw in the refrigerator. They should only partly defrost if they are to be stewed

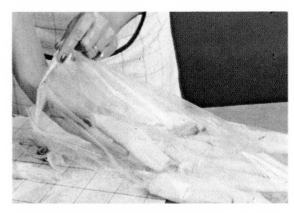

1 Squid and octopus: after cleaning, washing, and drying squid, place in a plastic bag...

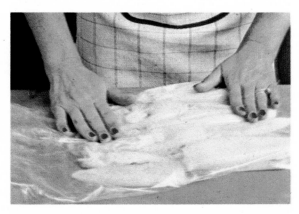

2 ...then press the bag flat with your hands to stop the squid from forming a block.

3 Use a straw to suck any remaining air out of the bag...

4 ...then tie with string or a plastic fastener.

or boiled, but they could completely thaw if they are to be fried.

In the case of mollusks with shells, too, be sure that they are fresh and uncontaminated. Wash and scrape mussels and clams thoroughly, then put over a hot flame to open. Remove the meat and strain the liquid produced during cooking through a cheesecloth (5). Now place in a small bag the amount of mollusks required either for a single portion or a whole meal (6), then add a little of the strained liquid (7). Seal the bag after first sucking out the air with a straw (8). Label and freeze. Shellfish can only be frozen for 3 to 4 months. Defrost

in the refrigerator either partly or completely, depending on the dish you have in mind. Oysters need a rather special freezing procedure if they are to stay good and fresh. It is worth buying them in quantity when they are at a good price. Wash the oysters several times in cold water, then open, reserving and straining the liquid in the shells. Soak the oysters briefly in lightly salted cold water so that they will expel any sand, drain, and dry on a cloth. Then seal in small sacks, 4 to 6 oysters in each one, adding some of the strained liquid. Place in the freezer. After thawing, the oyster should be cooked rather than served raw.

5 Shellfish: after heating the mollusks to open, strain their liquid...

6 ...and put the mollusks into bags.

7 Pour into each bag a few tablespoons of the strained liquid...

8 ...suck out any air inside with a straw, and seal.

Oysters on the half-shell

■ **Yield: 4 servings**
■ **Time needed: 20 minutes**
■ **Difficulty: ***

Ingredients: 12-16 very fresh oysters, 2 lemons, 8 slices bread, 4 tbsp unsalted butter.

First, scrub the shells to remove any algae or sand (1), then wash and dry. Using a special oyster knife with a short triangular blade, open as follows: protecting your left hand with a folded dish cloth, grip the oyster by the pointed end. Locate a space between the shells, insert the point of the knife (2), and twist the blade until the shell opens. Discard the flat upper shell to which the mollusk is not attached (3).

Spread the slices of bread with butter (4). Arrange the oysters on the half-shell on a glass plate (5), garnishing with lemon slices and a carved half lemon in the middle (6). Sprinkle with lemon juice (7). Crush a few ice cubes in a cloth (8), put the ice on a large plate (9), and put the plate of oysters on top (10). Serve at once with the slices of buttered bread.

1 Scrub the oysters with a stiff brush to remove any algae or sand.

2 Insert the knife between the shells, twist the blade...

3 ...and open the oyster completely, removing the upper shell.

4 Spread the slices of bread lightly with slightly softened butter.

5 Arrange the oysters on a glass plate...

6 ...garnishing with slices of lemon and a carved half lemon in the middle.

7 Sprinkle the oysters with the juice of the remaining lemon half.

8 Put some ice cubes in a cloth and crush.

9 Lay the crushed ice on a large glass plate...

10 ...and then put the plate of oysters on top. Serve at once.

Oysters on the half-shell

Mariscada

- **Yield: 4 servings**
- **Time needed: 1 1/2 hour**
- **Difficulty: ***

Ingredients: 3 lb mussels, 3 lb steamer clams, 1 1/4 lb shrimp, 1 lb peeled tomatoes, 1 finely chopped onion, 1 cup dry white wine, handful parsley, 1 clove garlic, pinch oregano, salt, pepper, toasted bread.

Scrub the mussel shells clean and wash repeatedly in running water. Wash the clams thoroughly too. Wash and dry shrimp but leave in the shell. Put the mussels and clams into a large pan (1) and open over a hot flame (2). Transfer with a skimmer to another pan (3). Add the shrimp (4), onions (5), the tomatoes either finely chopped or puréed (6), half the parsley chopped finely with the garlic (7), a little salt, and pepper (8). Put the pan over moderate heat and after a few minutes pour in the wine and let it reduce by half. Then add 1 cup water (9) and oregano and simmer for 40 minutes, stirring occasionally (10). A few minutes before taking the pan off the heat, sprinkle with the rest of the parsley, finely chopped. Serve if desired with slices of toast.

1 After thoroughly cleaning and washing mussels and clams, place in a large pan over high flame...

2 ...and stir until opened.

3 Transfer with a skimmer to another large pan.

4 Add the shrimp, still in shells, but washed and dried.

5 Add the finely chopped onion (more or less, according to taste).

6 Now add the peeled tomatoes, either finely chopped or puréed.

7 Chop half the parsley finely with the garlic and sprinkle over the dish...

8 ...then add a little salt and pepper.

9 Put the pan over the flame and pour in a cup each of wine and water.

10 Cook the mariscada for 40 minutes, stirring every so often with a wooden spoon.

Mariscada

Clam soup

- **Yield: 4 servings**
- **Time needed: 1 hour**
- **Difficulty: ***

Ingredients: 4½ lb steamer clams, 1 lb canned or peeled tomatoes, large handful chopped parsley, 3 cloves crushed garlic, 8 slices whole-wheat bread, 4 tbsp olive oil, salt, pepper.

Wash the clams repeatedly under running water, then drain in a colander and set aside to dry.

In a large deep pan lightly brown the crushed garlic in oil (1). Add the tomatoes, finely chopped (2), a pinch of salt and pepper, and simmer for about 10 minutes, stirring now and then. Add the clams (3) and cook over a high flame until the shells have opened (4). Just before removing them from the heat, sprinkle with the parsley (5).

Lightly toast the slices of bread (if you prefer, you can sauté the bread in a little olive oil). Arrange bread in soup bowls and, using a large ladle, fill the bowls with the clams and their broth (6).

If you like spicy dishes, you can sprinkle a little Cayenne pepper over each bowl.

1 In a deep pan brown the crushed garlic in oil...

2 ...then add the chopped peeled tomatoes.

3 When the mixture has reduced a little add the washed clams...

4 ...and cook over a hot flame, stirring constantly until they have all opened.

5 A couple of minutes before removing from the flame, sprinkle with chopped parsley.

6 Arrange the slices of bread in soup bowls and ladle in the clams and their broth.

Clam soup

Shellfish soup

- ■ **Yield: 4 servings**
- ■ **Time needed: 1 hour**
- ■ **Difficulty: ***

Ingredients: 4 ½ lb clams and mussels, 1 lb chopped peeled tomatoes, handful chopped parsley, 1 minced clove garlic, 1 small dried red chili pepper, 1 chopped onion, 1 cup dry white wine, 8 slices whole-wheat bread, ½ cup olive oil, salt, pepper.

Wash the shellfish repeatedly in running water, scrubbing the shells with a brush if necessary. Pour into a large pan and open over a hot flame, drain, and remove the empty shell halves (1). Set aside. Strain the liquid in the pan through cheesecloth and reserve.

Lightly brown the garlic and the chopped onion in oil (2), add the hot pepper, the reserved shellfish broth, and wine (3), and reduce slightly. Add the tomatoes (4) and a pinch each of salt and pepper, and return the shellfish to the pan (5). Heat almost to a simmer, sprinkle with the parsley (6), and remove at once from the flame. Arrange the bread in soup bowls and ladle on the soup.

1 Open the shellfish in a frying pan set over a hot flame and remove the empty shell halves.

2 Lightly brown the onion and garlic in oil.

3 Add the hot pepper, the shellfish broth, and the wine, and reduce.

4 Add the chopped peeled tomatoes...

5 ...then return the shellfish to the pan and cook just long enough to heat through.

6 Before removing from the flame, sprinkle the soup with plenty of chopped parsley.

Broiled mussels

- ■ **Yield: 4 servings**
- ■ **Time needed: 1¼ hours**
- ■ **Difficulty: ***

Ingredients: 20-24 very large mussels, handful chopped parsley, 1 clove minced garlic, ½ tsp thyme or marjoram, ½ cup very fine bread crumbs, about ½ cup olive oil, 1 tbsp grated Romano cheese (optional), salt, pepper.

Scrub the mussel shells with a stiff brush and wash repeatedly under running water. Pour mussels into a large pan and stir continually over a hot flame until opened (1). Remove the empty shell halves (2), and arrange mussels in a lightly oiled baking dish (3).

In a bowl mix the bread crumbs, garlic, parsley, and thyme (4). Add salt and pepper and about 2 tablespoons of the oil, drop by drop (5). The mixture should be thick. If you wish you can also add a tablespoon of grated Romano cheese. Fill the shells with the mixture, surrounding rather than covering the mussel itself (6). It is a good idea to use plenty of stuffing because it tends to diminish during cooking. Drizzle with remaining oil and brown under a hot broiler for just a minute or two.

1 Pour the well washed mussels into a large pan and stir over a hot flame until opened.

2 Drain and remove the empty shell halves.

3 Arrange the mussels in a lightly oiled baking dish.

4 In a bowl mix the bread crumbs, chopped parsley, garlic, and thyme...

5 ...then add enough oil to obtain a thick mixture.

6 Fill the half-shells with the mixture, leaving the mussels exposed in the center.

Broiled mussels

Stuffed scallops

■ **Yield: 4 servings**
■ **Time needed: 1 ½ hours**
■ **Difficulty: ***

Ingredients: 16 sea scallops, ½ lb cleaned squid, large handful parsley, 2 cloves garlic, 1 small onion, 1 small stalk celery, ½ cup fresh bread crumbs, 1 cup dry white wine, 1 small dried red chili pepper, ⅓ cup olive oil, salt, pepper.

Most people will start with cleaned scallops, but if you are lucky enough to be using scallops in the shell, here's how you deal with them. Scrub the scallop shells thoroughly with a wet, stiff brush (1), then wash repeatedly under running water. In a large pan put the onion and celery, cut into slices, a few sprigs of chopped parsley, and half the white wine (2). Arrange the scallops close together in the pan (3), and place over a high flame until the shells open just a crack. Remove from the flame and open the shells completely, then slip the blade of a knife underneath the scallops and detach from the shell (4). Remove the greyish beard around each scallop as well as the small blackish sac attached to the muscle (5). Then wash the scallops in plenty of cold water and drain. Set aside.

Cut the squid into slivers (6). Chop the remaining parsley finely with the garlic and chili pepper, turn half this mixture into a pan, and brown lightly in 3 tablespoons of the oil. Add the squid (7) and cook slowly for a few minutes. Pour in the remaining white wine (8) and cook over a moderate flame for 10-15 minutes.

In a bowl combine the scallops, a little chopped parsley (9), and the squid and their juice (10). Mix well and taste, adding salt if necessary. Fill 16 scallop shells with the stuffing (11), add plenty of freshly ground pepper (12), and sprinkle generously with bread crumbs (13). Sprinkle with the rest of the chopped parsley (14) and drizzle remaining oil over the top of the dish (15). Place the shells on a large baking sheet and bake in a 425° oven for about 15 minutes, or until lightly browned. Serve at once.

1 Scrub the scallop shells well with a wet, stiff brush.

2 In a large pan put the sliced onion and celery and a little parsley and white wine...

3 ...then place the scallops side by side and heat till open.

4 Pry the shells completely open and detach each scallop from the shell with a knife.

5 Remove the greyish beard and the small blackish sac attached to the muscle.

6 Wash the squid and slice finely.

7 Lightly brown the parsley, garlic, and red pepper in oil, add the squid...

8 ...stir for a moment, and then add a little white wine.

9 Put the scallops into a bowl, flavor with a little finely chopped parsley and garlic...

10 ....and add the cooked squid with their juice.

11 Fill scallop shells with the stuffing...

12 ...season with freshly ground pepper...

13 ...and sprinkle the top with bread crumbs.

14 Finish the dish by sprinkling chopped parsley over it...

15 ...drizzle with olive oil, and brown in the oven.

Stuffed scallops

Octopus stew

- **Yield: 4 servings**
- **Time needed: 2 hours**
- **Difficulty: ***

Ingredients: 2 lb octopus, 1 lb peeled tomatoes, 1 small dried red chili pepper, handful parsley, 3 tbsp vinegar, ½ cup olive oil, salt.

Fresh octopus must first be pounded with a wooden mallet before cooking to break down the fibers and make the meat tender and more digestible. Next remove the thin skin, peeling from the bottom of the sac (1) and working toward the tips of the tentacles. Pull away and remove the eyes and the horny beak, pushing upwards with your thumbs at the base of the tentacles (2). If the octopus is very large, separate the body sac from the tentacles. Finally, squeeze out the innards along with the sacs containing the black ink and the yellow liquid, then turn the body inside out and wash thoroughly. Bring plenty of salted water to a boil, add vinegar, and blanch the octopus for 3 minutes (3). Drain thoroughly.

Put the octopus in an earthenware pot (4), add the chili pepper, chopped parsley (5), peeled tomatoes, either chopped or cubed (6), oil (7), and a pinch of salt. Cover the pot with two sheets of baking paper (8) or aluminum foil. Press the lid down tight, and tie the paper or foil to the rim of the casserole with kitchen twine (9). The paper stops the juice from evaporating during cooking; octopus must always be cooked in a tightly covered pot or pan. Put the pan in a 350° oven and cook the octopus for a good hour. Instead of stirring, shake the pot gently from time to time to prevent sticking. When cooked, let stew stand at least 15 minutes before serving. This dish, which is excellent hot, warm, or cold, is traditionally served in the pot in which it was cooked.

1 Remove the skin, peeling from the bottom of the body sac.

2 To remove the horny beak, push up with your thumbs at the base of the tentacles.

3 Scald octopus in salted boiling water with a little vinegar added, then drain...

4 ....and place in a large pot, preferably earthenware.

5 Add the chili pepper, chopped parsley...

6 ...chopped or cubed tomatoes...

7 ...olive oil and a pinch of salt.

8 Cover the casserole with two sheets of baking paper or aluminum foil.

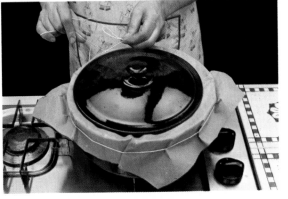

9 Lay the lid on top and tie paper to the rim of the casserole with kitchen twine.

Octopus stew

Ligurian style squid

- Yield: 1 liter/2 pint preserving jar
- Time needed: 2 hours
- Difficulty: *

Ingredients: About 4 1/2 lb small squid, 2 cloves crushed garlic, 3-4 small dried red chili peppers, 1/2 lb pitted green olives, 1 chopped onion, 1 chopped carrot, 1 chopped celery, 2 bay leaves, large pinch thyme, about 1 quart white vinegar, 1 cup olive oil, 1/8 tsp peppercorns, salt.

Clean, skin, and wash squid (1). Plunge in boiling salted water, adding a little vinegar plus the chopped vegetables (2). Boil 10 minutes or so, drain (3), and dry on a dish cloth (4). In a pan, lightly brown the garlic in the oil, add the squid (5) and olives (6), and cook for 5 minutes, stirring. Set aside and let cool.

In another casserole bring the vinegar to a boil with a pinch of salt, a few peppercorns, the thyme, and bay leaves (7). Put the squid and olives in a canning jar (8), cover with the boiling vinegar (9) and, straining out the garlic, add the oil used in cooking the squid (10). Last of all lay the chili peppers on top. Sterilize the jar for half an hour. Store in a cool dark place.

1 Clean the squid thoroughly and peel off the skin starting at the bottom of the body sac.

2 Parboil in plenty of salted water with vinegar and chopped vegetables added.

3 After about 10 minutes transfer to a bowl with a skimmer...

4 ...and then dry carefully with a dish cloth.

5 In a pan lightly brown the garlic in a cup of oil and add the squid...

6 ....and the pitted green olives.

7 Bring vinegar to a boil with a pinch of salt, some peppercorns, thyme, and bay leaves.

8 Fill a canning jar with the squid and olives...

9 ...pour in enough boiling vinegar to cover...

10 ...and then add the oil in which the squid have been cooked, omitting the garlic.

Ligurian style squid.

Stuffed squid

- ■ **Yield: 4 servings**
- ■ **Time needed: 2 hours**
- ■ **Difficulty: ***

Ingredients: 12-16 large whole squid, 1½ cups dry bread crumbs, 6 anchovy fillets, 1 tbsp capers, handful parsley, 1 clove garlic, 1 chopped onion, 1 lb puréed or chopped peeled tomatoes, ½ cup milk, 1 cup dry white wine, 5 tbsp olive oil, salt, pepper.

Clean the squid thoroughly and remove the bone inside the body (1). Starting at one end of the body, peel off the thin skin (2), then carefully detach the cluster of tentacles from the body (3).

Place the bread crumbs in a bowl, cover with milk (4), and set aside to soften. Chop the anchovies, capers, parsley (reserve about a tablespoon), and garlic, and add to the bread crumbs (5). Season with salt and pepper, add 2 tablespoons of oil, and mix well (6). If you like you can add various other ingredients to the stuffing. For example, you can replace some of the bread crumbs with leftover fish or shellfish or with the chopped tentacles of the squid. Fill the squid with the stuffing (7) generously. With a large needle sew up the openings of the squid bodies (8).

Using the remaining oil, sauté the onion until soft along with the reserved chopped parsley in a large pan. Add the squid and their tentacles (9) and brown over a high flame, stirring frequently. Pour in white wine (10), let it reduce by half over a high flame, then add the tomatoes (11). Cover the pan and cook over a medium flame for about 45 minutes. Do not remove the lid during cooking, but shake the pan lightly every so often to keep the squid from sticking to the bottom. Serve the stuffed squid with freshly cooked polenta, which will go well with the plentiful sauce.

1 Clean the squid thoroughly and remove the bone from the body.

2 Starting from one end of the body, peel off the thin skin...

3 ...and detach the tentacles from the body.

4 Place the bread crumbs in a bowl and cover with milk.

5 Chop the anchovies, capers, parsley, and garlic and add to the bread crumbs.

6 Season with salt and pepper, add a little oil, and mix well.

7 Fill the squid with the stuffing.

8 With a large needle and strong white cotton thread, sew up the openings of the bodies.

9 Arrange the stuffed squid and their tentacles in a pan containing sautéed onion and chopped parsley.

10 After browning the squid over a hot flame pour in a glass of white wine...

11 ...allow to reduce a little and then add tomatoes.

Stuffed squid

Fried squid

- ■ **Yield: 4 servings**
- ■ **Time needed:** ¹/₂ **hour**
- ■ **Difficulty:** *

Ingredients: 2 lb squid, ¹/₂ cup flour, oil for frying, 1 lemon, salt.

Remove the long thin cartilaginous bone from the body of each squid (1), detach the tentacles (2), and squeeze out the viscera. Peel off the thin dark skin (3). Open the cluster of tentacles by pressing lightly upwards with your fingers (4). Clean remaining squid in the same manner (5). Cut the bodies into rings using a large sharp knife (6). Wash and dry the rings carefully in a dish cloth (7).

Place the squid on a large sieve, cover with flour, and shake lightly to dust the rings evenly (8), letting any excess flour fall on the table. Heat 1 inch oil in a large pan and fry the squid a few pieces at a time until golden. Be careful not to cook squid too much or it will become hard and rubbery. Drain on a sheet of absorbent paper (9) and sprinkle with salt (10). Serve at once with lemon wedges.

1 Remove the bone from the squid...

2 ...detach the tentacles from the body...

3 ...and last of all remove the dark skin covering both the tentacles and the body.

4 Pressing gently upwards, open out the tentacles.

5 Clean remaining squid in the same manner.

6 Using a large sharp knife, cut the squid into rings.

7 Dry the squid carefully on a dish cloth.

8 Coat the rings by sprinkling with flour and shaking on a large sieve.

9 Fry in very hot oil and drain on absorbent paper when golden.

10 While still hot, sprinkle with salt.

Fried squid

Razor clam soup

- **Yield: 4 servings**
- **Time needed: 1 hour**
- **Difficulty: ***

Ingredients: 2 lb razor clams, 2 cloves garlic, handful parsley, 2-3 fresh ripe tomatoes, 8 slices whole-wheat bread, 1 quart fish stock or 3 cups bottled clam juice and 1 cup water, 3 tbsp olive oil, pepper.

With a stiff brush scrub the razor clams to remove any sand, then wash repeatedly under running water. Place in a pan, add $1/4$ cup water, and set over high flame. Remove clams as they open, discarding the empty shells. Strain the cooking liquid through cheesecloth and set aside. Chop the garlic with the parsley and fry gently in a casserole in the oil. Peel the tomatoes after scalding for a moment in boiling water, chop finely, and then add to the casserole along with the strained juice from the clams. Bring to a boil, stir the reserved clams into the sauce, and simmer for a few minutes.

In another fairly large casserole bring to a boil the fish stock and add the razor clams and their sauce. Stir well. Arrange the bread in the soup bowls and ladle the clam soup over it. Add pepper and serve.

Smothered mussels

- **Yield: 4 servings**
- **Time needed: 1 1/4 hours**
- **Difficulty: ***

Ingredients: 3 1/2 lb large mussels, 1 clove minced garlic, handful chopped parsley, 1 tbsp grated Romano cheese, 4 eggs, 1 cup milk, 2 tbsp olive oil, salt, pepper.

Scrub the mussels with a stiff brush, wash repeatedly under running water, and soak in salted water for at least 10 minutes. Drain and open with the point of a knife, working over a bowl to reserve the juice. Discard the empty shells and arrange the mussels on the half-shell in a large baking dish. Strain the reserved juice through cheesecloth and pour over the mussels. Moisten with oil, a little salt, and plenty of pepper. In a bowl beat the eggs with milk and add the cheese, the chopped parsley, garlic, and a little salt. Put the mussels over high heat. When they start to boil, pour on the beaten egg mixture, covering them completely, and bake in a 400° oven until the eggs are firm, about 30 minutes.

Risotto with squid

- **Yield: 4 servings**
- **Time needed: 2 hours**
- **Difficulty: ***

Ingredients: 1 1/4 lb squid, 1 cup rice, 1 chopped onion, 2 cloves minced garlic, handful parsley, a few fresh basil leaves or 1/2 tsp dried basil, 1 lb puréed peeled tomatoes, 1/2 cup dry white wine, 3 tbsp olive oil, salt, pepper.

Clean the squid, remove the bone from the body, peel off the thin skin, and detach the tentacles from the body. Set ink sacs aside, cut the bodies into slivers, and chop the tentacles. In a casserole, gently fry the onion, garlic, parsley, and basil in oil. When the onions are soft add the squid slivers and tentacles, mix well, and cook slowly for several minutes. Pour in the white wine, let it reduce a little, then add the puréed peeled tomatoes, a pinch each of salt and pepper, and 1 quart water. Bring to a boil and simmer slowly for about an hour.

Pour the rice into the casserole, mix well, and cook until tender, stirring occasionally and adding more boiling water if the rice dries out before it is cooked. A few minutes before removing the rice from the flame, add the ink obtained by rupturing the sacs with the back of a spoon.

Squid with artichokes

- **Yield: 4 servings**
- **Time needed: 1 1/4 hours**
- **Difficulty: ***

Ingredients: 1 1/2 lb squid, 4 artichoke hearts, 3 tbsp lemon juice, 1 clove minced garlic, 1 small chopped onion, handful chopped parsley, 1 lemon, 1/2 cup dry white wine, 1 cup chicken stock, 3 tbsp olive oil, salt, pepper.

Clean the squid, removing the bones and skin, wash, and dry. Cut the artichoke hearts into thin slices, and cover with 4 cups water to which lemon juice has been added. In the oil, fry the onion, garlic, and parsley until the onion is soft. Add the artichokes and squid, mix well, pour the wine and stock in, and season with salt and pepper.

Cook over a medium flame in a covered pan for about 30 minutes or until the squid is tender. Serve hot.

Spaghetti with clams

- ■ **Yield: 4 servings**
- ■ **Time needed: 1 hour**
- ■ **Difficulty: ***

Ingredients: 2 lb very fresh steamer clams, 1 lb spaghetti, 1¼ lb very ripe fresh tomatoes, 2 cloves crushed garlic, 3 tbsp olive oil, salt, pepper, handful coarsely chopped parsley.

Wash the clams very thoroughly under running water and place in a large pan over high heat. As soon as they open, drain and remove about two-thirds of the clams from the shells, leaving the remainder attached. Strain the clam broth in the pan through cheesecloth.

In a small casserole heat the oil, add the crushed garlic, and brown lightly. Add the clam juice and reduce on a hot flame until just a few tablespoons remain. Scald the tomatoes for a moment in boiling water, then peel. Slice in half, squeeze out the seeds, and cut into pieces. Add the tomatoes to the reduced clam juice, season with a little freshly ground pepper and a small pinch of salt, and simmer the sauce for 10-15 minutes.

Now add the clams (including those on the half-shell) and simmer for a few more minutes. Cook the spaghetti, drain, and cover with the clam sauce and the chopped parsley.

Spaghetti with clams

STUFFED VEGETABLES

Hot Stuffed Vegetables

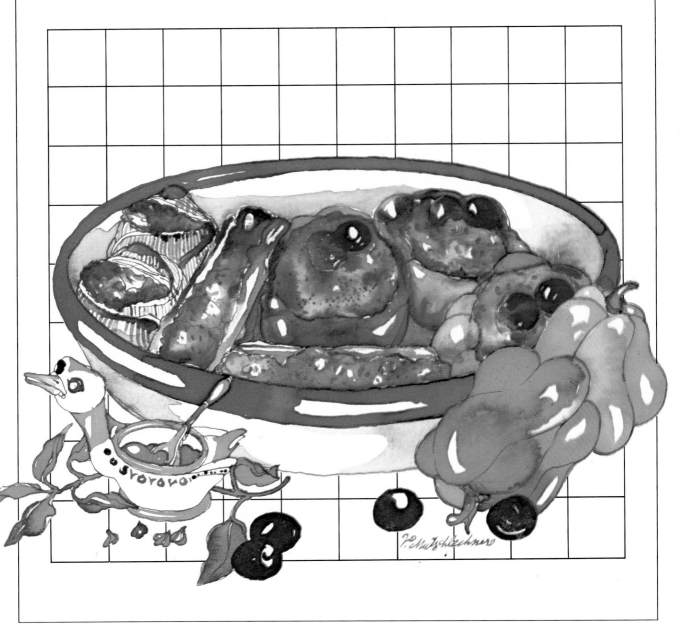

Man's first food on earth, vegetables, are an important source of minerals, vitamins, and enzymes, all indispensable for our health. In Italy, where both cultivated and wild vegetables flourish, they play an especially big role. But why a chapter devoted exclusively to stuffed vegetables? We felt that in a step-by-step cookbook such as this, we wanted to go beyond the usual basic recipes and spend time on more elaborate preparations in which vegetables are stuffed with various fillings and served as tempting antipasti, appetizing first courses, or savory accompaniments to the main course.

Vegetables can be divided into three groups according to the part of them that is used. In the first group are flowering and leafy vegetables, including cabbage and other greens, zucchini blossoms, and artichokes. In the second group are vegetables prized for their roots and stalks, such as onions, fennel, potatoes, cardoons, celery, and beets. The third group comprises tomatoes, squash, eggplants, and peppers, all of which are the fruits of the plant and are particularly well suited to stuffing. In a category by themselves are mushrooms, whose large caps are perfect for a delicate stuffing.

Stuffed vegetables are usually baked in a casserole dish and can often be brought from oven to table in the same container. They are frequently covered with a béchamel sauce and sprinkled with bread crumbs or grated cheese, though they can also be dipped in batter and fried or cooked slowly in tomato sauce. In all cases, the result is a very tasty dish which can also be economical if made with leftovers.

Stuffed onions with tomato sauce

How to stuff vegetables

Preliminaries — Before stuffing, the vegetables must be washed thoroughly under running water to remove every trace of dirt. Be careful, though, not to soak them in water or they will lose many of their nutrients. The exception here is the delicate zucchini flower, which should be washed quickly inside and out after the pistil is removed, and then gently shaken so that it doesn't wilt.

Some vegetables are not washed but scrubbed instead with a small stiff brush or scraped with a sharp knife. Mushrooms are only wiped with a damp cloth, because they are very porous and soft and would absorb too much water if washed. Most vegetables are cooked with their skins on to preserve nutrients. After trimming, some vegetables such as artichokes, cardoons, and Jerusalem artichokes should be immersed in acidulated water (water to which lemon juice or vinegar has been added) to keep them from turning brown.

To prepare artichokes, remove the tough outer leaves, the thorny tips, and the central choke before stuffing. The stringy filaments, the leaves, and the tough ends are removed from cardoons, celery, and fennel. Leafy greens, including cabbage, are cleaned leaf by leaf and soaked for a few minutes in a bowl of water to which a little vinegar or baking soda has been added. The soda acts as a disinfectant and also helps the greens to maintain their color during cooking.

Precooking — It is necessary to precook almost all vegetables that are to be stuffed either by simmering in water or by steaming. Those vegetables that must keep their light color, such as cardoons, celery, or fennel, and those that should remain green, such as artichokes, are precooked with a little so-called "special whitener". This is made by mixing about a teaspoon of flour with a little water and then adding, little by little, vinegar or lemon juice, and butter or another fat. Steaming is generally the best way to precook vegetables as they keep their shape better and lose fewer vitamins when steamed than when boiled.

How to stuff vegetables — Vegetables can be divided into two groups: those that must be hollowed out before filling and those that can be stuffed as they are. Potatoes, onions, zucchini, eggplants, and tomatoes are in the first group. If they have been previously boiled, they are drained and allowed to cool. Zucchini and eggplant are then simply cut in half and hollowed out. Vegetables like potatoes, onions, and tomatoes are given a more elaborate treatment which involves cutting a little cap off and removing part of the pulp with a spoon or a special scoop; the pulp is later added to the other ingredients in the filling. Care must be taken not to scoop out too much of the vegetable or the skin will break. Some vegetables, such as peppers and artichokes, are hollowed out in the same manner, but the pulp is inedible and is not used in the stuffing. These vegetables are rinsed out and left to drain upside down.

Among those vegetables that can be stuffed without removing any of the pulp are leafy greens, which can have stuffing placed between the leaves (and this works with artichokes as well) or can have a large leaf split in half and filled. Cabbage leaves can also be filled and rolled up into little bundles; celery and cardoons can be filled down the length of their trough-like stalks.

The different fillings — The most traditional fillings are those made of meat or fish, but fillings based on pasta, rice, bread, and cheese are also quite common. Broadly speaking, all stuffings can be divided into two groups: stuffings made with meat, and meatless stuffings. Meat stuffings are made with raw chopped meat or with cooked meats such as salami, sausage, mortadella, or ham, plus the vegetable pulp. Everything is finely chopped, sautéed with onion in a little oil, bound with egg and grated cheese, and seasoned with basil, parsley, marjoram, nutmeg, pepper, and paprika. Dried mushrooms, first softened in water, can be added to give a little more flavor to an otherwise bland vegetable. Among the meatless stuffings are those containing tuna, anchovies, capers, olives, or shrimp as well as those based on rice or small pasta. There are also fillings made of bread crumbs, garlic, parsley, oil, and the chopped vegetable pulp. Particularly popular in southern Italy, these fillings are usually served hot but are also very good cold.

Cooking stuffed vegetables

The necessary equipment

The most common way to cook stuffed vegetables is to bake them; this, like steaming, keeps them from drying out too much. The oven is first preheated to between 350° and 400°. After the vegetables have been allowed to brown, the baking pan is covered with aluminum foil to allow the vegetables to cook in their own juices without adding additional liquid. The vegetables are basted from time to time with these juices so they don't dry out.

Some stuffed vegetables are dipped in egg, rolled in flour or bread crumbs, and then fried in hot oil. Often two slices of a vegetable are sandwiched together with a filling between before being fried. Flat vegetables, like celery and cardoons, and larger vegetables, like fennel and eggplant, are especially well suited to that method. Some vegetables are dipped in specially prepared batters rather than flour or bread crumbs before being fried. Braising, which requires sautéed garlic or onion and usually a little tomato purée as well, is particularly suitable for stuffed leafy greens such as cabbage leaves.

Hot stuffed vegetables can be served as an antipasto, a first course, or as an accompaniment to the main course. Meatless stuffings based on fish, bread, or ingredients like capers, olives, or anchovies are particularly good for vegetables served as antipasti. Vegetables stuffed with rice or pasta are especially suitable as a first course. Vegetables simply filled with bread crumbs seasoned with oil, minced garlic, and parsley customarily accompany the main course, but stuffed vegetables topped with cheese or covered with a sauce, or *tortini* made up of layers of vegetables alternating with cheese, béchamel, and tomato sauce are even better side dishes.

For vegetables that need to be precooked before stuffing, there are two indispensable utensils: a steamer and a pressure cooker. The steamer has small holes in the base and fits inside another pan filled with simmering water. The steam generated by the simmering water cooks the vegetables. The pressure cooker must be carefully watched and timed so that the vegetables don't overcook.

Also available are many kinds of baking pans including decorated porcelain dishes, classic brown earthenware pots with a white interior, and various ceramic dishes that sometimes come with their own serving trivets.

Stuffed vegetables can also be sautéed on top of the stove, preferably using non-stick pans. In this case, previously warmed stainless steel plates may be used as attractive serving dishes.

A salad spinner and a colander are useful in preliminary cleaning operations, permitting the leaves to be washed without becoming bruised and getting everything else wet.

A small stiff-bristled brush and a small sharp knife are useful for scrubbing potatoes or removing the woody part of the stems of the mushrooms. The melon baller, a little tool with round deep scoops on each end, is very useful for hollowing out vegetables. For precooked vegetables, a serrated grapefruit knife is very handy.

One should also keep on hand a supply of aluminum foil and wax paper that can be used to cover a pan so that stuffed vegetables don't dry out or brown too quickly during cooking.

Rice-stuffed tomatoes

■ **Yield: 4 servings**
■ **Time needed: 1 hour**
■ **Difficulty: ***

Ingredients: 8 firm medium-sized tomatoes, 1 cup rice, 1 carrot, 1 small onion, 1 stalk celery, 1 clove garlic, 2-3 tbsp olive oil, 1¼ cups chicken broth, salt, pepper.

Cut a cap-like slice off the bottom of the tomato and set aside, then carefully scoop out the pulp (1). Mince the other vegetables and sauté them gently in two tablespoons oil. When they are transparent and soft, add the rice and mix well (2). Let it brown with the vegetables a few seconds, then add the hot broth and salt. Simmer until the broth has been absorbed, about 10 minutes, then remove the rice, which will still be a little hard, from the fire.

Fill the tomatoes loosely with the rice (3) and add a little of the seeded and chopped tomato pulp (4). Pour a little oil over them, add pepper, and arrange close together in a baking dish. Replace the caps on the tomatoes and spread the rest of the chopped tomato pulp on the bottom of the baking dish. Place in a preheated 350° oven for about 40 minutes, or until the tomatoes are cooked and the rice is completely tender.

1 Cut a small cap off the bottom of each tomato and remove the pulp.

2 Sauté the minced vegetables in two tablespoons oil and then add the rice.

3 Loosely fill the tomatoes with the cooked rice. Don't fill too full.

4 Spoon on a little of the chopped tomato pulp.

Rice-stuffed tomatoes

Tomatoes stuffed with cheese

■ **Yield: 4 servings**
■ **Time needed: 1 hour**
■ **Difficulty: ***

Ingredients: 20 plum tomatoes, 6 tbsp butter, 1/3 cup flour, 1/2 cup grated Parmesan or Gruyère cheese, about 2 cups hot milk, pinch nutmeg, salt, pepper.

Wash and dry the tomatoes. With a sharp knife, cut a cap-like slice off the bottom and set the caps aside. Scoop out the pulp, remove the seeds, chop the pulp coarsely, and put in a bowl.

Melt 4 tablespoons butter in a pan, add the flour, and stir to remove lumps. Add the hot milk and, stirring constantly, bring to a boil; the sauce will be very thick. Add salt, pepper, and a pinch of nutmeg, remove from the fire, and add the cheese and tomato pulp. Fill the tomatoes with this mixture and wedge together in a buttered baking dish so that they remain upright. Dot with the remaining butter and replace the caps. Bake for about 20 minutes in a 350° oven. Serve hot.

An unusual and appealing way of serving these tomatoes is inside a pie crust. The dish can be made quickly if you use a frozen ready-to-cook pie shell. Simply let it thaw and then pierce the bottom with a fork. Cover with foil, place some dried beans on top to keep the shell from buckling and bake for about 20 minutes in a 350° oven. Remove beans and foil. Spread some béchamel on the bottom of the shell and arrange the tomatoes, already stuffed and baked, inside. Return to the oven again for a few minutes, then serve at once.

Tomatoes stuffed with pasta

■ **Yield: 4 servings**
■ **Time needed: 1 hour 15 minutes**
■ **Difficulty: ***

Ingredients: 8 ripe tomatoes, 1/2 lb macaroni, 1 cup tomato sauce, 8 fresh basil leaves or 1/2 tsp dried basil, 1 clove garlic, 2 tbsp grated Parmesan or Romano cheese, 4 tbsp olive oil, salt, pepper.

Cook the pasta in boiling salted water until *al dente* (resistant to the bite). With a sharp knife, cut a cap-like slice off the bottoms of the tomatoes and set caps aside. Scoop out the pulp and reserve; remove the seeds. Finely chop the basil and garlic, put into a bowl, add the pasta, half the tomato sauce, the tomato pulp, cheese, 2 tablespoons of the oil, salt, and pepper.

Salt the inside of the tomatoes lightly, fill with the stuffing, cover with the caps, and arrange in a baking pan. Add the remaining tomato sauce to the pan and drizzle the tomatoes with the remaining oil. Bake in a 350° oven for about 30 minutes. If too much sauce evaporates, add a little water or broth. Serve hot, directly from the baking pan.

This dish may also be made with leftover pasta. A little sauce should be added to moisten it before stuffing the tomatoes.

Tomatoes stuffed with mushrooms

■ **Yield: 4 servings**
■ **Time needed: 1 hour 40 minutes**
■ **Difficulty: ***

Ingredients: 6 ripe salad tomatoes, 10 oz mushrooms, handful parsley, 1/2 small onion, 1 scallion, 1 minced clove garlic, 4 oz ham, finely chopped, 4 tbsp butter, 2 tbsp grated Parmesan, 2 tbsp bread crumbs, 1 beef bouillon cube, 1 tbsp tomato sauce, 3 tbsp dry white wine, 2 tbsp olive oil, salt, pepper.

Wash the tomatoes, cut a small cap off the bottom, scoop out the pulp, and remove the seeds. Salt and pepper the inside of the tomatoes and drizzle with a tablespoon of oil. Wipe the mushrooms clean with a damp cloth, set aside six of the smallest, and slice the rest thickly. Finely chop the onion and scallion and sauté until soft with 2 tablespoons butter and 1 tablespoon oil in a skillet. Add both sliced and whole mushrooms and the garlic clove and brown lightly. Sprinkle with white wine, season with salt and pepper, and add the tomato sauce and the bouillon cube, dissolved in 3 tablespoons hot water. Simmer slowly until the mushrooms are cooked. Just before removing from the fire, sprinkle on half the chopped parsley; off the heat, remove and set aside the six whole mushrooms, and blend remaining mixture with the chopped ham, bread crumbs, and cheese. Fill the tomatoes with this stuffing and place a whole mushroom on top of each one. Arrange tomatoes in a buttered baking pan, sprinkle with the remaining parsley, and dot with the rest of the butter. Bake in a 350° oven for about 25 minutes or until the tomatoes are cooked.

Stuffed fried artichokes

- ■ Yield: 4 servings
- ■ Time needed: 1 hour
- ■ Difficulty: *

Ingredients: 4 large artichokes, 1 lb mozzarella, flour, 1/2 lb mushrooms, juice of 1 lemon, 2 eggs, bread crumbs, 1 chopped sprig parsley, 1 clove garlic, minced, 3 tbsp olive oil plus additional oil for frying, 2-3 tbsp dry white wine (optional), salt, pepper.

Trim the artichokes by removing the tough outer leaves and the choke, then cut lengthwise into thick slices (1); immerse artichokes in water acidulated with half the lemon juice as they are cut, so that they don't turn brown. Parboil artichokes for five minutes in salted water to which you have added remaining lemon juice (2). Drain and pat dry with a towel (3).

Wipe the mushrooms clean with a damp cloth, slice, and sauté in a skillet with the parsley and garlic in three tablespoons of olive oil. Add salt, pepper and, if you wish, a little white wine. Continue to cook over a low flame until the mushrooms are cooked, stirring from time to time with a wooden spoon.

Lay half the artichoke slices in a single layer on a work surface. Cover with pieces of mozzarella about the same size as the artichokes (4), mask with the mushroom mixture (5), and top with remaining artichoke (6). Dip the artichokes first in flour, then in the two eggs beaten with a little salt (7), and finally in bread crumbs (8). Press the edges to seal so that the stuffing doesn't leak out. Heat 1 inch oil in a wide skillet and fry the artichokes a few at a time until golden, turning once. Drain on paper towels (9). Serve on a plate covered with a napkin or on a serving dish garnished with a little parsley. These go well with mixed grill, veal scalloppine, or turkey breast cooked in Madeira or white wine.

1 Wash and trim the artichokes, removing the tough outer leaves and sharp tips, and slice lengthwise.

2 Boil the artichoke slices for five minutes in salted water and lemon juice.

3 Drain and place on a towel to dry.

4 Lay half the artichoke slices on a work surface and cover with mozzarella.

5 Evenly mask the mozzarella with the mushroom mixture.

6 Cover each with another artichoke slice and press together.

7 Dip the artichoke sandwich first in flour, then in beaten egg...

8 ...and then in bread crumbs, being sure to coat the edges to keep the filling in.

9 Fry the slices a few at a time in hot oil until crisp and golden, and drain on paper towels.

Stuffed fried artichokes

Artichokes stuffed with meat

■ **Yield: 4 servings**
■ **Time needed: 1 hour**
■ **Difficulty: ***

Ingredients: 4 large artichokes, 4 oz ground veal, 1 ground chicken breast, 2 oz sliced pancetta or bacon, 1/4 cup shredded Gruyère, 2 tbsp butter, 1/4 cup grated Parmesan, handful parsley, 1 clove garlic, 1 egg, 1 cup broth made from a beef bouillon cube, juice of 1 lemon, 2 tbsp olive oil, salt, pepper.

Wash and trim the artichokes, removing the tough outer leaves and the sharp tips. Cut off the stems so that the artichokes will remain upright in a pan. Spread open and cut off the top of the dome with scissors to remove the thorns. Cover artichokes with water and lemon juice.

Chop the parsley and garlic and mix in a bowl with the veal, chicken, Gruyère, Parmesan, salt, and pepper. Add a beaten egg to bind the mixture. Drain the artichokes well and pack the stuffing between their leaves, starting from the center. Cover each artichoke with a slice of pancetta or bacon, then arrange them side by side in a baking dish. Moisten tops with oil and dot with butter. Bake in a 350° oven for about 45 minutes, occasionally basting with a little broth until done.

Artichokes with cheese and olive stuffing

■ **Yield: 4 servings**
■ **Time needed: 1 hour**
■ **Difficulty: ***

Ingredients: 4 large artichokes, 1/2 cup grated Parmesan, 1/2 lb shredded mozzarella, 1/2 cup chopped (plus 4 whole) pitted green olives, 4 anchovies, 1 egg, 1 tbsp bread crumbs, pinch oregano, juice of 1 lemon, 1 cup broth made from a beef bouillon cube, 3 tbsp olive oil, salt, pepper.

Wash and trim the artichokes, removing tough outer leaves and sharp tips and cutting away the stem. Spread open and clip off the thorny top of the pale inner leaves; cover artichokes with water and lemon juice. In a bowl, combine the mozzarella, Parmesan, chopped olives, bread crumbs, oregano, egg, salt, and pepper. Pack this mixture between the leaves. Place artichokes in a greased baking dish, sprinkle with oil, and top each one with an anchovy and a whole olive. Bake in a 350° oven for about 45 minutes, basting occasionally with broth until done.

Artichokes with red wine

■ **Yield: 4 servings**
■ **Time needed: 1 hour 20 minutes**
■ **Difficulty: ***

Ingredients: 8 medium-sized artichokes, 4 oz ham, 1 cup tomato purée, 1/2 onion, juice of 1 lemon, handful parsley, 1 cup dry red wine, 1/4 cup olive oil, salt.

Cut the stems from the artichokes and remove the tough outer leaves and thorny tips. Spread the artichokes open at the center and scoop out the pale inner leaves and the choke. As each one is trimmed, place it in water and lemon juice. Parboil artichokes in salted water for 5 minutes; drain well. Chop the parsley, onion, and ham together finely and fill the hollowed-out centers of the artichokes with this mixture. Arrange in a baking dish, moisten with oil, and pour the tomato purée and red wine over them. Sprinkle with salt to taste, cover, and bake in a 350° oven for about 35 minutes or until done.

Artichokes, Roman style

■ **Yield: 4 servings**
■ **Time needed: 1 hour 15 minutes**
■ **Difficulty: ***

Ingredients: 8 medium-sized artichokes, juice of 1 lemon, large handful parsley, 8 leaves fresh mint, 2 cloves garlic, 2 tbsp bread crumbs, 6 tbsp olive oil, salt, pepper.

Trim the artichokes: peel the stems deeply, then snap off the top portions of all the leaves. Spread the center of each artichoke, pull out the dome of pale inner leaves, and scrape the choke off the bottom with a spoon. As each artichoke is trimmed, place in a pot of water and lemon juice. Mince the mint, parsley, and one clove garlic together. Add the bread crumbs, moisten with 2 tablespoons of the olive oil, and add salt and pepper to taste. Using a spoon, stuff the hollowed-out centers of the artichokes with this mixture, then arrange on their sides in a baking dish that can go directly over a flame. Pour on remaining oil and turn to coat. Add enough water to the pan to reach halfway up the sides of the artichokes, add the remaining garlic, cover tightly, and simmer on top of the stove for half an hour, turn and place in a 350° oven for another half an hour, adding more water if necessary.

Artichokes, Roman style

Stuffed eggplant au gratin

- **Yield: 4 servings**
- **Time needed: 2 hours**
- **Difficulty: ***

Ingredients: Two 1-lb eggplants, 1/2 cup grated Parmesan, 1/2 lb mushrooms, pinches oregano, bread crumbs, 1 tbsp parsley minced with 1 clove garlic, 1 lb mozzarella, 1/2 cup olive oil, salt, pepper.

Wash the eggplants, cut off the ends, and slice in half lengthwise. Slash the inside of the eggplant to within 1/2 inch of the skin with a sharp knife. Sprinkle very generously with salt and arrange upside down on a triple layer of paper towels. Let stand for about an hour to drain off some of the bitter juice.

Meanwhile wipe the mushrooms clean with a damp cloth, chop coarsely, and cook thoroughly in 2 tablespoons of the oil. Set aside.

Firmly squeeze the eggplant halves, then hollow out with a sharp knife, leaving a shell about 3/8 inch around the edge (1), and finely chop the scooped-out pulp (2). In a skillet sauté the garlic and parsley in 4 tablespoons of the oil (3), then add the eggplant pulp (4) and season with pepper. Stirring from time to time, cook until the eggplant is soft and just beginning to brown. Remove the skillet from the heat and add the Parmesan (5), bread crumbs, sautéed mushrooms (6), oregano, and salt and pepper to taste.

Fill the eggplant shells with the mixture (7) and arrange in a greased baking dish. Cut the mozzarella into cubes, distribute over the eggplant (8), and moisten with remaining 2 tablespoons oil (9). Bake the eggplant halves at 350° for 50-60 minutes, or until they are fork tender and the mozzarella has turned golden brown. If the cheese browns too quickly, cover the dish with foil, removing foil a few minutes before taking the dish from the oven. This can be served as part of an antipasto or as an appetizing first course.

3 Sauté the garlic and parsley in a little oil in a skillet.

1 Cut the eggplants in half lengthwise and hollow out the pulp with a sharp knife.

2 After firmly squeezing eggplant halves to get rid of the bitter juice, cut out the pulp and chop it finely.

4 Add the chopped eggplant to the parsley and garlic and cook until soft.

5 Then add bread crumbs and grated cheese...

6 ...the cooked mushrooms, a few pinches of oregano, salt, and pepper.

7 Fill the eggplant shells with the mixture and place in a baking dish.

8 Distribute the cubed mozzarella over the top of the eggplants.

9 Moisten with a little oil and place in a preheated oven for about an hour.

Stuffed eggplant au gratin

Eggplant rolls

- **Yield: 4 servings**
- **Time needed: 1½ hours**
- **Difficulty: ***

Ingredients: Four 1-lb eggplants, 5 oz ground beef, 2 oz mortadella, ½ cup grated Parmesan, 2 eggs, 3 tbsp sweet sausage meat, 1 tbsp parsley, 1 clove garlic, one 8-oz can tomato purée, 1 chopped small onion, 6-8 tbsp olive oil, ⅛ tsp nutmeg, salt, pepper.

Wash the eggplants, trim the ends, and cut in lengthwise slices (1). Sprinkle generously with salt and let stand for 30 min. Mix together the beef, sausage meat, chopped mortadella, cheese, whole egg, egg yolk (2), parsley, garlic, and nutmeg, plus salt and pepper to taste. Dry the eggplant slices thoroughly (3). Brown in 4-6 tablespoons hot oil (4) on both sides (5); drain on paper towels (6). Lay out half the slices of eggplant on the work surface and place remaining slices on top to form a cross (7). Place a little stuffing in the center of the top slices (8) and close the ends of the top slices over the stuffing (9). Bring up the ends of the bottom slices to enclose the stuffing completely (10). Fasten rolls with toothpicks (11). Sauté onion in remaining oil, then add tomato purée (12), salt, and pepper, and simmer briefly. Place rolls in a baking dish, cover with sauce, and bake at 350° for half an hour.

1 Wash the eggplants, trim the ends, and slice lengthwise.

2 Mix the beef, sausage, mortadella, and cheese in a bowl and bind with egg.

3 Dry the eggplant in a towel, pressing firmly to get rid of the bitter juices.

4 Fry the slices a few at a time in hot oil.

5 When they are browned on both sides, remove with a spatula...

6 ...and drain on paper towels.

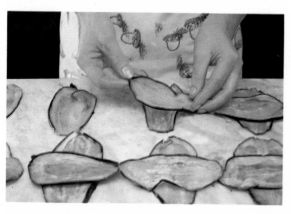

7 Lay out half the slices and place remaining slices crosswise over the top.

8 Put a little of the filling in the center of the top slices.

9 Enclose the filling by first folding the ends of the top slices...

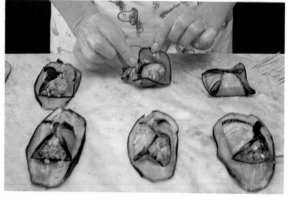

10 ...and then bringing up the ends of the bottom slices.

11 Secure the rolls with toothpicks so that they don't open during cooking.

12 Sauté the onion in oil, then add the tomato purée and simmer briefly.

Eggplant rolls

Spicy eggplant rolls

- **Yield: 4 servings**
- **Time needed: 1 hour**
- **Difficulty: ***

Ingredients: Two 1-lb eggplants, 1 small dried red chili pepper, 3 cloves garlic, 1 sprig basil or $1/2$ tsp dried basil, 3 tbsp bread crumbs, 4 anchovies, $1 1/2$ cups tomato purée, 1 chopped small onion, pinch oregano, 4-5 tbsp olive oil, vegetable oil, salt, pepper.

Wash the eggplant, trim the ends, and cut lengthwise into $1/4$-inch-thick slices. Salt and let stand on a triple layer of paper towels for at least 30 minutes. Fry the onion with one clove garlic until soft in 2 tablespoons olive oil; discard the garlic. Add the tomato purée and simmer for at least 20 minutes, or until reduced into a thick sauce, adding 2-3 tablespoons olive oil towards the end of cooking. Dry eggplant slices thoroughly between sheets of paper towels and fry in vegetable oil until lightly browned on both sides. Mince together anchovies, red pepper, remaining cloves of garlic, and basil. Add bread crumbs, mix well, and moisten with remaining tablespoon olive oil. Place some of this stuffing on each slice and roll up, securing with toothpicks, if necessary. Arrange rolls in the skillet containing the tomato sauce, sprinkle with oregano and pepper, and simmer slowly for 5-8 minutes. Serve hot.

Eggplant Parmesan

- **Yield: 4 servings**
- **Time needed: 1 hour 40 minutes**
- **Difficulty: ****

Ingredients: Three 1-lb eggplants, 1 small onion, $1 1/2$-2 cups tomato purée, 1 lb thinly sliced mozzarella, 1 cup grated Parmesan cheese, $1/2$ cup flour, oil for frying, 3 tbsp olive oil, $1 1/2$ tsp basil, salt.

Wash the eggplants, trim the ends, and cut lengthwise into slices-$1/4$-inch thick. Salt and let stand for an hour on a triple layer of paper towels. Meanwhile, slice onion and sauté in olive oil until soft. Add tomato purée, season with salt, and simmer slowly until thickened.

Dry the eggplant slices between sheets of paper towels, then coat lightly with a thin layer of flour. Fry in oil until lightly browned on both sides. Pour a thin layer of tomato sauce into a baking dish and cover with a slightly overlapping layer of eggplant slices. Spread with more sauce, cover with slices of mozzarella, and sprinkle with Parmesan and basil. Make additional layers until you have used up the ingredients, topping the dish with sauce and cheese. Place in a 375° oven and bake until bubbling and browned on top.

Fried eggplant "sandwiches"

- **Yield: 4 servings**
- **Time needed: 1 hour 20 minutes**
- **Difficulty: ***

Ingredients: Three 12-oz eggplants, 1 lb thinly sliced mozzarella, 2 eggs, $1/3$ cup sliced stuffed green olives, $1/2$ cup flour, 1-$1 1/2$ cups bread crumbs, pinches oregano, salt, oil for frying.

Peel the eggplant, trim the ends, and cut lengthwise into $1/2$-inch-thick slices. Sprinkle generously with salt and let stand for an hour on paper towels to drain off the bitter juices. Dry well between additional paper towels.

Cover half the eggplant slices with slices of mozzarella, sprinkle with olives and a little oregano, and cover with remaining slices of eggplant, pressing the edges firmly together. Dip the sandwiches first in flour, then in egg, beaten with a little salt, and finally in bread crumbs. Fry a few at a time in $1/2$ inch hot oil until golden brown on both sides, draining on paper towels.

Peppers stuffed with eggplant

- **Yield: 4 servings**
- **Time needed: $1 1/2$ hours**
- **Difficulty: ***

Ingredients: 4 green or yellow bell peppers, three 12-oz eggplants, 3-4 chopped anchovies, $1 1/2$ tbsp minced sour pickles, 1 tbsp parsley minced with 1 clove garlic, 1 egg, 2 tbsp grated Parmesan or Romano cheese, 2 tbsp bread crumbs, 8-10 tbsp olive oil, salt, pepper.

Wash the eggplants, trim the ends, peel, and cut into cubes. Sauté in 6-8 tablespoons olive oil until they begin to brown, then add the anchovies, chopped pickle, minced parsley and garlic, and bread crumbs. Add salt and pepper and, off the fire, the cheese and egg. Wash and dry the peppers. Cut off the tops, remove the seeds and ribs, and fill with the eggplant stuffing. Arrange peppers side by side in a greased baking dish. Moisten each with a little of the remaining oil and bake at 350° for about an hour, covering with aluminum foil about halfway through the cooking.

Fried eggplant "sandwiches"

Meat-stuffed zucchini

- **Yield: 4 servings**
- **Time needed: 1½ hours**
- **Difficulty: ***

Ingredients: 8 medium-sized zucchini, 10 oz ground beef, 4 oz chopped ham, 2 tbsp parsley minced with 1 clove garlic, ½ cup Parmesan, ¾ cup tomato purée, 1 egg, 3 tbsp olive oil, salt, pepper.

Scrub the zucchini, trim the ends, using either a knife or an apple corer, and remove the pulp (1). In a bowl, combine the meat, chopped ham, half the parsley-garlic mixture, egg, and cheese, and season with salt and pepper (2). Pack this stuffing in the zucchini (3). Heat the oil in a skillet, add the rest of the parsley and garlic (4), and let brown slightly. Add the zucchini to the pan in a single layer (5), cover, and cook slowly for 10 minutes to let them absorb the flavor. Pour the tomato purée over the zucchini (6) and add salt and pepper. Simmer over a moderate flame, partially covered, for about an hour, or until the zucchini are very tender.

1 Trim both ends of the zucchini, then hollow out with an apple corer or knife.

2 Mix ground beef, ham, half the parsley-garlic mixture, egg, and cheese in a bowl.

3 Fill the zucchini with the meat mixture.

4 Sauté the rest of the parsley and garlic in a little oil.

5 Arrange the stuffed zucchini in a single layer in the pan.

6 Pour tomato purée evenly over the zucchini.

Meat-stuffed zucchini

Peppers, country style

■ **Yield: 4 servings**
■ **Time needed: 1¹/₂ hours**
■ **Difficulty: ***

Ingredients: 4 large bell peppers, 8 oz ground beef, 4 oz mortadella or ham, chopped, 2 tbsp parsley minced with 2 cloves garlic, one 8-oz can tomato purée, 2 tbsp bread crumbs, 1 egg, ¹/₂ cup grated Parmesan, ¹/₄ cup cooked rice (optional), 8 oz mushrooms, 1 chopped small onion, 6 tbsp olive oil, salt.

Wash the peppers, cut off the tops, and remove seeds and ribs (1). Clean and slice the mushrooms and sauté until soft in 3 tablespoons oil with half the parsley and garlic (2). Mix the beef, chopped mortadella, the rest of the garlic and parsley, the cheese, rice, bread crumbs, and mushrooms. Add the egg, a pinch of salt, and a tablespoon oil and mix well (3). Fill the peppers with this mixture (4). In a large pan, sauté the onion in 2 tablespoons oil until soft, then add the tomato purée (5) and salt, and simmer for 5 minutes. Place the peppers in the pan with the tomato sauce, cover (6), and simmer gently for about 45 minutes or until tender, adding a little hot water or broth if needed.

1 Cut the tops off the peppers and remove the seeds and ribs.

2 Sauté the mushrooms in a little oil with the parsley and garlic.

3 Mix the stuffing ingredients in a bowl with a wooden spoon.

4 Divide the stuffing among the peppers, filling them generously.

5 After sautéeing the chopped onion, add the tomato purée.

6 Arrange the peppers in the pan and cover.

Peppers, country style

Stuffed potatoes in foil

Ingredients: 4 large oval-shaped baking potatoes, 8 oz sausage meat, 1 oz dried mushrooms, 4 tbsp butter, 1 tbsp parsley minced with 1 clove garlic, 1 egg, pinches nutmeg, white pepper, salt.

Cover mushrooms with warm water and set aside. Scrub the potatoes, prick well and bake for 45 min. or until tender in a 400° oven. Cut a lengthwise slice off the tops and set aside (1); hollow out potatoes (2), leaving a 3/8-inch-thick shell. Mash removed potato until crumbly. Cook sausage in 2 tbsp butter, adding mushrooms, drained, and seasoning with white pepper, salt, and nutmeg. Add mashed potato to sausage mixture and fill potato shells (3). Dot with rest of butter and wrap in aluminum foil (4). Bake at 400° for 25 min., opening the foil towards the end of cooking so that top browns. Before serving, cover potatoes with reserved lids.

- **Yield: 4 servings**
- **Time needed: 1 hour 45 minutes**
- **Difficulty: ***

1 Bake the potatoes, then cut off the tops to form lids.

2 Carefully hollow out the potatoes with a spoon.

3 Stuff the potatoes with the prepared filling, mounding it in the center.

4 Dot the potatoes with butter and wrap individually in aluminum foil.

Stuffed potatoes in foil

Mushrooms on toast

- **Yield: 4 servings**
- **Time needed: 1½ hours**
- **Difficulty: ***

Ingredients: 8 large boletus or regular mushrooms, 8 toasted slices French bread, large handful parsley, 1 tsp dried basil, 1 clove garlic, 1 tbsp bread crumbs, 5 tbsp olive oil, salt, pepper.

Wipe the mushrooms clean with a damp cloth. Remove the stems and chop finely; gently scrape the inside of the caps to hollow out slightly (1), reserving the shavings. Chop the parsley together with the garlic and basil.

Heat 2 tablespoons olive oil in a skillet, and add half the herb mixture plus the chopped stems and reserved shavings from the mushroom caps. Season with salt and pepper and cook over moderate heat, stirring occasionally, until the mixture begins to color. Let cool and chop finely. Combine the remaining herb mixture, bread crumbs, and the sautéed mushroom pieces in a bowl (2) and moisten with a tablespoon oil (3). Place the caps in a baking dish and divide the stuffing among them (4). Add salt and pepper (5), moisten with remaining 2 tablespoons oil (6), and bake in a 350° oven for 20-25 minutes, or until lightly browned. Serve on toasted bread slices.

1 Remove the stems and gently scrape the insides of the caps to hollow out slightly.

2 Mix the parsley, bread crumbs, and chopped cooked mushrooms in a bowl.

3 Add a little oil to the mixture and blend well.

4 Fill the mushroom caps with the mixture.

5 Season with salt and pepper.

6 Moisten with a little more oil and bake in a moderate oven.

Mushrooms on toast

Celeriac with cheese

- Yield: 4 servings
- Time needed: 2 hours
- Difficulty: *

Ingredients: Four 8-oz celeriac, two 2-oz sausages, 2 oz chopped mortadella or ham, 8 tbsp butter, 2 oz Fontina, 2 tbsp flour, juice of 2 lemons, 1 cup milk, 2 tbsp heavy cream, 1/8 tsp freshly grated nutmeg, salt, pepper.

One at a time, scrub the celeriac with a stiff brush, peel deeply, and immediately drop into water mixed with the juice of one lemon to prevent discoloration (1). Place peeled celeriac in a pot, cover with cold water, and add the juice of another lemon. Simmer slowly, partially covered, for 30-45 minutes, or until the roots give only slight resistance when pierced with a fork. Drain well before stuffing.

While the celeriac is cooking, slice one sausage and set aside. Crumble the other sausage in a skillet and sauté with the mortadella in two tablespoons butter (2); remove from the heat when the sausage is cooked and set aside.

In a saucepan, melt 4 tablespoons butter, add the flour (3), and mix well with a wooden spoon to get rid of lumps. Add the hot milk, stirring constantly (4). Still stirring, heat the sauce until it boils and becomes very thick (5). Add the Fontina, cut into cubes (6), and the cream. Remove from the fire as soon as the cheese has melted and season with salt, freshly ground pepper, and a little nutmeg (7). Set aside in a pan of hot water to keep warm.

Cut the celeriac in two, lengthwise, and scoop out a fairly deep depression in each half with a spoon (8). Divide the sausage and mortadella mixture among the hollowed-out celeriac (9) and top with the cheese sauce (10). Arrange the celeriac in a greased baking dish, scatter the reserved sausage slices over the top (11), and dot with the remaining 2 tablespoons butter. Bake in a 400° oven for 15-25 minutes. Serve at once.

1 Peel the celeriac and immerse in acidulated water.

2 Sauté one of the sausages and the mortadella in a pan with a little butter.

3 Melt 4 tablespoons butter in a sauce pan, add the flour, and mix well.

4 Add boiling milk, stirring constantly.

5 Still stirring, cook the sauce until it is thick and smooth.

6 Before removing it from the heat, add the cubed Fontina and stir until the cheese melts.

7 Season carefully with salt, pepper, and nutmeg.

8 Cut the celeriac in half and hollow out with a spoon.

9 Put a little of the mortadella mixture in each one.

10 Then cover with the cheese sauce.

11 Put the celeriac in a baking dish and top with sausage slices.

Celeriac with cheese

Cabbage rolls

- Yield: 4 servings
- Time needed: 1½ hours
- Difficulty: *

Ingredients: One 1½-lb cabbage, 8 oz ground beef, 4 oz finely chopped ham, 1 egg, 4 oz sausage meat, ½ cup grated Parmesan cheese, handful parsley minced with 1 clove garlic, one 8-oz can tomato purée, 2 tbsp butter, 1 small onion, ¼-½ cup chicken broth (if needed), 1 tbsp olive oil, salt and pepper.

Wash the cabbage and discard outer leaves. Remove inner leaves by cutting at the stem (1). Rinse the leaves, then blanch in boiling water for 2-3 min. (2), or until wilted and pliable. Drain and blot dry with a towel (3). Mix ground beef, crumbled sausage meat, ham, cheese, parsley and garlic, egg, salt, and pepper (4), blending well. Divide this mixture among the leaves (5), roll up (6), tuck the ends underneath to form little packages (7), and tie the bundles with string (8). Finely chop onion and sauté in oil and butter. Add cabbage rolls (9) and cook slowly for 10 min., turning once. Add tomato purée (10), cover, and continue to cook for half an hour, adding broth if necessary.

1 Remove the leaves by cutting them at the base from the central core.

2 Wash the leaves and blanch them for a few minutes in salted water.

3 Drain well and then blot dry with a towel.

4 Prepare a filling with ground beef, sausage, ham, cheese, parsley, and egg.

5 Divide the stuffing evenly among the leaves.

6 Roll the leaves up over the filling....

7 ...then fold the ends underneath, making a package.

8 Tie the cabbage leaves with string.

9 Sauté chopped onion in oil and butter and add the cabbage rolls.

10 Cook briefly, then add tomato sauce and simmer until tender.

Cabbage rolls

Stuffed zucchini au gratin

■ **Yield: 4 servings**
■ **Time needed: 1 hour**
■ **Difficulty: ***

Ingredients: Four 8-oz zucchini, 2 tbsp butter, 3 tbsp flour, 4 oz diced mortadella or ham, 2 tbsp shredded Gruyère, 1 cup hot milk, pinch nutmeg, 2 tbsp olive oil, salt, pepper.

Scrub the zucchini and pat dry. Trim the ends, cut in half lengthwise, and arrange in a baking dish, moistening with oil. Bake at 350° for 30-45 minutes, or until just tender enough to be pierced with a fork. Carefully scoop out some of the pulp with a spoon, forming little boats with walls about ³/₈ inch thick.

While the zucchini are baking, prepare the stuffing. Melt the butter in a saucepan, add the flour, and mix until completely smooth. Stirring constantly, add the hot milk and heat the sauce until it boils and has become very thick. Add salt, pepper, and nutmeg to taste, then stir in the mortadella and Gruyère. Spoon the sauce into the hollowed-out zucchini and bake in a 400° oven for 15-25 minutes, or until the top is golden brown.

Stuffed zucchini blossoms

■ **Yield: 4 servings**
■ **Time needed: 1 hour**
■ **Difficulty: ****

Ingredients: 16 zucchini blossoms, 1 egg, ¹/₃-²/₃ cup fresh bread crumbs, large handful parsley, 1 cup grated Parmesan or Romano cheese, 1 clove garlic, oil for deep-frying, salt.
For the batter: 1¹/₄ cups flour, 2 eggs, separated, 2-4 tbsp beer, pinch nutmeg, ¹/₄ tsp salt.

Remove the stems and the pistils from the zucchini blossoms. Gently wash and dry with a towel. Mince the parsley and garlic and combine in a bowl with the cheese, egg, and enough bread crumbs to form a filling stiff enough to hold its shape on a spoon. Stuff the zucchini blossoms with the bread crumb mixture, folding the petals over the filling.

To make the batter, put the flour, salt, and nutmeg in a bowl, make a well in the center, and add the egg yolks and 2 tablespoons beer. Mix with a wooden spoon until smooth, adding a little more beer if necessary to make a thick but fluid batter. Beat the egg whites till stiff and carefully fold into the batter. Using your fingers, dip the zucchini blossoms into the batter one by one and immediately drop into 2-3-inches hot oil. Fry until golden, remove with a slotted spoon and drain on paper towels. Salt and serve.

Stuffed grape leaves

■ **Yield: 4 servings**
■ **Time needed: 1 hour 15 minutes**
■ **Difficulty: ***

Ingredients: 12 large grape leaves, fresh or preserved in brine, 6 oz ground beef, 6 oz ground lamb, 2 tbsp flour, 3 tbsp butter, 1 egg, handful chopped parsley, 1 chopped small onion, 1 lemon, 1 cup chicken broth, salt, pepper.

If you are using fresh grape leaves, wash thoroughly, then boil until tender and drain and pat dry. Brine-packed grape leaves need only be rinsed and blotted dry with paper towels. Combine the beef and lamb, onion, parsley, egg, salt, and pepper in a bowl and mix well. Using two spoons dipped in water, form the mixture into 16 small oval shapes and place in the center of each leaf. Roll the leaves up and tuck the ends underneath to enclose the stuffing. Arrange the rolls in a large skillet and cover with salted water. Add the juice of half a lemon, cover, and simmer slowly for 30 minutes.

Meanwhile, prepare the sauce. Melt the butter in a saucepan, add the flour, and stir until smooth. Stirring constantly, add the hot broth, bring to a simmer, and cook for a few minutes. Add the juice of the remaining lemon half. When the stuffed grape leaves are cooked, drain well, arrange on a plate, and cover with the sauce.

Stuffed onions with tomato sauce

■ **Yield: 4 servings**
■ **Time needed: 2 hours**
■ **Difficulty: ***

Ingredients: 8 large yellow onions, 10 oz lean pork, 4 oz diced Gruyère, ¹/₂ cup grated Parmesan, 10 oz frozen peas, 2 oz diced prosciutto or smoked ham, 2 oz pancetta or bacon, 6 finely chopped scallions, 3 eggs, 1 cup tomato sauce, pinch sugar, lemon juice, 4 tbsp olive oil, salt, pepper.

Peel the onions, parboil for 5 minutes, and drain well. Chop the pork into small pieces and brown along with one-third of the finely chopped scallions in 2 tablespoons oil. Turn the flame down to low, and cook slowly for 5 minutes, stirring them from time to time. Add salt and pepper to taste, remove from heat, and set aside. Combine the peas in a pan with the pancetta or bacon cut into cubes, two tablespoons oil, a pinch of sugar, and the rest of the scallions. Add 2 tablespoons water and bring to a simmer. When the peas have cooked halfway, add the browned pork and diced prosciutto. Beat the eggs with half the grated Parmesan cheese and a few drops of lemon juice. Add this mixture to the peas and meat and mix well. Using a grapefruit knife, gently remove the inner sections of the onions. Fill the onions with the diced Gruyère, add the meat filling, pressing down firmly. Arrange the onions in an oiled baking dish, pour the tomato sauce over them, and sprinkle with the rest of the grated Parmesan and a little pepper. Place in a 400° oven and bake for 40 minutes, or until tender when pierced with a fork. (A photo of this dish appears on p. 134).

Fennel with ham au gratin

■ Yield: 4 servings
■ Time needed: 1 hour 15 minutes
■ Difficulty: *

Ingredients: 2 large whole fennel, 6 oz thinly sliced Fontina, 6 oz lean sliced ham, 4 tbsp butter, 1/2 cup heavy cream, salt, pepper.

Shave off the ends of the fennel stalks and remove any leaves. Wash well and boil in salted water until the fennel can be pierced with the point of a knife but still gives some resistance. Drain well and divide in half lengthwise. Melt the butter in a shallow metal baking dish, then lay in the fennel, cut side down, in one layer. Add salt and pepper to taste, pour on the cream, and simmer slowly, covered, until completely tender. Arrange the slices of ham and cheese over the fennel and bake in a 400° oven until the cheese has melted. Serve immediately.

Stuffed potatoes

■ Yield: 4 servings
■ Time needed: 1 1/2 hours
■ Difficulty: *

Ingredients: 4 baking potatoes, all the same size, 2 eggs, separated, 5 tbsp butter, 1 tbsp grated

Parmesan, 4 tbsp shredded Swiss cheese, 2 oz finely chopped ham, pinches nutmeg, salt, pepper.

Scrub the potatoes with a stiff brush and prick well. Bake in a 425° until tender when pierced with a fork. Cut potatoes in half lengthwise and hollow out, leaving a shell about 1/4-inch-thick. Mash the removed potato, add 3 tablespoons of butter, egg yolks, ham, and Parmesan, and season with salt, pepper, and nutmeg. Beat egg whites until stiff and gently fold them in. Stuff potato shells with mixture using a pastry bag fitted with a 1/2-inch star tip, if possible. Arrange potatoes in a baking dish, drizzle with remaining butter, melted, and sprinkle with grated Swiss cheese. Put them in a 400° oven until golden brown. Serve at once, with a roast or other similar dish.

Stuffed cabbage

■ Yield: 4 servings
■ Time needed: 2 hours
■ Difficulty: **

Ingredients: One 3-lb cabbage, 10 oz ground beef, 8 oz sausage meat, 1/2 cup grated Parmesan, 1 1/2 cups fresh bread crumbs, 3 tbsp butter, 2 beaten eggs, 1 chopped onion, 1/4 tsp dried basil, 1/3-1/2 cup milk, 1 1/2-2 cups chicken broth, pinches nutmeg, 2 tbsp olive oil, salt, pepper, 1/2 cup tomato sauce or 2 tbsp tomato paste.

Break off and discard the tough outer leaves of the cabbage. Using a long thin knife, remove the core, without detaching leaves. Drop the cabbage into boiling salted water for 5 minutes, then drain upside down in a colander. When cool enough, gently spread leaves and blot with paper towels.

Soak the bread crumbs in enough milk to cover for 15 minutes, then gently squeeze out. Mix bread crumbs with the ground beef, crumbled sausage, Parmesan, basil, salt, pepper, and nutmeg. Blend in the beaten eggs to bind. Sprinkle the cabbage leaves with salt, put some of the stuffing in the center of the cabbage in a ball, then spread the rest of the stuffing between the leaves, beginning with the inner leaves and working out.

In a deep pot just large enough to hold the cabbage comfortably, sauté the onion in the butter and oil until pale golden. Add the cabbage, season with salt, and let it brown very lightly on all sides, turning it carefully. Add 1 cup broth, cover, and cook over a moderately low flame for an hour and a half, occasionally basting with a little broth. If you want a richer sauce, add a little tomato sauce, or tomato paste diluted with broth.

Pommes Anna

■ **Yield: 4 servings**
■ **Time needed: 1 hour 15 minutes**
■ **Difficulty: ***

Ingredients: 2 lb boiling potatoes, 8 tbsp butter, 4 oz finely chopped ham (optional), salt, pepper.

Peel the potatoes and using a knife, carve them so that they are all the same size and shape (1). Cut in ⅛ inch slices, preferably using a vegetable slicer (2). Generously butter a spring-form mold about 7 inches in diameter (3). Arrange an overlapping ring of potato slices around the edge (4), then make a second ring of slices in the center going in the opposite direction (5). When the bottom is covered with potatoes, season with salt and pepper, dot with 2 tablespoons of the butter (6), and sprinkle on one-third of the optional ham. Make three more layers in the same manner, topping the final layer with butter, but not with ham. Cover the mold with aluminum foil and bake at 350° for about 45-60 minutes, or until the potatoes are very tender when pierced with a fork. Invert on a serving plate, unhinge the sides of the mold, and remove the bottom. Serve at once.

1 Peel the potatoes and carve them so that they are all the same size and shape.

2 Cut in ⅛ inch slices using a vegetable slicer if possible.

3 Generously butter a spring mold about 7 inches in diameter.

4 Arrange a ring of potato slices around the edge, overlapping them slightly.

5 Then make a second ring of slices going in the opposite direction.

6 When the bottom is covered with potato slices, dot with butter.

Pommes Anna

Potato pancake casserole

- **Yield: 4 servings**
- **Time needed: 1 hour**
- **Difficulty: ***

Ingredients: 1 lb all-purpose or baking potatoes, 1 cup flour, 4 eggs, 2 tbsp butter, $^2/_3$ cup grated Parmesan, $1^1/_2$-2 cups tomato sauce, 2-8 tbsp milk, salt, pepper.

Boil the potatoes in salted water until tender, then peel and mash. Mix in a bowl with the flour (1), eggs, salt, and pepper. Add enough milk to make a thick but pourable batter (2). Melt the butter in a 6-inch skillet and pour in a large spoonful of the batter. Tilt the pan to spread the batter thinly. Cook until brown on one side, then turn and brown the other. Make the rest of the pancakes in the same way (3). Generously butter a baking dish and stack the pancakes, alternating with boiling-hot tomato sauce (4) and cheese. Sprinkle the top with cheese and place in a 400° oven for 15-20 minutes. Serve at once.

Potato pancake casserole with ham and cheese

- **Yield: 4 servings**
- **Time needed: 1 hour**
- **Difficulty: ****

Ingredients: 16 potato pancakes (see Potato Pancake Casserole, above), $^1/_2$ cup flour, 12 tbsp butter, 4 oz Fontina, 6 oz diced ham, 2 egg yolks, 1 qt hot milk, $^1/_4$ tsp nutmeg, $^1/_2$ tsp salt.

Make the potato pancake batter as described in the recipe above, but prepare slightly larger pancakes using an 8-inch skillet. Set aside. Prepare a béchamel sauce. Melt 8 tablespoons of the butter in a saucepan, then add the flour and mix well with a wooden spoon to eliminate all lumps. Add the hot milk and, stirring constantly, bring the sauce to a boil and cook 1 minute. It will be extremely thick. Add salt and nutmeg, remove from the fire, and beat in Fontina and ham. Let the sauce cool for a few minutes, then add the egg yolks and mix well. Butter a baking dish the same diameter as the pancakes, and stack the pancakes with the sauce and dots of the remaining butter between. Mask the top and sides with sauce, sprinkle with cheese, and bake at 400° for about 20 minutes, or until golden. Serve directly from the baking dish.

Potato pancakes Miriam

- **Yield: 4 servings**
- **Time needed: 1 hour**
- **Difficulty: ****

Ingredients: 24 potato pancakes (see Potato Pancake Casserole, above), 10 oz boletus mushrooms*, 4 tbsp butter, 1 clove garlic, 1 cup chicken broth, $1^1/_2$ cups heavy cream, 1 tbsp flour, $^3/_4$ cup grated Parmesan, 3 tbsp brandy, 1 tbsp olive oil, salt.

Make the pancakes as described in the recipe above.

Trim off the woody ends of the mushroom stems, wipe mushrooms with a damp cloth, and cut into thin slices. Crush the garlic clove and brown lightly in a skillet in 1 tablespoon each butter and oil. Add the mushrooms and cook, stirring with a wooden spoon until they are firm. Sprinkle with the brandy and simmer until it has evaporated. Add 2 tablespoons additional butter, stir in the flour, and pour on the broth. Simmer the mushrooms slowly, stirring often, for about 20 minutes. Add the cream about 5 minutes before the end of cooking and continue to simmer until the mixture thickens slightly. Butter a round baking dish. Add 2 or 3 pancakes, spread with a little sauce, sprinkle with Parmesan, and dot with butter. Continue in this way until you have used all the pancakes, topping the final layer with Parmesan. Place in a 400° oven for about 25 minutes, or until browned. Serve at once.

* Note: you may substitute 1 ounce dried boletus mushrooms for fresh. Cover with tepid water first, and soak for 30 minutes, then dry and chop. The soaking water can be strained through cheesecloth and reduced over heat (add a bouillon cube for extra flavor), then added to the mushrooms while they cook.

1 Mash the boiled potatoes and mix with flour in a bowl.

2 Add eggs and enough milk to make a thick but fluid batter.

3 Fry the pancakes in a skillet with melted butter.

4 Arrange in layers in a baking dish, alternating with tomato sauce and cheese.

Potato pancake casserole

Cold Stuffed Vegetables

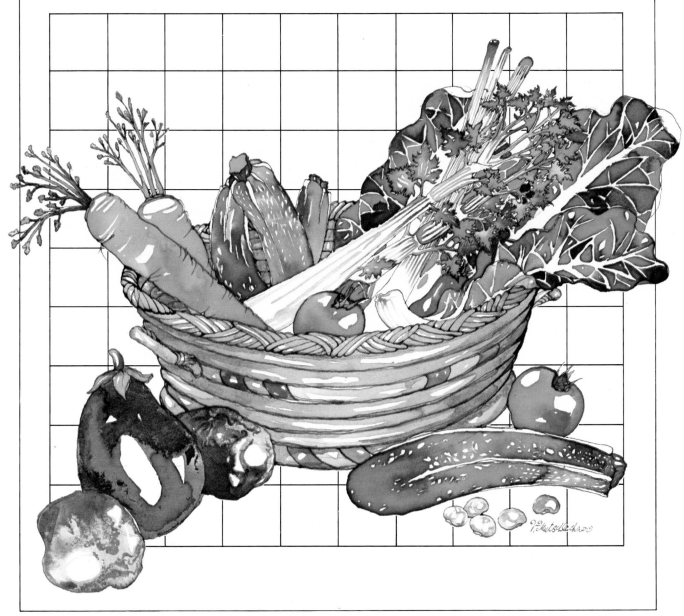

Tomatoes with green mayonnaise

C old stuffed vegetables include both raw and cooked vegetables stuffed with an uncooked filling, and vegetables stuffed, baked, and then allowed to cool before serving. Many vegetables are excellent cold and stuffed, including onions, which have been part of Mediterranean cooking since ancient times, and tomatoes, green peppers, and eggplants, all of which were introduced to Italian cooking after the discovery of America. These relatively recent arrivals are also key ingredients in many regional Italian recipes, with their fillings varying depending on regional tastes. Among the many regional recipes for stuffed vegetables are stuffed peppers, which are made with tomatoes in Campania and rice in Piedmont; both dishes are very good hot, but even better cold. Onions, artichokes, fennel, celery, zucchini, and

eggplants all lend themselves to being served at room temperature or chilled. How fortunate for the busy cook, who can make all these delightful dishes the day before. Indeed, only stuffed vegetables that are fried cannot be served cold.

Even though cold stuffed vegetables can make a perfect winter luncheon, their real moment of glory is in the summer, when freshly picked, perfectly ripened produce is abundant. Cooks with their own gardens can pick the vegetables still warm from the sun! Summer vegetables lend themselves well to a variety of different sauces and stuffings. All that is needed is a bit of imagination. Imagination also plays a role in the decoration and presentation of dishes. Just a simple garnish of an herb like curly parsley can give a finishing touch to a stuffed vegetable creation.

Some useful advice

The first step in preparing these recipes is to choose the vegetables with a certain critical eye. They should be neither too big nor too small, and all should be roughly the same size so that they cook at a uniform rate and make equal servings. They should also be unblemished, perfectly ripe, and absolutely fresh. Let's look at how to choose each vegetable to insure the success of these recipes.

Artichokes should have tightly closed leaves and stiff firm stems.

Cucumbers should be firm and not too large, with a dark green skin.

Onions should be either yellow or white, rather than red, and should be large, firm, and without sprouts.

Fennel should have tightly closed stalks and be meaty and white with no yellowish spots.

Eggplants should be small and firm, indicating that there are not too many seeds, and free from blemishes.

Peppers and tomatoes are the vegetables most commonly served stuffed and cold since they are very good raw and require little preparation. Peppers can be red, yellow, or green. Meaty and sweet, their flesh should be firm, thick, and unnicked.

Tomatoes should be round, firm, and neither too large nor too ripe. Their skin should be smooth and blemish-free.

In choosing celery to stuff, look for a green, tender, meaty stalk that is not too large.

Zucchini should be on the small side, fairly straight rather than curved, and without soft spots or blemishes.

Once you have chosen a vegetable, you must choose a stuffing, keeping in mind the amount of time you have to prepare it.

Many of the recipes mentioned in the section on hot stuffed vegetables are, in fact, equally good if not better served cold and make an excellent first course or even a main course in the summer. One example is stuffed peppers, which contain a succulent filling based on eggplant, anchovies, and bread crumbs (see on page 152). Another example is rice-stuffed tomatoes from the Campania region (see on page 138). Raw tomatoes are with seasoned rice and baked in the oven, then left to cool so that their full flavor can be enjoyed on a hot summer day. Artichokes packed with the famous stuffing of parsley, mint, garlic and bread crumbs are delicious served cold (see on page 144), as are onions and eggplants with meatless stuffings.

All of these vegetables make delicious accompaniments to a plate of cold meats, but they really shine when served as a first course.

There are a hundred different quick and easily prepared stuffings from which to choose. Artichokes are delicious with finely minced ham, tongue, or chicken dressed with mayonnaise; for tomatoes, a thick flavorful sauce based on tuna, anchovies, capers, and different kinds of pickles is sublime; cucumbers are beautifully complimented by a mixture of hard-boiled egg with anchovies or herring, pickles, mustard, and grated horseradish.

And there are still more stuffings: beet salad, fish salad, and cold rice with vegetables, pickles, and cheese. Raw stuffed vegetables can often be molded in gelatin and then the dish becomes an irresistable taste treat.

One final word of advice: as already mentioned, these dishes can be cooked ahead of time and, in fact, improve upon standing. They should be kept in the refrigerator but removed a few hours before serving.

Tomatoes stuffed with tuna

- ■ Yield: 4 servings
- ■ Time needed: 1 hour 15 minutes
- ■ Difficulty: *

Ingredients: 8 ripe tomatoes, 10 pitted green olives, 1 small can anchovies, drained, one 7-oz can chunk light tuna in oil, drained, one 2 to 3-oz jar capers, 2 tbsp chopped sour pickle, 2 hard-boiled eggs, 2 large egg yolks, lemon, parsley sprigs, 1⅓ cups good quality olive oil, salt, pepper.

Choose medium-sized tomatoes that are firm and meaty. Wash and drain, then cut a slice off the bottom (1). With a spoon or scoop, remove the pulp without breaking the walls (2). Place the tomatoes face down on a plate and let stand for 10 minutes to drain off excess liquid. Sprinkle the inside with salt and pepper (3).

Meanwhile make a mayonnaise. Beat two egg yolks in a bowl with ¼ teaspoon salt and a few drops of lemon juice until thick and pale. Beating with a wire whip or,

1 Slice off the bottoms of the tomatoes with a sharp knife.

2 Scoop out the pulp, being careful not to break the walls.

3 Let drain upside down, then sprinkle with salt and pepper.

4 To prepare the filling, mix tuna, capers, pickles, and anchovies into the mayonnaise.

better still, an electric mixer, begin by adding the olive oil drop by drop.

When the mixture begins to mount, add the oil by teaspoonfuls, still beating continuously, until very thick. Add lemon juice to taste, and thin if necessary with additional oil.

Chop the olives together with the pickles, anchovy fillets (reserve 8), capers (reserve a big spoonful), and the tuna. Set aside ⅓ cup of the mayonnaise for decoration and combine the rest with the chopped ingredients (4), mixing with a wooden spoon until perfectly blended.

Fill the tomatoes with the tuna mixture (5), dividing it evenly. Wrap each reserved anchovy around a caper and place an anchovy roll in the center of each tomato (6). Put the reserved mayonnaise in a pastry bag and, using a small star tip, decorate around the edges of the tomatoes (7). Place the tomatoes on a serving plate and garnish with slices of hard-boiled egg and parsley (8). Refrigerate until ready to serve.

These cold tomatoes may be presented as part of an antipasto or as a first course.

Note: If you like, the stuffed tomatoes may be glazed with aspic. Soften ½ envelope (1½ teaspoons) instant gelatin in 2 tablespoons chicken broth for 5 minutes, then add another cup broth and heat until gelatin dissolves. Let cool, then cover the tomatoes with several coats, refrigerating after each coat to set. Spoon remaining aspic onto a plate, chill until firm, cut into cubes, and serve with the tomatoes.

5 Fill the tomatoes with the tuna mixture, dividing it evenly.

6 Place an anchovy fillet wrapped around a caper in the center of each tomato.

7 Decorate each tomato with mayonnaise using a pastry bag.

8 Garnish the serving dish with hard-boiled eggs and parsley.

Tomatoes stuffed with tuna

Tomatoes with green mayonnaise

■ Yield: 4 servings
■ Time needed: ¹/₂ hour
■ Difficulty: **

Ingredients: 4 ripe but firm tomatoes, 3 hard-boiled eggs, 1¹/₄ cup mayonnaise, 1 packed cup spinach, 1 tbsp capers, 1 tbsp chopped sour pickle, 1 tsp anchovy paste, sprigs watercress, salt, white pepper.

Trim off the tough stems of the spinach and wash thoroughly. Boil until tender, then squeeze as dry as possible between your hands. Purée the spinach, capers (set aside 4), and pickles in a blender, then add the purée to the mayonnaise. Force two of the eggs through a sieve and add to the mayonnaise mixture along with the anchovy paste and a little pepper.

Cut a slice off the tops of the tomatoes, then cut tomatoes in half horizontally. Gently squeeze out some of the seeds and juice, sprinkle with salt and pepper, and spread the four bottom halves with a thick layer of mayonnaise. Cover with the top halves and decorate each tomato with a slice of the remaining hard-boiled egg and a caper. Finally, garnish the plate with sprigs of watercress or some other leafy green. See photo on page 176.

Tomatoes with pâté

■ Yield: 4 servings
■ Time needed: 1 hour
■ Difficulty: *

Ingredients: 8 medium-sized tomatoes, 4 eggs, about 4 oz goose-liver or chicken-liver pâté, 2 tbsp heavy cream, whipped, paprika, salt.

Wash the tomatoes and cut a slice off the bottom. Gently squeeze to remove seeds and juice, then scoop out the flesh. Liberally salt the inside of the tomato shells and let drain upside down for 30 minutes. Cook the eggs for 10 minutes in boiling water, then cool under cold running water and shell. Cut eggs in half and put one half inside each tomato.

Mash the pâté with a spoon until soft and perfectly smooth, fold in the whipped cream, and then place the mixture in a pastry bag fitted with a ¹/₄-inch star tip. Pipe this mixture over the tomatoes in a decorative fashion. Sprinkle with paprika and place the tomatoes in the refrigerator until ready to serve.

Tomato "sandwiches"

■ Yield: 4 servings
■ Time needed: ¹/₂ hour
■ Difficulty: *

Ingredients: 4 ripe but firm tomatoes, 16 oz mozzarella, about 12 sliced stuffed green olives, sprigs curly parsley, pinches oregano, mayonnaise or oil and lemon dressing (see below), salt, pepper.

Wash and dry the tomatoes, cut into thick slices, and let drain on paper towels for 15 minutes. Cut the mozzarella into slices approximately the same size as the tomato slices. Make "sandwiches" by covering half the tomato slices with slices of mozzarella; salt lightly and top with another slice of tomato. Season with salt, pepper, and a little oregano. Decorate the top of each tomato "sandwich" with sliced olives and tiny sprigs of parsley. Serve with mayonnaise or oil and lemon dressing (one part lemon juice to two parts oil, plus salt and pepper).

Dressed-up tomatoes

■ Yield: 4 servings
■ Time needed: ¹/₂ hour
■ Difficulty: *

Ingredients: 8 medium-sized tomatoes, 10 oz tuna in oil, 2 large egg yolks, ¹/₂ cup heavy cream, whipped, ¹/₂ lemon, 1 tbsp vinegar, 1¹/₄ cups olive oil, sour pickles, salt.

Cut a slice from the tops of each tomato. Loosen the insides lightly with a sharp knife, then scoop out the pulp. Turn tomato shells upside-down for 15 minutes to drain.

Prepare a mayonnaise. Put the egg yolks in a bowl, add salt and vinegar, and beat vigorously with a wire whip or electric beater until thick. Beating constantly, add the olive oil in a thin stream until the mayonnaise is thick and smooth. Add a few drops of vinegar to taste and fold in the whipped cream.

Drain and mash the tuna. Fill the tomatoes with the tuna, sprinkle with lemon juice, and completely cover with the mayonnaise. Place on a serving plate and decorate with pickles cut into fan-like slices.

Artichokes with poached eggs

1 Trim the artichokes, removing the stems and the tough outer leaves.

- **Yield: 4 servings**
- **Time needed: 1 hour**
- **Difficulty: ****

Ingredients: 4 large artichokes about the same size, 4 eggs, 1 sieved hard-boiled egg yolk, juice of 1 lemon, ¾ cup mayonnaise, 1 tbsp parsley minced with 1 clove garlic, 1 tbsp chopped capers, 1 tbsp chopped sour pickle, 3 tbsp white vinegar, salt.

Trim the artichokes by removing the tough outer leaves (1) and thorny tips (2), immersing each in water and lemon juice as it is finished. Cook in boiling salted water for 30-40 minutes, or until the bottoms are tender when pierced with a fork.

Meanwhile, bring 1 quart water to a boil in a large pot and add white vinegar and a little salt. Turn down the heat so that the water is barely simmering. One at a time break the four eggs onto a plate (3) and then gently slide each into the simmering water (4). With a wooden spatula or strainer, bring the whites up around the yolks (5). Adjust the flame so that the water remains at a bare simmer and cook three minutes. Remove each egg as it is done with the strainer (6) and place it on a cloth. Trim off ragged edges with a knife.

Drain the artichokes upside down on a cloth. When cool, spread the center leaves and scrape the choke off the bottom with a teaspoon (7). Sprinkle the hollows with the parsley-garlic mixture, capers, and pickles, and place an egg in the center (8). Transfer the artichokes to a serving plate (9), sprinkle the leaves with the sieved hard-boiled egg yolk (10), and spoon the mayonnaise over the eggs (11). To give this dish even more flavor, mix finely minced fresh herbs such as parsley, tarragon, chives, or chervil into the mayonnaise. Serve as part of an antipasto or as a first course.

2 Cut off the sharp tips and place the artichokes in cold water and lemon juice.

3 One at a time, break the eggs, onto a plate...

4 ...and gently slide into barely simmering water.

5 With a wooden spatula or a strainer, scoop the white around the yolk.

6 As the eggs are cooked, carefully remove them with a strainer.

7 Drain the boiled artichokes and spread the leaves with a spoon.

8 Place an egg in the center of each artichoke.

9 Arrange the artichokes in a ring on a serving plate.

10 Sprinkle the leaves with hard-boiled egg yolk.

11 Then cover each egg with a spoonful of mayonnaise.

Artichokes with poached eggs

Artichokes in a piquant sauce

■ Yield: 4 servings
■ Time needed: 1 hour 15 minutes
■ Difficulty: *

Ingredients: 8 artichokes, 1 tbsp capers, 1 tbsp chopped sour pickles, handful parsley, 4 tbsp olive oil, 2 lemons, 1 beef bouillon cube, salt, pepper.

Cut off the artichoke stems and remove the tough outer leaves, the thorny leaf tips, and the choke. As you finish trimming each one, drop the artichokes in water acidulated with the juice of one lemon.

Boil the artichokes in salted water about 10 minutes. Drain, then place upright on a cutting board and spread the leaves a little. Finely chop the capers, pickles, and parsley together, add the oil and the juice of the other lemon and season with salt and pepper. Spoon this mixture into the center of the artichokes, place in a pan, and add the bouillon cube plus enough water to come halfway up the sides of the artichokes. Simmer over a low flame until the bottoms are very tender. Watch that the broth doesn't cook away. Best served cold.

Tuna-stuffed peppers

■ Yield: 4 servings
■ Time needed: 1 1/2 hours
■ Difficulty: *

Ingredients: 4 red peppers, one 7-oz can tuna packed in oil, 1 tbsp capers, 2/3 cup fresh bread crumbs, 8 black olives, pinch oregano, 4 tbsp olive oil, salt, pepper.

Wash the peppers, slice off the tops along with the stems, and scoop out the ribs and seeds. Briefly soak the bread crumbs in water to cover, then squeeze out. Pit the olives and chop them together with the capers. Drain the tuna and crumble. In a bowl, mix the tuna, squeezed-out bread crumbs, capers, olives, and oregano. Add the oil, stirring well, and season with salt and pepper. Fill the peppers with this mixture and bake in a 350° oven until tender. Best served cold.

Stuffed celery hors d'oeuvre

■ Yield: 4 servings
■ Time needed: 20 minutes
■ Difficulty: *

Ingredients: 8-10 celery stalks, 3 1/2 oz sharp Gorgonzola cheese (or substitute Roquefort), 4 tbsp softened butter, 1/2 cup shredded Gruyère, 1/2 lemon, pepper.

Choose very tender celery stalks. Wash, peel off the toughest outer strings, and remove the top inch or so. Soak in ice water mixed with the lemon juice for 30 min. Meanwhile, prepare the spread. Beat the butter in a bowl with a wooden spoon until fluffy. Add the Gorgonzola and mash with a fork until smooth. Season with pepper. Drain and dry the celery. Pack the cheese mixture into a pastry bag fitted with a 1/2-inch star tip and pipe it down the middle of the grooved side of celery stalks. Arrange them on a serving plate. Scatter some of the Gruyère over the celery and mound the rest in the center of the plate.

Stuffed celery stalks

■ Yield: 4 servings
■ Time needed: 1/2 hour
■ Difficulty: *

Ingredients: 8-10 celery stalks, 1 hard-boiled egg, 1 large egg yolk, 1 lemon, parsley, 1 tbsp anchovy paste, 2/3 cup oil, 1 tbsp Dijon mustard, salt, pepper.

After removing the stringy filaments, cut the celery stalks into pieces about 3 inches long and put into a bowl of ice water mixed with the juice from half the lemon. Set aside for 15 minutes.

Proceed to make a mayonnaise: beat the egg yolk until thick with a few drops of lemon juice and a pinch each of salt and pepper. Very slowly add the oil, beating constantly with a wire whip or electric mixer. When the sauce is thick, add the anchovy paste, mustard, and lemon juice, mixing until ingredients are blended. Scoop the mayonnaise into a pastry bag fitted with a 1/2-inch star tip. Drain and dry the celery, then pipe the mayonnaise sauce down the center of the stalks. Arrange on a plate and decorate with the slices of hard-boiled egg and parsley. Serve cold.

Note: For a more flavored dish, fill celery with this mixture: mash 1/3 cup ricotta cheese with salt, pepper, 1 tbsp olive oil, 3-4 mashed garlic cloves, and 2 tsp anchovy paste or 4-6 mashed anchovy fillets. Pipe this mixture as indicated above and garnish celery with caper-stuffed anchovies or strips of marinated pepper.

Pepper rolls

■ **Yield: 4 servings**
■ **Time needed: 1 hour (plus 1 hour marinating time)**
■ **Difficulty: ***

Ingredients: 4 yellow or bell peppers, 1 small can anchovies, drained, 1 tbsp capers, 1/3 cup pitted green olives, 1 tbsp mustard, 1 envelope gelatin, 2 cups chicken broth, 2 lemons, parsley sprigs, 1 tbsp parsley chopped with 1 clove garlic, 1 bay leaf, 1 cup distilled white vinegar, 4-6 tbsp olive oil, salt, pepper.

Cut the peppers in half lengthwise, remove the seeds, ribs, and stems (1), and cut into large strips (2). Place under the broiler, skin side up, until the skin turns black, then remove and scrape off the skin with a knife (3). A few at a time, boil pepper strips for 3 minutes in 1 quart water to which you've added the vinegar, bay leaf, and 1 tablespoon salt (4). Dry and place in a deep dish. Sprinkle with a little lemon juice, the chopped parsley and garlic (5), 3-4 tablespoons oil, salt, and pepper; add sliced garlic if you wish (6). Let marinate about an hour.

Mash the pitted olives in a mortar with the anchovies, capers, and mustard, adding enough oil to make a paste (7). Lay the peppers out on a marble slab and spread each one with a little of the paste (8). Roll up each strip (9) and arrange on a plate (10). Decorate with lemon slices and parsley sprigs (11) and, if you like, sliced stuffed green olives. Refrigerate.

Combine 2 tablespoons strained lemon juice and 2 tablespoons of the chicken broth in a small saucepan. Sprinkle with the gelatin and let soften 10 minutes. Add remaining broth and stir over low heat until the gelatine completely dissolves. Let cool to room temperature, then spoon over the peppers (12). Return the plate to the refrigerator until the gelatin has completely set.

1 Cut the peppers in half lengthwise, removing the seeds, ribs, and stems.

2 Cut the halves into long strips all the same size.

3 Broil the peppers until charred, then scrape off the skins.

4 Bring vinegar and water to a boil and boil the pepper strips a few at a time.

5 Arrange peppers in a dish and sprinkle with lemon juice and chopped garlic and parsley.

6 Season with salt and pepper, moisten with oil, and add a few slices of garlic if you like.

7 In a mortar, mash the olives, anchovies, mustard, and capers, adding a little oil.

8 Spread the pepper strips out and cover with some of the paste.

9 Then roll each strip up around the paste.

10 Arrange peppers in a deep serving dish.

11 Decorate with lemon slices, parsley and, if you like, stuffed olives.

12 Cover the rolls with a layer of aspic and refrigerate until set.

Pepper rolls

Stuffed onions

■ Yield: 4 servings
■ Time needed: 1 hour 45 minutes
■ Difficulty: *

Ingredients: 8 large yellow onions, 2 bell peppers, one 8-oz can tomatoes, 4 tbsp butter, 1 anchovy fillet, ¼ cup pitted black olives, 2 tbsp bread crumbs, ½ tsp oregano, oil, salt, pepper.

Peel the onions and boil for 15-20 minutes, or until partially tender. Drain and dry on a towel (1). Cut the top off each onion, remove inner layers (2), and chop the pulp. Broil the peppers until the skins char, then scrape off the skins with a knife and cut peppers into thin strips. Drain the anchovies and chop them with the olives.

Heat 3 tablespoons oil in a skillet and gently sauté the reserved chopped onion until soft. Add the anchovy-olive mixture, the pepper strips, and the canned tomatoes, drained. Simmer until the mixture becomes a thick sauce, then remove from the fire and add the oregano, the bread crumbs, and salt and a little pepper to taste.

Fill the onions with the tomato mixture (3), arrange them in a greased baking dish, and dot with the butter (4). Bake in a 350° oven for about 40 minutes, or until is very tender.

This flavorful dish is best served cold. It makes a very good first course in the summer or an excellent accompaniment to roasts.

1 Boil the onions for 15 to 20 minutes, drain, and dry on a towel.

2 Cut off the tops and remove most of the insides with a spoon.

3 Make a stuffing and fill the boiled onions with it.

4 Arrange onions in a greased baking dish and dot with butter.

SALADS
AND DECORATIVE
GARNISHES

Salads

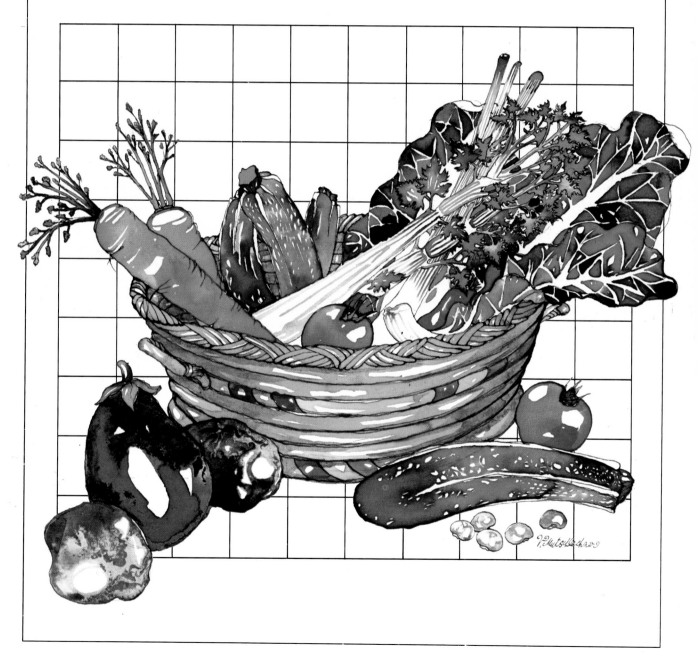

Usually made from raw vegetables, salads are full of vitamins, but also happen to be refreshing, colorful, and exciting dishes, especially in the summer. The origin of the word "salad" is probably the Latin verb "salare", meaning "to salt". The earliest mention of salad comes from ancient Greece, where vegetables were served with a dressing of oil and vinegar, or with other complicated dressings made with oil, crushed olives, eggs, and honey, or even with the ever-present "garum", a kind of fermented fish oil which the ancient Romans loved. In Rome the most popular salads were made with chicory and watercress, but some salads were also made with garlic and onion, gladiola bulbs, asphodels, and even orchids.

Pliny wrote that the Romans were familiar with vinegar, which was often diluted with water and given to soldiers during long marches to quench their thirst. Only occasionally was it used in salad dressings. During the medieval period a diet based on vegetables was very common. This was not by choice, but rather because wars and famine left little else available. Starting with the Renaissance, the average diet improved, especially as far as vegetables are concerned. Previously unknown vegetables began to appear and partly alleviated the problem of hunger. We can justly say that today, as in the past, raw vegetables greatly enhance our diet because of their nutritional qualities, especially their high content both of vitamins (A, C, B, E and K) and of precious minerals. Even the large amount of water that vegetables contain has a beneficial effect in protecting the body against dehydration. Vegetables are also high in fiber.

In closing it should be emphasized that the word "salad" refers both to green salads made with lettuce, endive, and chicory, as well as to salads made with such raw vegetables as fennel, celery, cauliflower, artichokes, zucchini, or spinach, and served with either traditional or unusual dressings.

How to make salads

Simple green salads — Green salads are composed of leafy vegetables of various kinds, used either singly or in combination.

There are many different varieties of greens, but the best known are the various members of the lettuce family. These include iceberg head lettuce, romaine lettuce, Boston and Bibb lettuce, and numerous leaf lettuces that may have large or small, curly or smooth, green, golden, or even reddish leaves.

Also considered greens are the favorite Italian salad vegetable, chicory, the expensive and highly prized white Belgian endive, and the ruby red radicchio, whose vivid color and bitter savor lend distinction to salads based on milder greens. Finally, watercress and dandelion leaves can also be used as salad greens.

Before greens are eaten, the tough outer leaves as well as any damaged ones should be discarded. The greens should then be washed in at least two or three changes of water and carefully lifted out of the water each time so that the dirt settles to the bottom of the sink. They are then dried with a cloth or in a salad spinner. This drying process should be done with extreme caution, especially when the leaves are thin and tender, or else they will be crushed and the salad will be full of wilted greens. If the leaves are large, it is a good idea to tear them with your hands, or cut them into pieces or thin strips.

Simple green salads often contain other tender raw vegetables like zucchini, baby spinach, artichokes, and carrots. These salads are served with the same dressings used for other salads, though often fresh herbs are added for flavor.

Tossed Salads — Tossed salads are made by combining raw vegetables and at times even meat, fish, eggs, or cheese. These salads often turn out to be creative new dishes combining foods that may never have been served together before. The best results are obtained when there is an interplay of strong and delicate flavors and contrasting colors. These salads always contain some greens along with a wide variety of unexpected vegetables and — why not? — even fruit.

The vegetables used in tossed salads are usually sliced in thin strips or rounds, and fruit is usually cut into wedges or cubes. Fruit and vegetables that have been cleaned and cut up may be stored in the refrigerator in a bowl of ice water and covered with aluminum foil or plastic wrap.

Besides being served as a side dish, a tossed salad can be served as part of an antipasto or even as a main dish if it is especially hearty and filling.

If pasta or rice is added, the salad can be served as a first course.

Cooked salads — Made with vegetables that have been cooked, these salads can be served with the same dressings used for green salads and may contain a combination of vegetables and other foods as well.

The "mayonnaise salads", so-called because mayonnaise is the basic ingredient and binds the salad together, belong to this group.

Gelatin salads are also included. The gelatin matrix not only holds all the ingredients together but also adds a glamorous touch.

To make these cooked salads, the vegetables must first be trimmed and washed, then boiled in lots of salted water and drained while they are slightly underdone. If you are using vegetables that tend to turn brown, you will have to soak them in acidulated water, then add a little white flour to the water they are cooked in. If the salad you are making calls for beets, they should be cooked separately or else they will stain all the other vegetables.

The choice of vegetables for a mayonnaise salad is ample because mayonnaise is compatible with a wide range of flavors. The choice is more difficult when you are making gelatin.

Salad dressings

"To make a proper salad, you must be a wise man with the salt, a miser with the vinegar, and a spend-thrift with the oil; toss it like a madman and eat it straightaway." This old saying sums up all the rules for a perfect salad dressing. The traditional ingredients used to make the famous "vinaigrette" are three parts oil, one part vinegar, a pinch of salt, and just a dash of pepper. If you're making a cooked salad or a raw salad comprised mostly of lettuce, you can use lemon juice instead of vinegar. A raw salad should be tossed with the dressing at the very last minute or the vegetables will wilt; a cooked salad should be tossed with its dressing a bit in advance so that the vegetables have time to absorb the flavor of the dressing. It is always better to use extra-virgin olive oil and top quality wine vinegar. You can obtain an unusual, original flavor by using an oil or vinegar steeped with herbs. The oil should be added last, a little bit at a time, or the dressing may not emulsify and thicken and the salt may not dissolve. In addition to the most commonly used ingredients there are many others used in different regions of Italy by different ethnic groups. A cheese dressing, for example, is widely favored in the countryside. This is made by adding a strong aged cheese, grated, to a dressing for a raw salad. A garlic dressing is made by rubbing the inside of the salad bowl with a clove of garlic which will impart its flavor to the whole salad. Instead of using oil, farmers in the countryside have a tradition of using bacon fat on raw salads. Used in the same proportions as oil, bacon fat is melted in a pan and diluted with vinegar. Finally, for lettuce and other tender greens there is a very fancy dressing made with light cream and flavored with mustard and grated horseradish. Many popular dressings have raw or hard-boiled eggs as their main ingredient. These include tartar sauce and other kinds of mayonnaise.

The necessary equipment

When we are talking about salads, the most important piece of equipment is of course the salad bowl. There are many different kinds: crystal bowls for fancy dinner parties, glass or ceramic bowls for everyday use, bowls of glazed porcelain and more modern materials like plexiglass, traditional wooden bowls, and even a special kind of aluminum bowl that doesn't react in the presence of lemon juice or vinegar. Serving forks and spoons may be made of bone or wood, never of silver or ordinary aluminum. When the salad is a side dish that accompanies meat or fish it may be brought to the table in salad plates, which are set to the left of the dinner plate. Salad plates can either match the salad bowl or be part of a separate complete set. The only exception is molded gelatin salad, which should be presented on a serving platter and served up on small plates at the table. Raw vegetables can be served in sectioned fondue plates. Every person has a small bowl of dressing of his own and then dunks the vegetables in the dressing. A very simple and elegant touch is serving a colorful mixed salad in long-stemmed glass fruit cups set at each place. Serve any sauce that is to accompany raw vegetables or exotic fruits in a mustard dish, which resembles a miniature soup tureen, comes with a small spoon, and is often included in a set of dishes. Finally, in presenting salads at the table, remember to use handsome cruets for oil and vinegar, as well as attractive salt shakers and pepper mills. Before the salad is made, the greens must be washed well and thoroughly dried. A kitchen towel will do but a metal mesh basket with a handle or a salad spinner makes the whole process easier. Various small kitchen gadgets are handy if not essential. Among these are the olive pitter, the grater, the garlic press, and the parsley mincer. Vegetables that are firm but not hard may be sliced very thinly with an electric or manual vegetable slicer.

Russian salad

- **Yield: 4 servings**
- **Time needed: about 1 hour**
- **Difficulty: ***

Ingredients: 8 oz potatoes, 6 oz string beans, 6 oz carrots, 6 oz shelled peas, 2 oz assorted marinated vegetables, 2 egg yolks, 2 tsp fresh lemon juice, about 1¼ cups olive oil, freshly ground pepper, salt.

Clean all the vegetables and boil them in salted water until tender, adding the vegetables that need a longer cooking time to the pot first. Drain well. Cut the potatoes and carrots into cubes and the string beans (1) and marinated vegetables into small pieces.

Place the egg yolks in a bowl with 1 teaspoon of the lemon juice and a pinch of salt and pepper and beat with a whisk until thick. Beating constantly, add the oil a drop at a time. When the mayonnaise becomes too thick to beat, add a few drops of the remaining lemon juice (2). Continue adding the oil and lemon juice alternately until you have used them all up.

Place all the vegetables in a bowl and mix in the mayonnaise (3). Mound the salad on a serving dish covered with lettuce leaves (4). You may also add diced chicken, fish, ham, or tongue to the salad.

1 Cut the cooked potatoes and carrots into cubes and the string beans into pieces

2 Add the oil little by little to the beaten yolks; then add the lemon juice.

3 Place all the cooked and marinated vegetables in a bowl and mix in the mayonnaise.

4 Mound the salad on a serving dish that has been covered with lettuce leaves.

Russian salad

Zucchini
salad
with mint

- ■ **Yield: 4 servings**
- ■ **Time needed: 20 minutes (plus 3 hours soaking time)**
- ■ **Difficulty: ***

Ingredients: 1 lb small firm zucchini, 1 tsp fresh chopped mint, $^1/_3$ cup olive oil, salt, 3-6 sliced radishes (optional).

Wash the zucchini but do not peel. Soak in ice water for three hours so that zucchini will become hard and crispy.

Drain the zucchini, cut off the ends, and slice very thinly (1). Dry well with a kitchen towel (2).

In a small bowl beat together the oil and a pinch of salt (3). Place the zucchini slices in a large salad bowl, then pour on the oil mixture (4). Mix carefully. Just before serving, sprinkle the chopped mint over the zucchini.

If you want, you can garnish this simple salad with some sliced radishes.

1 Trim the ends of the zucchini and thinly slice with a slicing tool.

2 Put the zucchini slices on a clean kitchen towel and dry well.

3 In a small bowl beat together oil and a pinch of salt with a fork.

4 Place the zucchini in a large salad bowl, pour on the oil, and mix carefully.

Zucchini salad with mint

Spinach salad

- ■ **Yield: 4 servings**
- ■ **Time needed:** ¹/₂ hour
- ■ **Difficulty:** *

Ingredients: 8 oz tender small spinach, 8 oz mushrooms, 1 heart romaine lettuce, 1 head Boston or Bibb lettuce, 1 lemon, 1 tbsp chopped parsley, 1 tbsp mustard, ¹/₄ cup olive oil, salt.

Trim, wash, and dry the lettuce and put the leaves in a salad bowl. Wash the spinach very well under running water and dry with a cloth (1). Break the leaves off the stems and put these into the salad bowl (2). Trim away the dark outer leaves of the romaine and save for some other purpose. Wash and dry the pale, crispy heart, cut it in half lengthwise (3), slice into thin strips (4), and add to the other vegetables. Peel the mushrooms and remove the dried bit at the end of the stems, placing the trimmed mushrooms in water acidulated with lemon juice. Slice mushrooms (5) and put them in the salad bowl (6). Put a pinch of salt in a bowl, add the oil (7), parsley, mustard (8), and the juice of half a lemon (9). Beat until smooth and thick, then spoon the dressing over the salad (10), mix carefully, and serve.

1 After washing the spinach well under running water, dry it on a cloth...

2 ...and break the leaves off the stems one by one and place them in a salad bowl.

3 After trimming off the tough outer leaves, wash and dry the romaine lettuce and cut in half lengthwise...

4 ...then slice crosswise into small strips.

5 Trim the mushrooms, placing them in water acidulated with lemon juice, then slice...

6 ...and add the slices to the other vegetables already in the salad bowl.

7 In a small bowl, blend salt, olive oil...

8 ...chopped parsley, mustard...

9 ...and the juice of half a lemon, mixing well.

10 Spoon the prepared dressing over the spinach salad.

Spinach salad

Crispy salad

3 tbsp chopped parsley, 6 slices white bread, about 1 cup olive oil, 1-2 tbsp red wine vinegar, salt.

Using a grater, shred the cheese (1). Trim and wash the lettuce, dry the leaves well, tear them into pieces with your hands, and place in a large salad bowl (2).

In a small bowl, combine a pinch of salt, 3 tablespoons olive oil, the chopped parsley, and the vinegar (3). Mix well until the dressing is very thick and thoroughly blended (4).

Remove the crusts from the bread (5) and cut bread into strips, then into cubes (6). Sauté the bread in remaining oil, heated to the verge of smoking, and drain when nicely browned and crisp (7). Add the cheese (8), croutons (9), and anchovies to the salad and toss with the parsley dressing (10).

■ Yield: 4 servings
■ Time needed: ½ hour
■ Difficulty: *

Ingredients: 1 head leaf lettuce, 1 head romaine lettuce, 3 oz Gruyère, 3 drained anchovy fillets,

1 Shred the cheese using the large-hole side of the grater.

2 Tear the lettuce leaves into pieces and put in a salad bowl.

3 In a small bowl combine a pinch of salt, olive oil, chopped parsley, and vinegar...

4 ...and beat until the dressing is thoroughly mixed and quite thick.

5 Stack the slices of white bread and slice off the crusts with a long knife.

6 Cut bread into even strips, then cut crosswise to make cubes.

7 Sauté the croutons in very hot oil and drain on paper towels when nicely browned.

8 Strew the cheese over the salad...

9 ...then add the sautéed croutons and anchovy fillets.

10 Before you serve the salad, toss with the parsley dressing, adding it to the salad by spoonfuls.

Crispy salad

Vegetables in aspic

- ■ **Yield: 4 servings**
- ■ **Time needed: 1 hour (plus setting time)**
- ■ **Difficulty: ***

Ingredients: 4 oz cooked chicken breast, 2 oz ham, 4 oz cabbage, ⅓ cup stuffed green olives, 6 oz cauliflower, 2 tbsp sugar, 1 green pepper, 1 red or yellow pepper, handful cooked peas, 1 celery heart, a few strips marinated peppers, 3 tbsp white vinegar, 1 envelope (1 tbsp) gelatin, 1 lemon, 1 tsp salt.

This is a rather simple dish to prepare and looks great when you serve it, but you must use very fresh, top quality ingredients for the best results (1).

Cut the celery into pieces. Cut the chicken, ham, peppers, and cabbage into strips (2). Cut the olives and the marinated pepper into thin slices. Break the flowerets off the central core of the cauliflower (3), then slice thinly (4). Mix all the ingredients in a large bowl (5). Put a 1-quart mold with smooth walls into the freezer.

To make the aspic, sprinkle the gelatin over the lemon juice and vinegar and let soften for 5 minutes (6). Add 1¾ cups boiling water plus the salt and sugar and stir until the sugar and gelatin dissolve. Let cool to room temperature. Pour a little of the cooled liquid gelatin into the mold and tilt the mold in all directions to coat evenly (7). (When the gelatin comes in contact with the chilled mold it will solidify immediately.)

Fill the mold nearly to the rim with the vegetable mixture (8) and pour the rest of the cooled but still liquid gelatin over the mixture (9). The vegetables should be completely covered. Cover the mold with foil and refrigerate for about 2 hours, or until the gelatin has set.

Just before serving the salad, invert it onto a round plate (if the aspic doesn't unmold, dip the mold in very hot water for a split second). Decorate the plate with lettuce leaves or rings of leek.

1 Use only the freshest, top quality vegetables for an attractive, savory aspic salad.

2 With a sharp knife cut the celery into small pieces and the pepper and cabbage into strips.

3 Cutting with a sharp knife, detach the cauliflower flowerets from the central core...

4 ...then cut into very thin slices (don't forget that these are to be eaten raw).

5 Mix the prepared vegetables with the chicken and ham in a large bowl.

6 Sprinkle the gelatin over the lemon juice and vinegar and set aside to soften.

7 Pour a little aspic into the mold and tilt the mold in all directions to coat evenly.

8 Fill the mold almost to the rim with the vegetable mixture (do not press down)...

9 ...then pour the rest of the still liquid aspic over the mixture, covering everything.

Vegetables in aspic

Salade niçoise

- Yield: 4 servings
- Time needed: 45 minutes
- Difficulty: *

Ingredients: 8 oz string beans, 10 oz boiling potatoes, 8 oz tomatoes, 8 drained anchovy fillets, 2 tbsp drained capers, 1/2 cup black olives, sprig parsley (optional), 5 tbsp olive oil, 2 tbsp wine vinegar, pepper, salt.

Start by preparing the cooked vegetables. Boil the potatoes in their skins in a large quantity of salted water. In another pot, boil the string beans. Cut the potatoes into cubes and the string beans into pieces (1). In a small bowl, combine a pinch of salt and pepper, vinegar, and the oil. Beat with a fork until thick and emulsified (2). Place the potatoes and the string beans in a salad bowl (3) and toss them with the dressing. Assemble all the remaining ingredients: the capers, olives, anchovies, and tomatoes, cut into uniform wedges (4). When you are ready to serve the salad, top the potatoes and beans with the assembled ingredients in a decorative way, and sprinkle with chopped parsley if you wish.

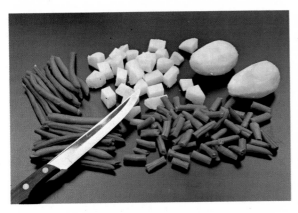

1 Boil the potatoes and string beans, then cut the potatoes into cubes and the string beans into pieces.

2 Make a dressing by mixing the oil and vinegar, a pinch of salt, and a few peppercorns.

3 Place the potatoes and string beans in a salad bowl, with the center slightly raised.

4 Prepare garnish by cutting tomatoes into wedges and setting out the capers, olives, and anchovies.

Salade niçoise

Mixed salad with yogurt dressing

- ■ Yield: 4 servings
- ■ Time needed: 1 hour 15 minutes
- ■ Difficulty: *

Ingredients: 3 boiling potatoes, 4 carrots, 1 leek, 1 tbsp capers, 1 tbsp mushrooms marinated in oil, 3 small sour pickles, ¼ cup black olives, 8 oz lean ham, 1 egg yolk, ½ lemon, ½ cup yogurt, 3 tbsp olive oil, salt, pepper.

Boil the potatoes and carrots until tender and cut into cubes (1). In a small bowl beat the egg yolk with a pinch of salt, pepper, and the juice from the lemon (2).

Place the cooked vegetables in a salad bowl and add the ham, cut into cubes, the pickles, sliced, the mushrooms, capers, and olives (3). Pour on the egg sauce (4) and mix. Spoon the yogurt over the top (5) and add the oil (6). Garnish with the white part of a leek cut into rings. Let stand for a few minutes to allow the vegetables to absorb the dressing.

1 Boil the potatoes and the carrots, drain, cool, and cut into cubes.

2 In a small bowl beat the yolk with a pinch of salt, pepper, and the juice of half a lemon.

3 In a salad bowl mix the vegetables, ham, pickles, mushrooms, capers, and olives.

4 Dress the salad with the egg sauce, mix well...

5 ...then spoon the yogurt evenly over the top.

6 Lastly, add olive oil and garnish with leek, cut into rings.

Mixed salad with yogurt dressing

Mushroom and shrimp salad

■ **Yield: 4 servings**
■ **Time needed: ½ hour**
■ **Difficulty: ***

Ingredients: 8 oz mushrooms, 10 oz shrimp, 1 bay leaf, 1 cup dry white wine, 1 head leaf lettuce, 2 tbsp ketchup, 2 tbsp sherry, 2 tbsp heavy cream, 1 tsp Worcestershire sauce, 1 tsp Dijon mustard, dash paprika, 1 cup mayonnaise, ½ tsp peppercorns, salt.

Clean the mushrooms and cut into thin slices. Wash the shrimp. Simmer white wine, a bay leaf, peppercorns, and salt for 5 minutes. Add the shrimp, cover, and steam for 3-5 minutes or until curled and pink. Drain, let cool, and shell.

Put the mayonnaise in a bowl and add the mustard, a little ground pepper, paprika, ketchup, Worcestershire sauce, sherry, and cream.

Line four small bowls with lettuce leaves. Put some of the sliced mushrooms in each bowl and cover with the sauce. Hook the shrimp over the rims of the bowls and serve as a first course.

Kiwi salad

■ **Yield: 4 servings**
■ **Time needed: 20 minutes**
■ **Difficulty: ***

Ingredients: 3 kiwis, the pale heart of 1 small head romaine lettuce, 2 grapefruits, juice of 1 lemon, 3 tbsp olive oil, salt, pepper.

Peel and slice the kiwis. Peel the grapefruits; cut one into cubes, the other into slices. Wash the lettuce and slice it into shreds.

Line the bottom of a glass salad bowl with shredded lettuce. Line the sides of the salad bowl with the fruits, alternating slices of kiwi with slices of grapefruit. Mound additional lettuce plus the grapefruit cubes in the center.

Dress the salad with a mixture made by beating together a pinch each of salt and freshly ground pepper, lemon juice, and olive oil.

(A picture of this salad is on page 192).

Midsummer salad

■ **Yield: 4 servings**
■ **Time needed: ½ hour**
■ **Difficulty: ***

Ingredients: One 16-oz can white beans, 5 oz bologna or mortadella, 5 oz Gruyère cheese, 5 oz ham, 4 small frankfurters, cooked, 2 scallions or pearl onions, 1 tbsp Dijon mustard, Worcestershire sauce, 1 red onion, 6 sliced radishes, juice of 1 lemon, 3 tbsp olive oil, salt, pepper.

Drain the beans in a strainer and rinse under running water, letting the water run off.

Dice the bologna or mortadella, the ham, and the cheese. Slice the onions thinly. Arrange the beans, bologna, ham, and cheese in a ring on a serving dish or salad bowl. Put the radishes and the sliced frankfurters in the center and garnish with the onion rings along the outside. In a small bowl, make a dressing by beating together a pinch each of salt and pepper, the lemon juice, mustard, a few drops Worcestershire sauce, and the oil. Spoon the dressing over the salad.

Note: you may substitute leftover meat or chicken, cut into thin strips, for some of the ingredients called for above.

Capricious salad

■ **Yield: 4 servings**
■ **Time needed: 1 hour**
■ **Difficulty: ***

Ingredients: 8 oz cooked chicken, 4 oz ham, 2 boiling potatoes, 2 carrots, 2 cooked artichoke bottoms, 2 celery hearts, 1 small white truffle (optional), juice of 1 lemon, 1 tbsp Dijon mustard, 1-2 tsp ketchup, ½ cup olive oil, salt, pepper.

Peel the carrots and potatoes and boil in salted water until tender. Let cool, then cut into cubes. Cut the chicken into slices and the ham into cubes; slice the artichoke bottoms and the celery hearts. Place all the ingredients in a salad bowl. Proceed to make the dressing. Beat the lemon juice with a pinch of salt, add the mustard and ketchup, beat in the oil, and season with freshly ground pepper. If you wish, top with slices of white truffle. Toss the salad with the prepared dressing.

Lettuce and fennel salad

- **Yield: 4 servings**
- **Time needed: 20 minutes**
- **Difficulty: ***

Ingredients: 1 large head romaine lettuce, 2 small tender fennels, 2 hard-boiled eggs, 1/2 cup pitted green or black olives, 1 tsp fennel seed, 1/3 cup olive oil, 2 tsp red wine vinegar, salt, pepper.

Trim off the tough outer leaves of the lettuce. Wash and dry the leaves without bruising them. Then cut into shreds. Remove the hard outer stalks of the fennel and any feathery leaves, and cut the hearts into nearly transparent razor-thin slices. Use a truffle slicer if you have one. In a small bowl, beat the oil with vinegar and a pinch each of salt and pepper. Put the lettuce, fennel, fennel seed, and olives in a salad bowl and toss the salad very carefully with the dressing. Cut the hard-boiled eggs in wedges, arrange them decoratively over the salad, and serve.

Sliced-egg salad

- **Yield: 4 servings**
- **Time needed: 1/2 hour**
- **Difficulty: ***

Ingredients: 1 small head Boston or Bibb lettuce, 1 head romaine lettuce, bunch chicory, 5 large eggs, 1 chopped scallion, 4 chopped drained anchovies, 1 tbsp Dijon mustard, 1 tbsp white vinegar, 3 tbsp olive oil, 1 cup mayonnaise, salt, pepper.

Boil the eggs for 14 minutes. Drain and let cool. Slice one egg into rounds, cut two eggs in half horizontally, and slice the remaining two into wedges. Wash the greens, drain, and dry the leaves well. In a small bowl, dissolve a pinch of salt in the vinegar, then add the mustard and a few pinches of freshly ground pepper. Stir this into the mayonnaise. Place the greens on a large serving dish to form a bed. Dress with oil and salt, then place the halved eggs in the center and cover with a little mayonnaise. Place the egg slices and wedges all around, overlapping slightly. Sprinkle chopped scallion and anchovies on top. Serve the salad with the dressing on the sides. To vary this salad, add small capers, sliced stuffed olives, or a few tomato wedges.

Grilled radicchio salad with anchovies

- **Yield: 4 servings**
- **Time needed: 1/2 hour**
- **Difficulty: ***

Ingredients: 1 lb radicchio, 4 drained anchovy fillets, 1 tsp capers, 1/4 cup olives, bunch parsley, 1/3 cup olive oil, 1 tbsp red wine vinegar, salt, pepper.

Trim the radicchio, removing the bottom of the stem and any wilted leaves. Cut all the heads in half lengthwise (cut very big ones into quarters). Wash and dry carefully, place on a dish, and oil lightly. Cook on a hot grill until wilted and nicely browned, turning often with a spatula.

In the meantime, make the dressing. Finely chop the anchovies, parsley, olives, and capers. Put the chopped mixture in a bowl and add the vinegar, a pinch of salt, and a goodly amount of pepper.

Place the grilled radicchio on a platter, pour the dressing over it, and serve.

This salad goes nicely with mixed grilled meats or with roast veal, pork, or chicken.

Grapefruit and avocado salad

- **Yield: 4 servings**
- **Time needed: 1/2 hour**
- **Difficulty: ***

Ingredients: 2 large grapefruits, 2 avocadoes, 2 oranges, 1 tart juicy apple, 1/4 cup chopped walnuts, 1 small head romaine lettuce, 4-5 tbsp mayonnaise, 1 tbsp yogurt, a few drops Worcestershire sauce.

Cut the grapefruits in half horizontally and remove sections with a grapefruit knife. Scrape all membranes out of the grapefruit skins and set skins aside. Peel the oranges, pulling off the white pith, and divide into sections. Slice the sections of oranges and grapefruit in half. Cut the avocado meat and apple meat into cubes. Mix all the fruit in a salad bowl and sprinkle the chopped nuts on top.

Add the Worcestershire sauce and yogurt to the mayonnaise. Pour the dressing over the fruit and mix.

Trim the lettuce, discarding the dark green outer leaves. Wash and dry. Line the empty grapefruit skins with lettuce leaves and fill with the salad. Refrigerate until serving time.

Endive and orange salad

■ **Yield: 4 servings**
■ **Time needed: 15 minutes**
■ **Difficulty: ***

**Ingredients: 4 heads Belgian endive, 2 oranges,
1 tbsp pitted black olives, 1 lemon, 5 tbsp olive oil,
pepper, salt.**

After removing any damaged leaves, cut the endive into thin strips. With a very sharp knife, peel one of the oranges, removing both skin and white pith, and cut the sections free of the membrane sacs, discarding any seeds.

Put the endive, orange sections, and the olives, cut in half, into a salad bowl. Sprinkle the grated zest of half of the remaining orange all around.

In a bowl, beat the oil with a pinch each of salt and pepper, then add the strained juice of the remaining orange and the lemon. Pour the dressing over the salad and mix carefully before serving.

Endive and orange salad

Triple delight salad

■ **Yield: 4 servings**
■ **Time needed: 1½ hours**
■ **Difficulty: ***

Ingredients: ½ small chicken, 6 oz ham, 10 oz mushrooms, juice of 2 lemons, 1 egg yolk, 1 lemon, 1 chopped carrot, 1 chopped stalk celery, ½ chopped onion, handful parsley, ⅔ cup olive oil, salt.

Simmer the chicken in salted water flavored with the carrot, celery, onion, and a few sprigs of parsley. After about 30 minutes, remove the chicken from heat, let cool, then remove the skin and bones and slice the chicken into strips. Cut the ham into strips also. Wash the mushrooms. Cut off the dried piece at the ends of the stems and carefully peel. As you proceed, drop the trimmed mushrooms into water acidulated with the juice of one lemon so that they don't turn brown. Cut the mushrooms into thin slices. Beat the yolk in a bowl with a pinch of salt. Drop by drop, add a few tablespoons of the oil, beating constantly till thick. Thin with a few drops of lemon juice, then add remaining oil a little at a time, still beating. Flavor to taste with lemon juice. The mayonnaise should be thick. Put the chicken, mushrooms, and ham in a salad bowl and fold in the mayonnaise dressing.

Corn salad

■ **Yield: 4 servings**
■ **Time needed: 20 minutes**
■ **Difficulty: ***

Ingredients: 1 cup canned corn, 3 heads Belgian endive, 1 avocado, one 2-oz slice Swiss cheese, juice of 1 lemon, ⅓ cup olive oil, salt, pepper.

Drain the corn. Wash the endive, dry, and cut into thin strips. Peel the avocado and cut into cubes. Cut the cheese into cubes too. Mix the ingredients in a salad bowl. Now, in a small bowl beat a pinch of salt together with the lemon juice. Add some pepper and slowly beat in the oil. Pour the dressing over the salad, mix and serve.

California salad

■ **Yield: 4 servings**
■ **Time needed: ½ hour**
■ **Difficulty: ***

Ingredients: 2 oranges, 1 cucumber, 1 grapefruit, 4 small sour pickles, sliced, 1 large red pepper, handful chopped parsley, 2-3 tbsp wine vinegar, ⅓ cup olive oil, pepper, salt.

Peel the oranges and cut into thin slices. Peel and slice the cucumber. Peel the grapefruit and cut it into sections. Arrange the orange slices in an overlapping circle in the center of a round plate. Surround the oranges with the grapefruit sections, then place the cucumber slices around the edge of the plate. Cut the pepper in half lengthwise, remove the core, seeds, and whitish ribs, and cut the pepper into thin strips. Garnish the salad with the pepper strips, pickles, and parsley. Dissolve a dash of salt in the vinegar. Slowly beat in the oil plus a little pepper, and pour the dressing over the salad.

Pepper and eggplant salad

■ **Yield: 4 servings**
■ **Time needed: 1 hour**
■ **Difficulty: ***

Ingredients: 1 lb green or yellow peppers, one 1-lb eggplant, ⅓ cup sliced green olives, 8 chopped drained anchovy fillets, 3 bay leaves, bunch chopped basil, ½ stick cinnamon, 6-7 whole cloves, bunch chopped parsley, 1 minced clove garlic, 1½-2 cups top quality distilled white vinegar, ½ cup olive oil, ¼ tsp peppercorns, salt.

Wash the peppers well and dry them with a kitchen towel. Cut them in half, remove the core, seeds, and ribs, and cut into small pieces. Wash the eggplant, cut into thick slices lengthwise, sprinkle liberally with salt, and let stand for at least 30 minutes on paper towels. Blot firmly with additional towels.

Place the vegetables in a non-corroding pot and add enough vinegar to cover. Add a pinch of salt, peppercorns, bay leaves, cinnamon, and cloves. Place over high heat and boil for 3 minutes. Drain the vegetables and dry with a paper towel. Cut eggplant slices into strips.

In a salad bowl, combine the peppers and eggplant with the olives, anchovies, basil, parsley, and garlic. Dress the salad with oil and season with salt and pepper. Serve the salad as part of an antipasto. If you wish, you may place it in an airtight jar, sterilize it, and store in a dark, cool place for later use.

Decorative Garnishes

It is a challenge to decorate a platter or the dinner table in such a way as to appeal to the eye as well as to the palate. But once you have learned how, you will find it extremely satisfying. Even for informal dinners, serving platters should be decorated; for formal dinner parties, elegant garnishes are an absolute must. When you are at the supermarket, remember to buy the items you need to prepare decorative garnishes even if the recipe does not call for a garnish, as is usually the case. It is up to the cook to know the art of decorating, despite what the recipe may leave unsaid. The first question is: What kind of garnish should you use? The basic rule is that the garnish should highlight the food but not overwhelm it. A vegetable garnish, whether raw or cooked, lends itself very nicely to most dishes because it is colorful and its taste blends well with many different foods. Generally speaking, raw vegetables are used to garnish cold platters, and cooked ones, hot platters, but this rule may be broken, as long as the garnish is attractive. The vegetables you choose must be of top quality, very fresh and at their ripest. They must also be cleaned well and dried. When using vegetables that tend to discolor, cover them with water that has been acidulated with lemon juice once they are peeled and cut, and keep them in the water until you are ready to use them. All vegetables that have been carved to resemble flowers should be kept in cold water so that they will open as much as possible.

It is a good idea to start with the easier garnishes and work your way up to the more complicated ones. Raw vegetables like tomatoes and carrots are so colorful that they need only minimal carving to create effective garnishes. Just a few thin slices or wedges of tomato or a carrot cut into geometric shapes will provide a marvelous garnish. These are especially nice for cold platters that lack color such as cheese and tuna dishes and rice salads. You can make other rather simple decorative garnishes with leeks, mushrooms, radishes, artichokes, and potatoes. Lemons are an especially decorative food. They can be used whole or cut into halves, slices, wedges, or fancy shapes. Marinated and pickled foods also make fine garnishes. Sliced olives, either stuffed or unstuffed, pickles cut into fan shapes, and sprinklings of capers are other possibilities. You can make very easy garnishes with herbs. A sprig of curly-leaf parsley or basil looks lovely on a platter of cold foods or hors d'oeuvres. In this chapter we will show you how to make fancier garnishes: delicate radish or artichoke flowers, playful tufts of leek, attractive cabbage and potato baskets, and many more.

The necessary equipment

Even if you have a delicate hand and lots of patience, it is difficult to make exquisite garnishes if you don't have the right equipment.

Above all, you must have a short paring knife that is pointed and well sharpened. In addition you need several special knives. A knife with a grooved blade that cuts hard vegetables like carrots and celery into pretty, crinkly slices is essential. You also need a swivel-bladed vegetable peeler that removes the peel of radishes and carrots and even makes thin strips of lemon peel. Also, a serrated knife is ideal for thinly slicing soft vegetables like tomatoes. A lemon-peel stripper is ideal for making verticle grooves on the lemon peel at regular intervals so that you can cut decorative slices from the whole lemon. A serrated and curved grapefruit knife is used not only for grapefruit but also for removing pulp from the skin of any citrus. Lastly, a utility knife with a rounded point and a large wide blade is useful for cutting big vegetables like a head of cabbage. And we cannot forget the hand-cranked vegetable slicer, made of stainless steel, that comes with several different size discs so that you can cut vegetables into shreds or thick slices. Another slicing device is the truffle slicer, which can also be used for other vegetables and which can be regulated to produce slices of varying thicknesses. For slicing tomatoes there is the tomato slicer, composed of closely spaced sharp vertical blades with a handle to press. It resembles an egg slicer, except that the egg slicer has a concave base so you can rest the hard-boiled egg in it.

Let's not forget the many different small cookie cutters which can be used to make decorative shapes from raw or parboiled vegetables. And then there is the melon baller, with two different sized round scoops at either end of the handle, to make uniform potato or carrot balls.

Carrot garnishes

used with boiled or baked fish, eggs, all kinds of salads, and barbecued and roasted meats. Naturally, there are many different ways to present a carrot. It is always a better idea to peel raw carrots with a swivel-bladed vegetable peeler than to scrape them with a knife. Here are some of the ways you can cut carrots and present them.

To make **flowers,** use carrots that are tender and rather long and cut them into pieces about 4 inches long (1). Using a sharp knife, round off one end of each piece of carrot (2), then with an apple corer or similar tool, bore into each piece but do not cut all the way through (3). Then cut into the outside section of the carrot lengthwise, using a paring knife. Make the cuts fairly close to each other. Next, in the same direction, cut each strip again, into thinner strips, so the flower will look like it has many petals (4-5). Open the petals

Carrots, whether raw or cooked, are one of the most widely used vegetables for making garnishes. They are

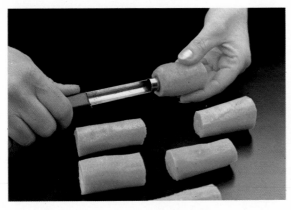

1 Flowers: cut tender carrots into pieces about 4 inches long...

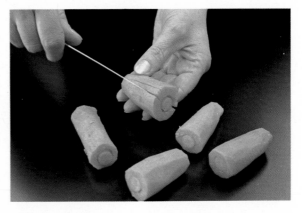

2 ...and, using a sharp pointed knife, round the pieces off at one end.

3 With an apple corer or similar tool, bore into the central section without cutting through to the end.

4 Make lengthwise cuts in the carrot using the point of the knife.

5 Now slice the cut section again into thin strips.

6 Open the petals carefully with your fingers so they don't break.

with your hands as much as you can, letting the inner part show (6). Now you have a lovely flower. To make **pinwheels,** which can also be used as daisies, take nicely shaped carrots and cut them into pieces 4 to 6 inches long. Cut away part of the carrot using a lemon stripper, making vertical grooves that are ¼ inch apart (7). If you don't have a lemon peel stripper, make the grooves with a paring knife, by making V-shaped cuts and removing the cut section with the point of a knife (8). Then slice the ribbed piece of carrot into pinwheels (9).

To obtain a rectangular-shaped ribbed carrot, with a serrated knife cut strips from the carrot lengthwise to form a square (10). Then cut the carrot into slices about ⅛ inch thick (11).

Roses are made by sculpting a carrot with the tip of a paring knife. Begin by making fan-shaped cuts about

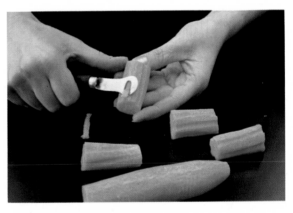

7 To make pinwheels, make long grooves in the carrot with a lemon stripper.

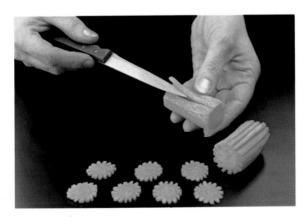

8 You can also make V-shaped cuts with a sharp paring knife...

9 ...then cut the ribbed carrot into ¼ inch slices.

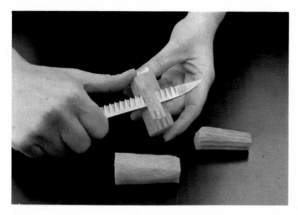

10 Ribbed rectangular slices: with a serrated knife, cut long strips to make a square...

11 ...then cut them into ¹/₈ inch slices.

³/₈ inch from the base of a small piece of carrot. Now, just above your cuts, cut ¹/₈ inch into the carrot (12) and remove a layer from there to the tip of the carrot. Next make another fan-shaped layer around the circumference, and then remove another ¹/₈ inch layer above that (13).

The carrot will gradually get narrower as you cut away layers. When you are finished, even the bottoms so the carrot-flower will sit upright (14).

To make **heart shapes, stars** and **flowers** with cookie cutters, slice large carrots into rounds, and cut with sharp metal cookie cutters (15).

To make **balls,** take large long carrots and, with a melon baller, scoop out different sized balls along the length of the carrot (16). These little carrot balls are usually boiled first and then used as decoration.

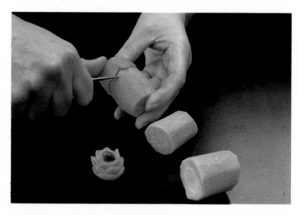

12 Roses: after making fan-shaped cuts around the base, cut ¹/₈ inch into the carrot.

13 Then remove a layer ¹/₈ inch deep above the cuts.

14 Even out the bottoms so the carrots will sit upright.

15 Make hearts, stars, and flowers with cookie cutters.

16 Balls are made by scooping out large carrots with a melon baller.

Artichoke flowers

To make flowers, buy artichokes that are rather tender and cone shaped. Remove the tough outer leaves till you come to the softer, slightly pink ones of the cone. Follow the instructions given below each photograph explaining how to make the various artichoke flowers.

1 Dahlias: remove the tough outer leaves, and cut off the top of the artichoke.

2 Make 5 or 6 cuts from the center to the edge, about ¾ inch apart.

3 Insert strips of carrots, radishes, hard-boiled eggs, or whatever you like into the cuts.

4 Roses: beginning at the outer edge, fold each leaf back and under...

5 ...and when your reach the center, cut away the thorny tips.

A bouquet of radishes

This garnish calls for round or oval-shaped radishes. If you have oval-shaped ones, you can make **buds.** Using a sharp paring knife, begin at the top and cut a narrow length-wise strip from the radish, taking care not to detach it at the bottom. Lift the strip to form a petal (1).

Continue doing this all around the radish, leaving a tiny strip of red peel intact between each petal (2). Finish the bud by cutting off a small slice at both ends.

If you have round radishes you can make different kinds of flowers, such as **roses, love-in-a-mists,** and **tulips.** Cut off the roots (3), then make several thin parallel slices without cutting to the end (4). Holding the radish firmly in your hand, make thin parallel slices perpendicular to the first ones (5). Put the radish in ice water so the petals will open. To make love-in-a-mist, cut a circular strip all around the radish with a lemon stripper (6). Then cut some strips perpendicular to the circular cutting you have made, leaving the red peel between cuttings intact (7). To make tulips, cut V-shaped notches in the top half of the radish (8) and remove the white part between the petals formed by the V's (9).

1 Buds: make vertical cuts, and then lift up the peel so it forms petals.

2 Continue cutting the radishes, leaving a strip of red peel intact between petals.

3 Roses: remove the tips of round radishes with a sharp paring knife.

4 Make very thin parallel slices without cutting all the way through.

5 Hold the radish firmly in your hand and make parallel slices perpendicular to the first ones.

6 Love-in-a-mist: remove the root, then cut a circular strip all around, using a lemon stripper.

7 Then make vertical cuts leaving some of the red peel intact.

8 Tulips: cut V-shaped notches in the top half of the radish.

9 Remove the white part between the petals.

Tomato flowers and baskets

Tomatoes are often used to make garnishes because of their bright color. Since there are many varieties of tomatoes on the market, choose the right kind of tomato for your garnish. The tomato garnishes illustrated on this page, made with mozzarella, hard-boiled eggs, and basil, can be served as an antipasto, especially in the summer.

To make these garnishes, you will need round tomatoes that have smooth skins. Make parallel cuts using a sharp knife, without cutting all the way through the tomato (1). Select a mozzarella approximately the same size as the tomato and slice it. Place a slice into each tomato cutting (2).

Sprinkle some oil, vinegar, pepper, and salt over the tomato before you serve it. A mixture of chopped basil and parsley can be sprinkled on as well.

A tomato trimmed with slices of hard-boiled egg makes an appetizing first course. Take a tomato and make several vertical cuts without cutting through to the center (3). Slice the hard-boiled egg with an egg slicer and insert a slice into each of the tomato cuttings (4).

1 Make parallel cuts on a round tomato without cutting all the way through.

2 Open the cuttings slightly and insert a slice of a mozzarella in each one.

3 Make several vertical cuts with a sharp knife.

4 Insert a slice of hard-boiled egg into each cutting.

Place the end slice of the egg on top of the core of the tomato, together with a few tiny fresh basil leaves.

Pour a dressing of oil, vinegar, pepper, salt, and chopped herbs over the tomato and egg before you serve it.

Tomato baskets. Slice off the top of a firm round tomato (5). Make V-shaped cuts all around with a paring knife (6). Remove the V-shaped sections you cut out and then scoop out the pulp (7). You can use these baskets for any recipe that calls for stuffed tomatoes and serve them hot or cold.

Little roses. The skin of a tomato, once it is delicately removed from the fruit, can be wound around itself to form a flower. Select tomatoes that are very fresh and firm and that have smooth skins. Start at the top of the tomato and peel off the skin in a spiral motion, going all around the tomato, the way you peel an apple (8). Make

5 Baskets: slice off the tops of firm round tomatoes.

6 Make V-shaped cuts around the tomato with a sharp paring knife.

7 Carefully remove the V-shaped wedges and pulp.

sure you end up with one long strip of tomato skin.

Take one end of the strip and begin winding it around itself to make the inner petals of the flower (9). Continue winding the strip around till you have a little rose (10). Naturally, the longer your strip is, the bigger your rose will be.

To make your rose even prettier, insert two toothpicks into the bottom of the flower to anchor it. Then cover the rose with a thin coating of aspic. When the rose hardens, remove the toothpicks.

You can make different colored roses by choosing tomatoes at various stages of ripeness, such as underripe green or yellow tomatoes, slightly ripe pink ones, or fully ripe deep red ones. Once you have made different colored roses, place some fresh basil or parsley around the roses to resemble leaves.

8 Little roses: cut the skin from the tomato in a spiral motion, as if you were peeling an apple.

9 Take one end of the strip and begin winding it around itself.

10 Continue winding the strip around till you have formed a small rose.

Pickle flowers and fans

You will need small, firm, sweet or sour gherkins. These garnishes go nicely with cold antipasto, dips, rice salads, mixed tossed salads, pâtés, mousses, aspic platters, and hors d'oeuvres.

To make a **fan,** begin at one end of a pickle and make several very thin slices lengthwise (1). Hold the other end of the pickle and carefully spread open the sections to form a fan (2).

To make a **boat,** remove a thin strip of pickle by cutting a wedge the length of the pickle. Remove it (3), then fill the boat with a strip of green, red, or yellow pepper. Tiny **flowers** can be made from pickles as well. Slice the pickles horizontally into thin round slices, then group several slices together to form the blossom. To make the stem, use a strip of marinated pepper (4).

Besides decorating the outside of platters with slices of pickles, you can also use them to garnish many cold salads and aspic dishes by spreading them directly on top of the food.

1 Miniature fans: make thin lengthwise cuts parallel to each other.

2 Hold the uncut end and press it down to open the sections.

3 Boats: remove a small wedge of pickle and fill it with a strip of red pepper.

4 Flowers: cut pickle into slices and group together to form a flower, using peppers strips as stems.

A bouquet of leeks

Choose tender leeks, half white and half green, and not too thick. Remove the roots and most of the green part before you begin making these highly original garnishes. Follow the procedure given beneath each photograph.

1 Flowers: make lengthwise cuts in pieces of leek without cutting the base.

2 Open the cut sections with your hands to form little flowers.

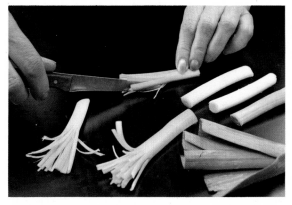

3 Brushes: use a whole trimmed leek and proceed as above cutting only one end.

4 Bundles: slice rings from the white part and slip one over the middle of a piece of leek...

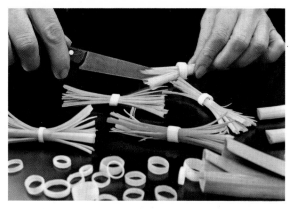

5 ...then slice both ends, making several parallel cuts.

6 Little towers: cut a leek into 1-inch pieces and push up the inside sections to form domes.

7 Rings: slice both the white part and the green part into rings and separate the layers with your fingers.

A cabbage basket

This unusual garnish is made by carving out a head of cabbage to form a basket. You can fill the basket with mixed vegetable salad or cold rice salad and include it on your summer buffet table. You will need a cabbage that is firm, fresh, and nicely rounded.

The instructions given under each photograph explain how to make this garnish.

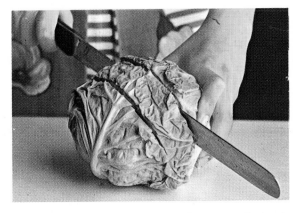

1 Start from the center and make two vertical cuts halfway down, 1½ inches from each other.

2 Make two perpendicular cuts, leaving the central section intact.

3 Carve out an arch in the central piece to form a handle.

4 Carefully cut away the inside of the basket and remove it.

5 Once it has been washed and dried you can fill the basket.

Potato garnishes

Before we discuss the innumerable ways you can use potatoes to garnish a platter of meat or fish, you must first know which variety of potatoes to use. For the garnishes described in this chapter, use Idaho or russet potatoes, which have a lovely mealy texture, and are also ideal for roasting, baking, and frying. New potatoes are better for making soups, mashed potatoes, and gnocchi.

A word on what to look for when you select your potatoes.

The potato skins should not be wrinkled or soft, nor should they have greenish spots or sprouts. The flesh, when cut, should be crisp and very firm.

Choose potatoes that are roughly the same size when you make these garnishes. Peel them just before you use them. Once peeled, keep them in a bowl of cold water till you are ready to use them so they don't turn brown.

Before you cook them, dry them thoroughly. You can cut a potato into numerous shapes and forms with the help of a few handy kitchen utensils.

Balls: Use potatoes that are large and well shaped and scoop out balls with a melon baller (1). Fry them in very hot oil or cook them in butter.

Use the leftover pieces to make mashed potatoes.

Crinkle-cut slices: Select potatoes that are long and narrow, peel, and cut them into round slices using a knife that has a notched blade (2). Try to cut the slices as thin as possible. They can either be fried in hot oil or sautéed in a little butter.

French fries: First, cut the potatoes into slices about 1/8 inch thick, then slice them again into sticks about 4 inches long and 3/8 inch wide (3). A sharp paring knife

1 Balls: scoop out the inside of a potato with a melon baller.

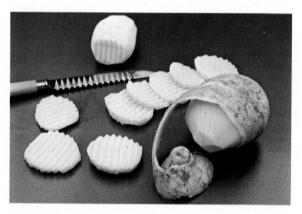

2 Crinkle-cut slices: slice a potato thinly using a notch-bladed knife.

3 French fries: first slice a potato, then cut the slices into sticks 4 inches long.

4 Cones: make a spiral cut around a potato using a lemon stripper.

5 Wedges: cut a potato in half, then cut each half into 3 or 4 wedge-shaped sections.

6 Homemade potato chips: cut the potatoes into very thin, nearly transparent slices, with a slicing device.

7 Straw potatoes: use the julienne disc of the vegetable slices to obtain matchstick-thin strips.

does this nicely. If you deep fry them in very hot oil the outside will be crisp while the inside will stay soft.

Cones: Select oval-shaped, medium-sized potatoes. Using a lemon stripper, start at one end and make a spiral cut, continuing on to the other end (4). These "cones" can be steamed and served either with melted butter and chopped parsley or with a creamed mushroom sauce.

Wedges: Cut medium-sized potatoes in half and then cut each half into 3 or 4 wedges (5).
Potato wedges can be fried or baked.

Homemade potato chips: Peel the potatoes and round them off so they are smooth, even, and well shaped.

Cut them into nearly transparent slices, using a "mandolin" or similar tool (6). Dry them well and fry them in a large amount of very hot oil so they become crisp and resemble the potato chips you buy in stores.

Straw potatoes: Imported from France, the vegetable slicing machine or "mouli" comes with 5 disks with various shaped holes to cut vegetables into small pieces, shreds, strips, etc. It also has a disk that grates cheese and makes bread crumbs.
Using the julienne disk of a "mouli" or food processor, make matchstick-thin potato strips (7). Deep-fry them in hot oil, using a deep-fat fryer or a pan into which a wire basket can be inserted and removed easily. Be sure to remove all the potatoes at once so that they are all cooked to the same point.

A potato basket

To make baskets you will need a special device consisting of two interlocking strainers, one slightly larger than the other, that are held together at the handle by a moveable ring. With this device, you can make baskets that look like flowers using sliced potatoes, and baskets that resemble bird's nests using shredded potatoes. To make flower-shaped baskets, select long, even-shaped potatoes (1). Peel and trim the potatoes, so they are perfectly smooth and oval-shaped, then use a "mandolin" or food processor to make thin round slices (2). Place a slice of potato on the bottom of the bigger strainer (3), then place other slices around the sides of the strainer, overlapping slightly, to form a flower (4). Put the smaller strainer into the larger one to hold the slices in place (5), and run the metal ring over both handles to hold them in place. Lower the device into hot oil (6). When the potatoes are golden brown, remove the device from the hot oil (7) and open it, carefully removing the potato baskets (8). They can be filled with mixed buttered vegetables (9).

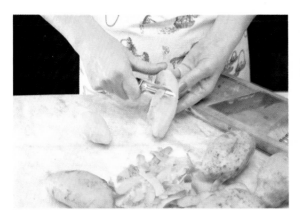

1 Peel and trim long, even-shaped potatoes.

2 After shaping the potatoes, slice them with a "mandolin" or food processor.

3 Place one slice of potato on the bottom of the larger strainer.

4 Then place more slices around the sides of the strainer to form a flower.

5 Lower the smaller strainer into the larger one to hold the slices in place.

6 Run the metal ring over both handles and put the device into very hot oil.

7 When the potatoes are golden brown remove them from the hot oil.

8 Open the strainers and carefully remove the baskets.

9 Fill the baskets with mixed buttered vegetables or puréed spinach.

10 To make bird's nests cut julienne-thin strips. Place them in the larger strainer.

11 Then close the device as explained above and put it in very hot oil.

12 Fill the nests with peas and carrots, string beans, or sliced mushrooms.

Mushroom flowers

Select tiny mushrooms with firm caps. Remove the dirt from the end of the stems, rub clean with a cloth, and flute the caps as explained under each photograph. These mushroom flowers can be cooked whole in butter or with cream, or cut into slices and cooked with garlic and parsley.

1 Make wedge-shaped cuts on the mushroom caps, using a sharp pointed knife.

2 Start from the center of the cap and cut outward, making the cuts as small as possible.

3 Remove the tiny wedged section with the point of your knife.

4 Mushroom caps can be decorated another way by making flower-shaped cuts with a lemon stripper.

5 You can also make spiral-shaped cuts on the mushroom caps using a lemon stripper.

Lemon garnishes

Lemons are used as garnishes more than any other fruit or vegetable. They can attractively grace almost any serving platter, from hors d'oeuvres to dessert.

Whole lemons, nicely decorated, can be placed at the edges of a platter, or they can be cut into thin slices and arranged around the rim of the platter.

1 Scalloped slices: make lengthwise strips with a lemon stripper...

2 ...then with a knife, cut the lemon into thin slices.

3 Half-moons: cut the scalloped lemon slices in half.

4 Place the lemon halves together, slightly misaligning them.

5 The slices and half-moons can be decorated with olives, cherries, anchovies, pickles, or parsley.

Before you begin, it's a good idea to scrub the lemons well with a brush under running water, rather than merely rinsing them. This removes any trace of pesticides or preservatives.

Scalloped lemon slices: Use the lemon stripper to make ⅛ inch strips on the lemon peel (1), then with a smooth or serrated knife, cut the lemon into thin slices (2).

Half-moons: Cut the slices of notched scalloped lemon in half (3). The slices can be placed around the edge of a serving plate as they are, or the two halves can be arranged facing each other and slightly misaligned (4). These garnishes are particularly recommended for platters of fried fish or seafood. Both the scalloped lemon slices and the half-moons can be decorated with an-

6 Waves: slice a lemon very thinly with a sharp knife.

7 Cut each slice in half and make a cut through the fruit up to the rind.

8 Twist one end to the right and one to the left to look like waves.

9 Little baskets: slice a lemon thinly and remove half the pulp, leaving the rind intact.

10 The letter "P": cut one end of the handle of the little basket and curve it inwards.

11 Curls: cut most of the zest from a round slice of lemon, leaving one end attached.

12 Curl the strip of zest around itself and knot it.

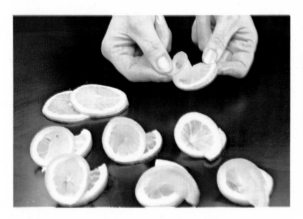

13 Twists: make a cut in a lemon slice and twist both ends of the zest in opposite directions.

14 Rocking horses: first cut a lemon slice in half...

chovies, cherries, capers, olives, pickles, and chopped parsley. These fanciful garnishes add color to a platter of hors d'oeuvres or cold antipasto (5).

Waves: Slice a lemon very thinly (6), otherwise you won't be able to twist the ends. Then cut each slice in half and make a cut through the fruit but not the rind (7). Now, turn one end of the slice to the right and the other end to the left to look like waves (8).

Little baskets: Slice a lemon thinly and remove half the fruit, leaving the rind intact (9). Once you have made a little basket you can make the letter "P" by cutting one end of the handle of the basket and curling it inwards (10).

Curls: Start with a round slice of lemon and cut the zest from around the edge, leaving one end attached (11),

then curl the zest around itself and loosely knot it (12).

Twists: Make a cut in the center of a slice of lemon. Then hold the ends and twist them in opposite directions (13).

Rocking horses: Starting with round lemon slices, cut a slice in half (14). Take one of the halves and make a slit in the pulp (15), then wedge the other half in the slit (16).

Butterflies, Little towers, etc.: Using round lemon slices, cut each one into 8 sections (17) and then make whatever you want with each piece. For example, you can join 2 sections with a piece of cherry to form a butterfly (18).

Wedges: Cut a lemon in half lengthwise, then cut each half into 4 or 5 wedges (19). To decorate these wedges, press one side into chopped parsley (20).

15 ...and slit the pulp of one of the halves to the rim, leaving the rind intact.

16 Then wedge the other half into the slit.

17 Butterflies, Little towers: cut each lemon slice into 8 sections.

18 Use the sections to make butterflies or design your own garnish.

19 Wedges: cut a lemon in half, then cut 4-5 wedges from each half.

20 Press one side of each wedge into chopped parsley.

Lotus flowers: Before you begin, score the circumference of the lemon lightly with the tip of a sharp knife, and use this line as a guide to keep hte cut straight (21). Now carefully cut the lemon in half by making V-shaped cuts and separate the two halves (22). You will have a lovely flower that you can decorate with capers, cherries, or sprigs of parsley (23). Use these flowers to garnish platters of meat or fish or to decorate a lemon tart or mousse.

Baskets: Begin by carving the handle.Make two parallel cuts through the fruit on one side, starting at the tip and going halfway down (24). Slide your knife under the zest of the strip you have just cut to free it from the fruit (25). This will form the basket's handle. Repeat the same procedure on the other side of the lemon to com-

21 Lotus flowers: score the circumference of a lemon and use the line as a guide when you cut.

22 Cut the lemon by making V-shaped cuts all around and separate the two halves.

23 Decorate these lovely flowers with capers or cherries.

24 Baskets: cut a strip on the upper part of a lemon.

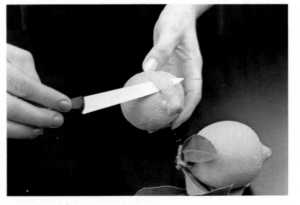

25 Carefully slip your knife under the peel you have cut and lift up the strip.

26 Make V-shaped cuts across the circumference.

27 Remove the pieces you have cut away to form a basket with jagged edges.

28 If you want to fill the basket, scoop out the fruit with a melon baller...

29 ...then, using a teaspoon, fill the baskets with mayonnaise or another sauce.

plete the other half of the handle. Now make V-shaped cuts along the circumference, cutting through to the center, as explained in making the lotus flower, taking care to leave the handle intact (26). Carefully remove the two parts you have cut away, using your knife to loosen the pieces you take out (27). If the baskets are to be filled, scoop the fruits out delicately using a melon baller (28). Then, using a teaspoon, fill the baskets with mayonnaise or another sauce (29).

These baskets add an attractive touch to buffet tables, summer salad platters, barbecues, or any outdoor parties.

Baby roses: Lemon peel, just like tomato peel, can be used to make very attractive garnish. Select a lemon that is nicely shaped and has a smooth, unblemished peel.

30 Baby roses: remove peel by cutting top to bottom in a spiral with a lemon peeler.

31 Wind one end of the strip to form the center of a flower...

32 ...and finish by winding the rest of the strip to form a rose.

33 Place a radish in the middle.

34 Lilies: make two incisions close together that meet at the top.

35 Carefully slide your knife under the cuttings and lift the zest.

36 Fold the tip of each petal in towards the fruit.

37 Make more petals using the white pith under the peel.

38 Fold the tips of these petals in towards the fruit for a fuller flower.

Using a lemon peeler or sharp knife, begin at one end and cut a single long thin strip, going from top to bottom in a spiral direction (30).

Take one end of the strip and wind it around itself to form the center of the flower (31). Then wind the rest of the strip around, in a spiral, to complete the rose (32). Place a radish in the middle (33).

Lilies: Begin by making the petals. For each petal make two long incisions close to each other which meet at the top of the lemon. Continue around the lemon this way, forming more petals (34). Now slide your knife under the cuttings and carefully lift up the thin layer of yellow zest, releasing the petals (35). Fold the tip of each petal in so the petal curls towards the fruit (36). You may either leave the remaining zest on the lemon or remove it

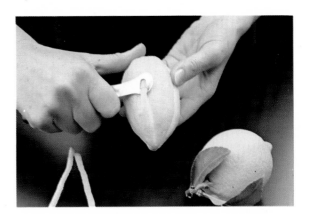

39 Mock pineapples: use a lemon stripper to cut lengthwise strips.

40 Then cut strips around the lemon, intersecting the other strips.

41 Slice off the tips from both ends of the lemon.

42 Make several lengthwise cuts in a piece of leek, taking care not to cut all the way through.

43 Place this tuft in the hole you have made in the tip.

44 Tulips: use a lemon stripper and cut a spiral strip from one end to the other.

45 Decorate further, sticking whole cloves in the grooves.

and then peel strips of the white pith to make additional petals (37), curling them in towards the center as well (38).

These garnishes can be used as centerpieces as well as decorations for serving platters. Use your imagination to add the final touches. Lemon leaves or sprigs of fresh mint add a note of contrast.

Mock pineapples: With a lemon stripper cut away ⅛ inch strips from the lemon peel. First cut the strip lengthwise from one end to the other (39), then cut strips around the lemon, intersecting the other strips. Slice off the tip of one end of the lemon so it stands upright (40). Then slice off the opposite tip (41). Now that the fruit of the pineapple has been carved you will need some pineapple leaves. Make a hole for the leaves on the up-

per tip of the fruit, with the point of a sharp knife. You can insert any green leaves that you wish. To make leaves from a leek, as shown in the picture, choose a piece that contains some of the white and some of the green part. Using a sharp knife, make several lengthwise cuts, without cutting all the way through (42). Place this tuft in the hole you have made in the tip (43).

Tulips: Using a lemon stripper, begin at the top of the lemon and cut a spiral strip from one end to the other (44). Slice off a small piece of the tip of the lemon so that it will stand upright. You can decorate it further if you wish, by sticking whole cloves into the grooves you made (45).

These tulips make an attractive garnish for pork and game dishes. They also add interest to a punch bowl.

SFORMATI, SOUFFLÉS, AND CROQUETTES

Sformati
and Tortini

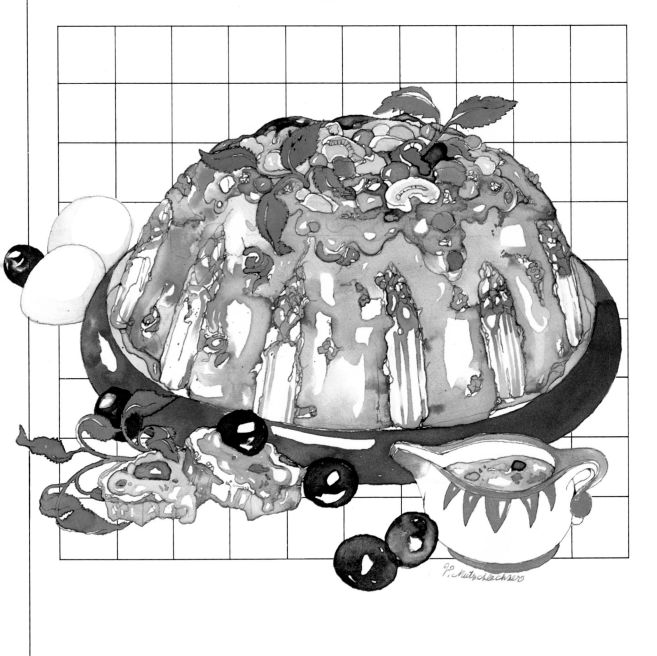

When you are looking for a new and different way to serve vegetables and cheese that is still simple and economical, why not try one of the many savory molds, called *sformati,* which are abundant in regional Italian cooking? *Sformati* are a cross between a soufflé and a pudding, normally using a base of puréed or finely chopped cooked vegetables, often seasoned with cheese, and bound with an egg or béchamel sauce. Delicious *sformati* can also be made using dried beans, rice, meat, or fish. The mixture is then poured into a mold with tall sides and baked either directly on the oven rack or in a bain-marie, until it has puffed up and is cooked to the right consistency. *Tortini* differ from *sformati* in that the vegetables, cheese, or meat need not be puréed or finely chopped; they can simply be cut into small pieces. Many *tortini* also have a final layer of bread crumbs or pastry covering the filling, which is always highly seasoned but not necessarily bound with either an egg or béchamel sauce. A *tortino* can serve as a one-dish meal. Both *sformati* and *tortini* are delicate, appetizing, light, and nutritious dishes that bring together the nutritional components of their various ingredients. In this sense they are especially good for those whose nutritional needs are particularly high.

Cheese sformato

The basic ingredients

As we've seen, the base for *sformati* is always thick and creamy since it is made up of puréed or finely chopped ingredients to which a thick béchamel sauce or egg yolks are added. The béchamel sauce should be well blended and smooth; for best results, always add hot milk to the butter and flour mixture. When the sauce is completely smooth and free of lumps, it is cooked over direct heat or in a double boiler until it reaches the right consistency. Cheese is added while the sauce is still hot so that it melts easily; the egg yolks are gently stirred in to the cooled mixture one at a time, with care taken to mix each one in well before adding the next.

If the base ingredient is a purée, a few spoonfuls of cream are added instead of béchamel sauce to make it creamier, as well as the usual egg yolk to bind it. When the *sformato* is composed of meat or fish, béchamel is often not used at all; bread crumbs soaked in milk and then squeezed out are added instead, along with the egg yolks. Sometimes, after all the ingredients have been mixed, stiffly beaten egg whites are carefully folded in to make a lighter, more delicate *sformato*. Then the entire mixture is poured into a casserole or mold which has been previously buttered and rolled with bread crumbs (the best come from white bread because they give the *sformato* a typical golden crust which not only looks attractive but makes it easier to turn out on a plate). The mold is filled three-quarters of the way. Often it is cooked in a bain-marie, i.e. placed inside a larger oven-proof pan which is then filled one-third of the way up the side of the mold with boiling water, placed over direct heat until the water comes back to a boil, and then put into a preheated oven. While the dish bakes, the heat should be adjusted so that the water just barely simmers, without coming to a boil or splashing into the mold (if it should boil, simply add a little cold water). When the dish is cooked, turn it onto a heated serving plate and serve with a suitable sauce.

The most common *sformati* are made of vegetables that are boiled, then puréed, chopped, or simply cut up, according to the recipe, and then sautéed in butter. Classic *sformati* are made of spinach, artichokes, or cauliflower, but equally good are those made with carrots, chicory, or pumpkin. More elegant and flavorful are those using mushrooms or several vegetables whose flavors and colors blend. Vegetable *sformati* are served with a sauce that complements the vegetable flavoring: a simple tomato sauce, a ragù, a *financière* sauce (or any other mixture based on mushrooms and peas), even a somewhat piquant sauce based on anchovies, or a cheese sauce such as *fonduta alla piemontese*. You can also make meat-based *sformati*: ground pork or minced veal plus mortadella and ham; finely chopped cooked pork, veal, chicken, or even beef plus ham; finely chopped game and ham; or the ground meat of small game birds.

As we've said, bread crumbs soaked in milk and then squeezed dry are often used instead of béchamel to bind the ingredients, and seasonings are added along with egg yolks, for texture, and beaten egg whites, for lightness. There are many sauces to accompany the *sformati*, from various béchamels to tomato sauces to mayonnaise for *sformati* made with cold meats. And don't forget the *sformati* made with smoked salmon or tuna and served cold, or with cooked fish and served hot. Cheese *sformati* often come very close to being proper soufflés. Several types of easily melted cheeses are used; and minced salami, fresh or dried mushrooms, peas, etc. are often mixed in to give it more flavor when a soft cheese like ricotta is used.

One can consult any Italian cookbook to see the infinite variety of traditional and fanciful recipes available to make *tortini*. These are often open-faced vegetable pies, such as the *scarpazza,* a typical spinach dish from Milan, or the *gattò* of potatoes from Neapolitan and southern kitchens, whose derivation is obviously French. In this kind of *tortino,* puréed vegetables are arranged in alternate layers with other ingredients, from tiny cubes of salami or cheese to other vegetables and aromatic herbs. Another kind of *tortino* is made in a spring-form mold that is lined with pastry dough and then filled with a mixture of precooked vegetables, cheese, and bits of other ingredients. Often a beaten egg, cream, or simply a little seasoned milk, is brushed over the top of the mixture. These *tortini* are all baked in the oven; some are unmolded and sliced before serving, while others are brought to the table in their baking pan and each person serves himself.

Serving sformati

The necessary equipment

These dishes often form part of the first course because they are light and appetizing. They can also serve as a luncheon entrée as well as one of those courses which *haute cuisine* calls *entremets*. The *entremet* is served (as its name indicates) between courses, such as between the fish and the meat course or between the meat and the salad. In such cases, close attention must be paid to the menu selected, keeping the various ingredients in mind so that nothing is repeated and everything works well together. For example, after a first course of rice or pasta, one would not serve a savory pie but would instead choose a vegetable *sformato*. The same mold would go well between a fish and meat course, while a fish *sformato* can be served between a soup course and a meat course served with vegetables. Cheese and salami *sformati* make wonderful antipasti followed by a light first course such as soup. These suggestions are most suitable of course for important occasions, where formality requires a more elegant and refined selection of courses than usual.

For family meals, where courses are much simpler, the *sformato* can replace the soup course or first course, especially when a savory pie or *tortino* is served. Vegetable *sformato* and *tortini* make perfect light and nutritious main courses for an evening meal or a very delicate first course followed by a roast or stew. The *sformati* and *tortini* made of meat or vegetables with cheese and eggs and covered with pastry can easily be served as a second or main course, or as meals in themselves; in the latter case, they are best accompanied by a tossed green salad. Finally, cold *sformati* such as those based on tuna or salmon are very good as an antipasto, as are some of the vegetable *tortini*, which are best hot but also delicious when served at room temperature or chilled, especially in the summer.

For dishes that call for finely chopped or puréed ingredients, manual or electric meat grinders or food processors are extremely useful. Both come equipped with interchangeable blades or disks to adjust how finely chopped you want the ingredient to be.

Among electric grinders, those operated by pressing the feeder with one's hand are good for meat and vegetables, though less good for cheese, as they tend to mash and pack it.

Wooden spoons and spatulas, and a set of nesting bowls are also useful.

The bowls can be earthenware, ceramic, fireproof porcelain, or pyrex and can be used for both casseroles and *tortini*.

Usually *sformati* are baked in round dishes with high sides, which can be made of various materials. *Tortini*, on the other hand, are often cooked in rectangular baking dishes made of pyrex, fireproof porcelain, or metal with a non-stick lining.

Sformati that will hold their shape when cooked and *tortini* baked in a pastry crust can be cooked in a spring-form pan. *Sformati* can also be baked in small individual molds.

To roll out the pastry crust to line a terrine there are rolling pins that can be filled with ice water. The dough should be rolled out quicky so that it stays chilled.

To prepare the béchamel and other sauces, measuring cups of different sizes are very useful, as are small fireproof lidded sauce cruets in which the sauces can be heated and kept warm. Finally, don't forget pot holders and heavy oven gloves, and hot pads and trivets on which the casserole, fresh from the oven, can be placed.

Spinach sformato

■ **Yield: 4 servings**
■ **Time needed: 1¹/₂ hours**
■ **Difficulty: ***

Ingredients: 2 lb spinach, 7 tbsp butter, 4 eggs, ¹/₃ cup flour, ¹/₂ cup grated Parmesan or shredded Gruyère cheese, 2 cups milk, 1 clove garlic, crushed, nutmeg, salt, pepper.

Clean the spinach, rinsing it thoroughly under cold water. Drain in a colander without drying. Cook it as is in a pot placed over high heat. Do not add more water. When it has wilted, drain well and let cool. Then finely chop (1) or force through a food mill. Melt 2 tablespoons butter and add the crushed garlic. When it has browned, remove it and add the spinach. Stir well for a few minutes until its water evaporates. Remove from the fire and put into a bowl.

To make the béchamel, melt 4 tablespoons butter in a saucepan. Add the flour all at once, stirring well so no lumps form. Let it cook briefly over low heat (2). Heat the milk and add it to the butter and flour, stirring constantly to avoid lumps (3). Bring it slowly to a boil, then let it simmer a few minutes till it thickens and is smooth. Season with salt, pepper, and a little nutmeg and remove from the heat.

Add the béchamel to the spinach (4) and mix well (5). Add the grated cheese (6), then the whole eggs (7). Taste the mixture and add more salt if necessary. Generously butter a ring mold. Spoon the mixture into it (8), filling it three-quarters full so the *sformato* has room to rise during cooking. Smooth the surface with the back of a spoon. Place it in a slightly larger pot and add enough water to come one-third of the way up the sides of the mold (9).

Bake for about 45 minutes in a 350° oven. If the water begins to boil during cooking, add a little cold water. When it is done, let it rest a few minutes, then carefully turn it out on a platter. Serve as an accompaniment to veal scalloppine or other veal dishes.

1 Boil the spinach, drain well, squeeze out excess water and chop finely.

2 Melt the butter, add the flour all at once, and let it cook gently.

3 Slowly add the hot milk little by little.

4 Turn the chopped spinach into a bowl and add the béchamel sauce.

5 Stir well with a wooden spoon.

6 Season the mixture with grated Parmesan or Gruyère.

7 Bind the mixture with whole eggs, added one at a time; beat well.

8 Butter a ring mold and pour in the spinach mixture.

9 Place it in a pot partially filled with water and bake.

Spinach sformato

Pumpkin sformato

- **Yield: 6 servings**
- **Time needed: 1 1/2 hours**
- **Difficulty: ***

Ingredients: 3 lb pumpkin, 6 oz mushrooms, 1/2 cup grated Parmesan cheese, 2 eggs, separated, 3 tbsp butter, 3 tbsp heavy cream, 1 minced clove garlic, 2-3 tbsp bread crumbs, salt, pepper.

Slice the pumpkin, removing the seeds and pith, then bake at 350° for about 30 minutes or until you can pierce it easily with a fork (1). Scrape out the pulp and force it through a sieve or a food mill (2). Wipe the mushrooms with a damp cloth (3). Slice them (4) and sauté in 2 tablespoons of the butter along with the garlic (5), cooking until their moisture has evaporated (6). Then add the pumpkin purée (7), mixing well, and cook until thick. Season with salt and pepper, then remove from heat and pour into a bowl. Beat the egg whites until stiff. Add the cream (8), cheese, and egg yolks (9) to the pumpkin mixture, then gently fold in the egg whites (10). Butter a high-sided 9- or 10-inch cake pan and sprinkle with bread crumbs (11). Pour in the mixture (12) and dot the top with remaining butter and bread crumbs. Bake in a 350° oven for about 1 hour.

1 Place the pumpkin slices in the oven and cook till you can pierce them easily with a fork.

2 Remove the pulp and force through a sieve or food mill with a spoon.

3 Wipe the mushrooms gently with a damp cloth so as not to damage them.

4 Cut the mushrooms into thin slices and dry them with a cloth.

5 Briefly sauté the garlic in the butter and stir in the mushrooms.

6 Continue to cook the mushrooms till their moisture has evaporated.

7 Mix the cooked mushrooms with the pumpkin purée and cook the mixture down a little.

8 Pour the mixture into a bowl and add the cream.

9 Add the egg yolks, incorporating each one well before adding the next.

10 Gently fold in the stiffly beaten egg whites.

11 Butter a cake pan and sprinkle with bread crumbs.

12 Pour the mixture into the pan and smooth the top with the back of a spoon.

Pumpkin sformato

Golden dome sformato

- Yield: 4 servings
- Time needed: 2 hours
- Difficulty: **

Ingredients: 2 lb all-purpose potatoes, ½ cup chopped cooked spinach, 4-5 frankfurters, 2 egg yolks, 2 hard-boiled eggs, 7 tbsp butter, ⅔ cup Parmesan cheese, 3½ oz Fontina cheese, ¾ oz dried cèpe mushrooms, 1 tbsp flour, 1 tbsp tomato sauce, bread crumbs, 3 tbsp dry Marsala, 3 tbsp chicken or beef broth, nutmeg, salt, pepper.

Boil potatoes in salted water. Peel and force through a potato ricer or food mill (1) into a large saucepan. Place over a low heat to evaporate some of excess moisture, stirring constantly with a wooden spoon. Remove from heat and stir in 4 tablespoons butter (2), 2 tablespoons of the grated cheese (3), a pinch of nutmeg, salt, and pepper. Let cool a moment, then add the egg yolks, one at a time, and mix thoroughly (4). Add the flour and blend well to form a dough-like mixture. Butter a deep mold (5). Sprinkle with bread crumbs, shaking out the excess (6). Coat the sides with a beaten egg, tilting and turning the mold so that the egg thoroughly covers it (7), and mixes with the bread crumbs. Now sprinkle on a second coating of bread crumbs (8) and tap out the excess. Cut off a piece of dough and set aside. Line the inside of the mold with the rest (9).

Melt 1½ tablespoons butter and sauté the chopped spinach (10), frankfurters, sliced in rounds (11), and the cleaned and sliced mushrooms. Add the grated cheese, salt, pepper, Marsala (12), and finally the tomato paste diluted with hot broth (13). Let this cook for 15 minutes, then add the Fontina, cut into small pieces (14). Fill the mold with part of the filling (15), arrange the cooked and peeled hard-boiled eggs on top (16) and cover with the rest of the filling (17). Pat the remaining bit of dough into a circle. Cover the top of the mold (18), smoothing it with a spatula (19). Press the edges together (20) and spread with the remaining butter. Sprinkle with bread crumbs (21) and place in a 375° oven for about 40 minutes.

1 Boil the potatoes, peel, and force through a ricer while still hot.

2 Let the potatoes dry out a little over heat, then add butter.

3 Season with salt, pepper, nutmeg, and a little grated cheese.

4 When the potato mixture has cooled a little, add two egg yolks.

5 Grease the inside of the mold with a little melted butter.

6 Sprinkle with bread crumbs and shake out the excess.

7 Coat the mold with a beaten egg, tilting to cover completely.

8 Sprinkle the walls of the mold with more bread crumbs.

9 Line the inside of the mold with the potato dough so it is about 3/4 inch thick.

10 Sauté the previously cooked and chopped spinach in a little butter.

11 Add the sliced frankfurters to the spinach...

12 ...along with the sliced mushrooms, the rest of the grated cheese, salt, pepper, and Marsala.

13 When the Marsala has evaporated, add the tomato paste diluted with a little hot broth.

14 When the sauce has reduced, add the chopped Fontina and mix well.

15 Fill the mold with some of the mixture.

16 Place the two hard-boiled eggs in the center.

17 Cover with the rest of the mixture.

18 Pat the remaining dough into a circle and place it on top of the mixture.

19 Smooth it gently with a spatula.

20 Press the edges together to seal.

21 Spread a little butter over the top and sprinkle with bread crumbs.

Golden dome sformato

Tricolor sformato

■ **Yield: 6-8 servings**
■ **Time needed: 2 hours**
■ **Difficulty: ****

Ingredients: 2 lb peas, 1 lb carrots, 1 small cauliflower, ¾ cup flour, 1 stick butter, 6 eggs, separated, ¾ cup grated Parmesan cheese, 5½ cups milk, nutmeg, salt, pepper.

Shell the peas, reserving the shells. Clean and trim the other vegetables. Boil them separately in salted water until tender. Drain well. Cut the carrots into rounds and separate the cauliflower into flowerets (1). Sauté each vegetable separately in 1½ tablespoons butter (2) and force each one through a sieve or food mill (3). (You can also use a blender or food processor). To give more color and flavor to the puréed peas, parboil a handful of shells, then pound them in a mortar, force the pulp through a food mill, and add to the puréed peas (4).

Melt 10 tablespoons of the remaining butter in a saucepan. Add the flour all at once and mix well with a wooden spoon to eliminate the lumps. Add hot milk and bring slowly to a boil, stirring constantly. Cook the béchamel for a few minutes, stirring constantly. When it has thickened, add salt, pepper, and a little nutmeg and remove from the heat. Add the cheese and divide sauce into three parts. Mix one of the three vegetables into each part (5), then add 2 egg yolks, one at a time, to each (6). Be sure each yolk is mixed in well before adding the next one. Beat the egg whites till stiff and fold in gently (7). Butter a deep ring mold, then pour in the carrot mixture first (8) and smooth it out. Cover with the pea mixture (9). Smooth it and finish with the cauliflower mixture (10). The three mixtures can also be divided into three sections instead of layers. Use a deep tube pan and divide sections with buttered pieces of cardboard (11). Remove cardboard after filling.

Place the mold inside a larger container and add enough boiling water to come halfway up the sides of the mold. Bake in a 350° oven for about 1 hour. If the water begins to boil, add a little cold water. When the *sformato* is done, remove it from the bain-marie and let it rest a few minutes before unmolding it.

1 After boiling the vegetables, separate the cauliflower into flowerets.

2 Sauté the carrots, peas, and cauliflower separately in 1½ tablespoons butter.

3 Force each vegetable through a sieve or food mill.

4 Pound some of the pea shells in a mortar and add the pulp to the puréed peas.

5 Divide the béchamel sauce into three portions and add to each of the three vegetable purées.

6 Add 2 egg yolks to each mixture, stirring well, then...

7 ...gently fold in the beaten egg whites.

8 Butter a ring mold and spread in the carrot purée first.

9 Smooth it with a spatula, then add the pea purée.

10 Finish filling the mold with the cauliflower purée.

11 You can also use a tube pan and divide the mold into three sections instead of layers.

Tricolor sformato

Cheese tortino

- ■ Yield: 4 servings
- ■ Time needed: 1 hour
- ■ Difficulty: *

Ingredients: Enough puff pastry or filo dough for a 10-inch pie shell, 8 oz ricotta, 8 oz mascarpone or cream cheese, 2 eggs, 2 tbsp butter, 1/2 cup shredded Gruyère cheese, 1/4 cup heavy cream, 1/2 tsp fresh ginger, flour, salt.

Force the ricotta through a sieve or food mill (1). Mix in the mascarpone (2) and a pinch of salt. Add the eggs, one at a time (3), then the cream, and Gruyère. Mix well until smooth. Grate fresh ginger into the mixture for flavor (4).

Butter and flour a 10-inch pie pan. Roll out the dough 1/8 inch thick and line the pan (5). Form a rim with the edge of the dough using your thumbs and flute with a knife. Pour the filling into the pie shell (6), smoothing it with a spoon. Bake in a 350° oven for about 40 minutes, or until puffed. Unmold and serve. This is also delicious served cold.

1 Force the ricotta through a sieve or food mill.

2 Add the mascarpone, season with a pinch of salt, and mix with a wooden spoon.

3 Add the eggs one at a time and beat until they are blended.

4 After adding the cream and Gruyère, grate in a little fresh ginger.

5 Roll out the pastry crust to a thickness of 1/8 inch and line a buttered pie pan.

6 Pour the filling into the pan and smooth top with a spoon.

Cheese tortino

Spinach and potato casserole

- ■ **Yield:** 4-6 servings
- ■ **Time needed:** 1½ hours
- ■ **Difficulty:** *

Ingredients: 1¾ lb spinach, 1 lb baking potatoes, 1 cup milk, 4 oz bacon, 4 oz slivered Fontina, ½ cup grated Parmesan cheese, 5 tbsp butter, salt.

Trim the spinach. Wash in cold water, drain, but do not dry. Place in a large pot and cook, without adding more water, until wilted. Drain well, let cool, squeeze out the excess water and force through a sieve or food mill (1). Dice bacon and sauté in 2 tablespoons butter. Add spinach (2) and cook for a few minutes. Boil unpeeled potatoes in salted water. Let cool, then peel and slice. Grease the insides of a baking dish. Pour on ⅓ cup of the milk and add a layer of potatoes (3), then a layer of spinach (4) and some of the Fontina (5). Sprinkle with Parmesan. Alternate layers of potatoes, spinach, and Fontina, finishing with Fontina and Parmesan (6). Spoon remaining milk over the top and dot with remaining butter. Bake at 400°, until bubbling hot.

1 Boil the spinach, drain well, squeeze out moisture, and force through a food mill.

2 Brown bacon in butter and add the spinach.

3 Butter a baking dish, pour in a little milk, and arrange a layer of potatoes over the bottom.

4 Spread a layer of spinach over the potatoes.

5 Cover the spinach with some of the Fontina.

6 Before baking, sprinkle with the remaining Fontina and Parmesan.

Spinach and potato casserole

Mushroom tortino

- Yield: 4-6 servings
- Time needed: 1 hour 15 minutes
- Difficulty: *

Ingredients: 1 1/2 lb cèpe mushrooms, 9 tbsp butter, 4 oz cubed ham, 5 tbsp flour, 12 slices homemade-type white bread, 2 eggs, separated, 1 3/4 cups milk, 1 1/4 cups heavy cream, 2 tbsp grated Parmesan cheese, nutmeg, salt, pepper.

Clean mushrooms and slice thin. Melt 4 tablespoons butter in a skillet and cook mushrooms thoroughly. Add salt. In another skillet, melt the rest of the butter. Add flour, mixing well, and then add 1 1/4 cups milk, heated, stirring till smooth. Cook béchamel a few minutes, then add cream, salt, pepper, and a little nutmeg. Remove from the heat and add the Parmesan, then, one at a time, the egg yolks. Remove crusts from the bread. Sprinkle 6 of the slices with remaining 1/2 cup milk and line the bottom of a buttered baking dish with them. Cover with half the ham, half the mushrooms, another bread layer, and then the rest of the ham and mushrooms. Finally cover with remaining bread. Spread béchamel on top and bake at 350° until browned and bubbly.

Swiss chard pie

- Yield: 4 servings
- Time needed: 1 1/2 hours
- Difficulty: *

Ingredients: 3 lb Swiss chard, 10 oz mushrooms, 6 tbsp butter, 2 tbsp grated Parmesan, 1 tbsp chopped parsley, 2 eggs, 3 tbsp heavy cream, 1 chopped clove garlic, 4-6 tbsp bread crumbs, salt, pepper.

Trim chard. Rinse well and boil until tender in a little lightly salted water. Drain, squeeze out excess water, and chop coarsely. Clean and slice the mushrooms. Melt 5 tablespoons butter in a skillet with 1 tablespoons oil. Add mushrooms and garlic and sauté until mushrooms are well cooked. Add chard and cook slowly for 10 minutes, stirring frequently. Before removing from the heat, sprinkle with parsley. Pour chard mixture into a bowl. Stir in cream, cheese, salt, pepper, and finally the eggs, beaten. Mix well. Grease an 8-inch baking pan with butter and sprinkle with bread crumbs. Add filling and smooth the surface. Sprinkle more bread crumbs on top and dribble oil over the surface. Bake at 350° until set. Serve hot or cold.

Potato tortino

- Yield: 4 servings
- Time needed: 1 1/2 hours
- Difficulty: *

Ingredients: 1 1/4 lb boiling potatoes, 7 tbsp butter, 8 oz chopped cooked sausage, 3/4 cup grated Parmesan, 3 eggs, separated, flour, salt, pepper, nutmeg.

Boil potatoes until tender in salted water. Peel and force through a potato ricer. Place purée in a saucepan with 1 tablespoon butter and stir with a wooden spoon over moderate heat to remove excess moisture.

Beat the egg whites till stiff. Add the sausage, cheese, nutmeg, egg yolks, salt, and pepper to the potatoes. Fold in the egg whites. Butter and flour a 9-inch, deep round baking dish, then pour in the potato mixture. Place in a 350° oven till the top is puffed and brown, 30-40 minutes.

Cheese delight

- Yield: 6 servings
- Time needed: 2 hours
- Difficulty: **

Ingredients for the dough: 2 1/2 cups flour, 13 tbsp butter, 1 egg yolk, salt.
For the filling: 1 1/4 cups grated Parmesan, 4 tbsp butter, 4 eggs, separated, 2 cups milk, 2/3 cups flour, pinch nutmeg, salt, pepper.

First, make the pastry dough. Place the flour on a pastry board. Make a well in the center and mix in the butter, cut into small pieces, the egg yolk, and a pinch of salt. Add just enough water to make a cohesive dough, then wrap in plastic and let rest in a cool place for half an hour. Roll dough out into a sheet 1/4 inch thick and use it to line the bottom and sides of a deep 10-inch pie pan, or better, a false-bottom tart pan. Prick the bottom with a fork and bake in a 400° oven for 15 min. Let cool and then carefully slide it out of the pan.

Bring the milk to a boil with the butter, a pinch of salt, a sprinkling of freshly ground pepper, and the nutmeg. Remove from heat, add the flour all at once, and beat vigorously until smooth. Add egg yolks and the Parmesan cheese. Beat egg whites till stiff, then gently fold in. Pour the filling into the pre-baked crust and bake in a 350° oven for about 25 minutes or until puffed and golden.

Cheese delight

Bread and mozzarella pie

- **Yield: 4 servings**
- **Time needed: 1 hour**
- **Difficulty: ***

Ingredients: 8 slices homemade-type white bread, 1 lb sliced mozzarella, 6 drained anchovies, 4 tbsp butter, 1/2 cup grated Parmesan cheese, 1/2 tsp oregano, 1 cup milk, salt, pepper.

Pour the milk into a flat-bottomed pan large enough to hold the bread in a single layer. Add bread and let it soak, then drain off excess milk. Place the bread in a single layer in a buttered baking dish and cover with the sliced mozzarella. Chop the anchovies and sprinkle them over the mozzarella. Add the grated cheese, oregano, salt, and freshly ground pepper. Cover the top with small bits of butter.

Bake in a 350° oven for about 30 minutes. Unmold and serve immediately.

This dish is very good as an appetizer or even as a light meal.

Spinach timbales

- **Yield: 4 servings**
- **Time needed: 40 minutes**
- **Difficulty: ***

Ingredients: 1 lb frozen spinach, 4 oz chopped ham, 1/2 cup shredded Gruyère cheese, 4 tbsp butter, 3 eggs, 1 cup milk, salt, pepper.

Defrost the spinach and squeeze out moisture. Place it in a saucepan with 1 tablespoon of the butter. Cook until dry. Add salt and pepper. Break the eggs into a bowl and add the milk, cheese, and ham, beating well with a fork. Then add the spinach and mix well.

Butter 4 individual ramekins and fill each one almost to the top with the spinach mixture (if there is any left over, you can use additional ramekins). Place in a baking dish and add enough hot water to come halfway up the sides of the molds. Bake in a 350° oven for about 30 minutes or until a knife inserted near the center comes out clean. Serve the timbales as a first course, as an accompaniment to a roast, or as the main course of a fancy lunch.

Ham and onion sformato

- **Yield: 4 servings**
- **Time needed: 1 1/2 hours**
- **Difficulty: ****

Ingredients: 2 large onions, 14 oz ham, 4 oz bacon, 7 oz cooked turkey breast, 1 1/2 tbsp butter, 1/2 cup fresh bread crumbs, 2 beaten eggs, 1/3 cup milk, salt, pepper, nutmeg.

Chop the turkey with the ham and bacon. Soak the bread crumbs in milk for 15 minutes, then squeeze out and mix with the meats. Bind with the eggs and add salt, pepper, and nutmeg to taste. Mix the ingredients with your hands until blended. Generously butter a 6-cup mold. Spread half the chopped onion on the bottom, press in the meat mixture, and scatter the rest of the onion on top. Bake in a 350° oven for about 1 hour. Unmold, draining off the accumulated juices, and serve immediately. Salami can be used in place of bacon in this *sformato*.

Cheese sformato

- **Yield: 4 servings**
- **Time needed: 1 hour 15 minutes**
- **Difficulty: ***

Ingredients: 1 3/4 cups shredded Gruyère or Fontina cheese, 1/2 cup semolina flour, 1/2 cup grated Parmesan cheese, 4 tbsp butter, 1 small onion, 2 eggs, separated, 1 1/4 cups hot milk, salt, pepper, nutmeg.

Chop the onion and sauté until tender in all but one tablespoon of the butter. Pour the milk over it and bring to a boil. Stirring constantly, gradually add the flour and cook for 10 minutes, still stirring with a wooden spoon. Season with salt, pepper, and nutmeg, and add the Gruyère and Parmesan, stirring till they melt. Off the heat, add the beaten egg yolks. Beat the egg whites till stiff, then gently fold into the mixture. Pour into a buttered 9-inch baking dish. Bake for 40 minutes in a 350° oven, or until puffed and firm.

Place the *sformato* on a hot plate and serve directly from the baking dish at the table.

See page 258 for a picture of this dish.

Soufflés
and Timbales

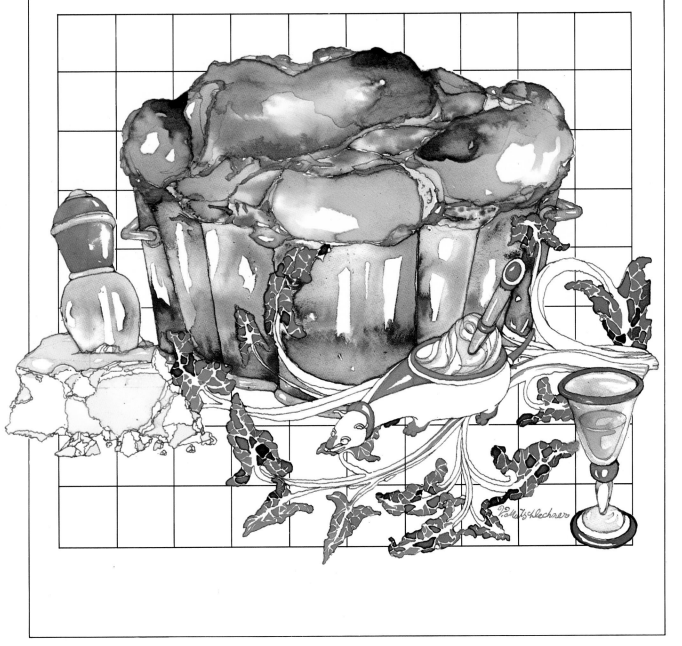

Soufflés and timbales command a great deal of respect and awe, especially from novice cooks. We will try to explain what they are, so people will know just what we're talking about. *Soufflé* is a French word meaning "blown-up" and it refers to a preparation based on puréed vegetables, cheese, or finely chopped meat mixed with a thick béchamel sauce; egg yolks and stiffly beaten egg whites are then added so that it puffs up during cooking. Timbales were also originally French dishes encompassing all kinds of sweet and savory custards. For Italians, a timbale generally refers to a *sformato,* especially one which, because of its creamy consistency, is baked in a ring mold to help the filling to firm up during cooking. While a soufflé requires some special treatment, especially in the cooking stage, a timbale should not present any problems because basically it is just another *sformato* that is baked in a bain-marie according to the instructions we have already given. On the other hand, a soufflé is baked directly on the oven rack, and to have it puff up and brown evenly, you should be mindful of certain things, especially the temperature of the oven, so that there are no last-minute disasters. But don't get discouraged, because even if everything goes wrong and the soufflé just doesn't rise, you can still serve a dish that your guests will appreciate for the delicacy of its ingredients.

Both these preparations were invented in the royal kitchens of France during the 18th century when the monarchy was in full glory and cooks often found themselves asked to prepare fabulous banquets and needed to serve dishes of an extraordinary variety and decorativeness. It is entirely possible that these very refined cooks suffered their own disasters from time to time and that timbales were invented to save the remains of an unsuccessful soufflé. The timbale is a little masterpiece in itself, the center filled with some delicate morsel and served with a succulent sauce. Soufflés and timbales are satisfying from a nutritional point of view as they can include vegetables, meats, fish, or cheeses and are served with sauce containing milk, eggs, flour, cream, and herbs and spices. They are not widely found in the Italian kitchen as Italian dishes tend to be simpler and heartier, but this is a pity because once the procedures are learned, soufflés and timbales are not very difficult to make and they are always impressive and delicious.

Preparation and cooking

Generally, soufflés and timbales consist of a béchamel sauce to which the main ingredient is added that gives the recipe its name. The ingredient can be a vegetable purée, finely chopped meat, fish, or poultry, or a grated cheese. We say "generally" because there are also some that do not call for a béchamel sauce, such as those that contain starchy vegetables or that are made with a paste of flour or cornstarch and water, which is diluted at a later stage with a little milk or cream and seasoned with butter. Whatever its precise nature, the basic sauce for these dishes should not be too liquid since it must solidify during cooking. Once it has cooled a bit, egg yolks are added one at a time (each must be well incorporated before the next is mixed in), then the main ingredients and the seasonings. The beaten egg whites are added just before the preparation is put in the oven; they are folded in a spoonful at a time, the mixture stirred gently from the bottom to the top so that the whites are not broken down. The proportions among the ingredients are fairly consistent: the amount of béchamel will be more or less half the amount of the main ingredient; the number of whole eggs varies according to the weight of the béchamel plus the main ingredient (one egg for about every 3 ounces batter). An extra egg white is added for every one to three whole eggs used, depending on the recipe. The basic ingredients for timbales are similar to those for the soufflés but the extra egg whites are not added. Soufflés and timbales are baked in buttered molds and floured or sprinkled with bread crumbs. The mold is filled two-thirds full so the mixture has room to rise. It is then placed in the center of an oven preheated to 350° for about 20 minutes. It is important not to open the oven door during cooking; a draft can make it fall. Timbales are cooked in a bain-marie in similar fashion to that for *sformati*.

How to serve soufflés and timbales

The necessary equipment

When the airy soufflé is ready, bring it to the table directly from the oven. A little trick for beginners, to keep the soufflé from spilling over the rim during the first stage of cooking, is to make a small collar, about 4 inches high, of foil or baking paper to go around the rim. Tie it in place with a piece of string and butter the inside. At the end of cooking, cut the string and remove the collar. Serve the soufflé immediately before it begins to fall. If it is pierced right away with a long needle, it will stay puffy a bit longer. Carry it out on a tray or a plate covered with a napkin.

A timbale is unmolded into a serving dish and its center is filled with a sauce or ragù, such as a *financière* sauce. Small individual timbales can also be served as an accompaniment to veal or other white meat. Soufflés are usually served as a first course. Delicate savory cheese soufflés made with Gruyère or Parmesan and enriched with other ingredients such as mushrooms, truffles, baby peas, or tomato sauce make especially good first courses. Ham and some fish soufflés made with salmon, tuna, or shellfish are exquisitely elegant and simple. Vegetable soufflés such as spinach, artichoke, asparagus, mushroom, and pea make excellent dishes whether served before or along with an important meat dish. Meat and fish soufflés are worth a chapter in themselves; they range from a simple first course to a light main course.

As for timbales, they may be served, depending on their ingredients, as a first course, an accompaniment to a meat course, or even as a meal in themselves, since as we have mentioned, they can be served with a very rich and filling sauce.

Old recipes for soufflés describe them baked in silver molds, brought directly to the table and served using silver spoons and spatulas. Today there are many decorative and probably more practical containers to use instead of silver ones. One can find modern soufflé molds, both decorated and plain, of heat-tempered glass and heat-resistant porcelain and pyrex; they just must have high smooth sides which will allow the soufflé to rise. There are also individual molds in which you can make small soufflés, *sformati,* or sweet steamed puddings.

Timbales, on the other hand, require a classic ring mold with a center hole, or a spring-form mold, generally made of aluminum and sometimes lined with a non-stick material like Teflon. A soufflé mold must be set on a hot plate; these are usually made of cork or wood and some soufflé molds come with their own.

For recipes calling for stiffly beaten egg whites, a good mixer is essential. The best, of course, is an electric one with large circular beaters for egg whites, flatter straight ones for softer mixtures, and a dough hook for stiff mixtures.

Equally good, but more tiring, are manual egg beaters, from wire whisks to the simple hand-held rotary beater.

Other useful items are a large heat-resistant glove to remove the soufflés and timbales from the oven, and aluminum foil or brown paper for making collars to raise the height of the soufflé molds and to cover the top if it is browning too fast.

Another very useful item for absent-minded or very precise people is an oven timer.

Cheese soufflé

- **Yield: 4 servings**
- **Time needed: 1 hour 15 minutes**
- **Difficulty: *****

Ingredients: ¾ **cup grated Parmesan cheese,** ½ **cup flour, 1 cup shredded Gruyère, 6 tbsp butter, 4 eggs, separated, 2 cups hot milk, salt, pepper, nutmeg.**

Melt the butter in a saucepan, add the flour, and stir well with a wooden spoon to avoid lumps. Now add hot milk, stirring constantly. Cook the béchamel for a few minutes (1), then season with salt, freshly ground pepper, and a pinch of nutmeg and remove from heat.

Add the Parmesan (setting aside one tablespoon), the Gruyère (2) and, one at a time, the egg yolks (3), beating until the sauce is smooth and velvety (4). Beat the egg whites until stiff and gently fold them into the sauce (5). Butter a 2-quart soufflé mold, sprinkle the inside with the remaining Parmesan, and pour the mixture in, filling the mold two-thirds full (6). Bake in a 375° oven for about 40 minutes or until puffed and brown.

1 Prepare a béchamel sauce with butter, flour, and milk. It should be smooth and velvety.

2 Remove the béchamel from the heat, add the cheese while the sauce is still hot...

3 ...and, one at a time, add the egg yolks, stirring the mixture vigorously for a few minutes...

4 ...until it forms a satiny ribbon when dropped from a spoon.

5 Fold in the stiffly beaten egg whites.

6 Pour the mixture into a soufflé mold that has been buttered and sprinkled with cheese.

Cheese soufflé

Tomato soufflé

1 Clean the tomatoes, place them in boiling water a moment, peel, and remove seeds.

- ■ **Yield: 4-6 servings**
- ■ **Time needed: 1½ hours**
- ■ **Difficulty: ***

Ingredients: 2 lb ripe tomatoes, 1 cup flour, 13 tbsp butter, 4 eggs, separated, ½ tsp sugar, 1 bay leaf, 3 cups milk, a few pinches nutmeg, salt, pepper.

Wash the tomatoes. Drop them in boiling water for a moment, then peel and seed (1). Force through a sieve or food mill (2) and put the purée into a pot. Add the bay leaf and sugar (3). Reduce the sauce, stirring constantly until it begins to thicken (4).

Now prepare the béchamel sauce: melt the butter (except for 1 tablespoon) in a saucepan, add the flour, and let it cook a moment. Add salt and pepper and the hot milk. Let the sauce boil for a few minutes. Then add the reduced tomato sauce (5), first removing the bay leaf.

Off the heat, add the egg yolks, one at a time (6), mix well, and season with nutmeg.

Beat the egg whites till stiff, then fold them gently into the cooled sauce (7), stirring up from the bottom to the top (8).

Butter a 2-quart soufflé mold and lightly flour the interior.

Pour in the mixture (9) to within ½ inch of the rim. Smooth the top, place in a bain-marie, and put in the oven. Bake at 350° for about 40-50 minutes, or until slightly puffed.

A cake needle inserted in the center should come out clean. Serve immediately (it is important to carry it to the table while it is still hot and puffy). It makes an elegant hot antipasto or first course.

2 Force through a sieve, put the purée in a pot, and add...

3 ...the bay leaf and half a teaspoon sugar, which helps cut the acidity of the tomatoes.

4 Reduce the sauce over heat, stirring constantly.

5 Prepare a thick béchamel sauce and mix in the thickened tomato sauce.

6 Add the egg yolks one at a time to the béchamel, then mix in the tomato sauce.

7 Beat the egg whites till stiff and carefully fold into the sauce...

8 ...bringing the batter up from the bottom to the top so as not to deflate the whites.

9 Pour the mixture into a buttered and floured soufflé mold.

Tomato soufflé

Mixed vegetable soufflé

- **Yield: 4 servings**
- **Time needed: 2 hours**
- **Difficulty: *****

Ingredients: 8 frozen artichoke bottoms, 1 cup shelled peas, 5 tbsp butter, $^1/_2$ cup hot water or chicken broth, $^1/_3$ cup flour, 1 onion, 2 tbsp chopped parsley, 4 eggs, separated, $^1/_2$ cup milk, 1 tbsp oil, salt, pepper.

Chop the onion and sauté it in a pan in the oil. When it is translucent, add the thawed artichoke bottoms, sliced, the peas, salt, pepper, and hot water or broth. Cook the vegetables till tender, then force them through a food mill or purée in a blender or food processor. Melt 4 tablespoons butter in a pan, add the flour, and mix well. Cook this a moment, then remove from the heat and add the vegetable purée, chopped parsley, and the half cup of milk. Place over a low flame and stir well till it is smooth and free of lumps. Season to taste with salt and pepper. Let the mixture cool a little, then add the egg yolks, one at a time. Carefully fold in stiffly beaten egg whites.

Butter and flour a 6-cup soufflé mold. Pour the mixture in, filling it to within $^1/_2$ inch of the rim. Place soufflé in a larger baking dish and add enough hot but not boiling water to come halfway up the sides of the soufflé mold. Bake in a preheated 350° oven for about 40 minutes or until puffed. If it is browning too fast on top, cover with a sheet of aluminum foil. The top should be golden brown when served.

Toasted almond soufflé

- **Yield: 4 servings**
- **Time needed: 2 hours**
- **Difficulty: ****

Ingredients: $1^1/_4$ lbs mealy potatoes, 2 oz blanched slivered almonds, $^2/_3$ cup shredded Gruyère cheese, 5 tbsp butter, 6 eggs, separated, 3 tbsp bread crumbs, nutmeg, salt, pepper.

Toast the almonds lightly in the oven. Boil the potatoes until tender, then peel and force through a potato ricer. Stir over moderate heat and evaporate excess moisture, then mix in 3 tablespoons of the butter, the cheese, salt, pepper, and nutmeg. Let the purée cool slightly, then add the egg yolks, one at a time, and the toasted almonds. Beat the egg whites till stiff, then gently fold them into the purée. Butter a mold and sprinkle the inside with bread crumbs. Pour in the soufflé mixture and dot with remaining tablespoon butter, then place in a large pan filled with boiling water and cook the soufflé in a preheated 350° oven for about 40 minutes.

Remove it from the oven and serve immediately while it is still puffy.

Spinach and carrot soufflé

- **Yield: 4-6 servings**
- **Time needed: $1^1/_2$ hours**
- **Difficulty: *****

Ingredients: 1 lb fresh or frozen spinach, $^1/_2$ lb carrots, 10 tbsp butter, $^3/_4$ cup flour, 6 eggs, separated, 2 cups hot milk, salt, pepper, nutmeg.

Trim the spinach and wash well under running water. Cook in a large pan until wilted without adding more water. Drain well, squeeze out excess moisture, and force through a food mill or purée in a blender or food processor.

Peel the carrots, boil until tender, purée. Melt all but 1 tablespoon of the butter in a saucepan, then add the flour, mixing until perfectly smooth. Let this cook a moment without browning, then add hot milk. Mix well and cook this sauce for 5 minutes over low heat. It will be extremely thick. Remove the sauce from the heat and let it cool, stirring occasionally so that it doesn't form a skin. Then add the egg yolks, one at a time, and season with salt, pepper, and nutmeg. Divide the sauce into two parts. Add the spinach purée to one and the carrot purée to the other.

Beat the egg whites till stiff, and add a pinch of salt. Add half the whites to the spinach sauce and half to the carrot sauce, folding them in carefully so they don't fall. Butter and flour a 2-quart soufflé mold and pour in first one mixture, then the other. Bake the soufflé in a 350° oven for 30-40 minutes.

Serve the soufflé at once.

(A photo of this dish is on page 284.)

Green pea timbale

- **Yield: 4-6 servings**
- **Time needed: 1¹/₂ hours**
- **Difficulty: ****

Ingredients: 3 cups fresh or frozen peas, 3 tbsp flour, 3¹/₂ tbsp butter, ¹/₂ cup grated Parmesan cheese, 6 eggs, separated, 1 cup milk, 1 tbsp bread crumbs, nutmeg, salt, pepper.

Boil the shelled peas in salted water. Drain and force them through a food mill or sieve (1) or purée in a blender or food processor. Melt 3 tablespoons of the butter in a saucepan, then add the flour, mixing well to get rid of lumps. Add hot milk and bring to a boil, stirring constantly. Cook for a few minutes (2), then add salt, pepper, and nutmeg and remove from the fire. Add the pea purée (3) and the grated cheese. Bind the mixture with the egg yolks, adding them one at a time (4). Beat the egg whites till stiff and gently fold them into the mixture (5). Butter an 8-cup ring mold, then sprinkle the inside with bread crumbs. Pour in the mixture (6) and cook in the oven in a bain-marie for 45 minutes at 350°.

1 Boil the peas in salted water, drain, and force through a sieve or foodmill.

2 Make a béchamel sauce with butter, flour, and milk and cook a few minutes.

3 Remove from the heat, let cool a moment, and add the puréed peas.

4 Bind the mixture with egg yolks, adding them one by one.

5 Beat the egg whites till stiff and delicately fold them in.

6 Pour the mixture into a buttered pan sprinkled with bread crumbs.

Green pea timbale

Timbale with peas and ham

- **Yield: 4-6 servings**
- **Time needed: 1 hour 45 minutes**
- **Difficulty: ****

Ingredients: 2 ²/₃ cups shelled fresh or frozen peas, 3 tbsp flour, 6 tbsp butter, 2 oz ham, 6 oz slab bacon, 1 tbsp bread crumbs, 1 cup milk, 4 eggs, separated, 1 small onion, salt, pepper.

Boil the peas in salted water until they are just tender. Drain. Chop the onion finely and put in a deep skillet with 2 tablespoons of the butter. Sauté until translucent (1). Add the ham, cut into small cubes, to the onions (2) and then add the peas (3). Salt lightly and let cook for a few minutes, stirring with a wooden spoon (4).

In a pan, melt 3 tablespoons butter, add the flour, and mix well to avoid lumps. Add salt, pepper, and the hot milk, and simmer, stirring constantly, till you get a thick sauce. Add sauce to the peas and ham (5), and then add the egg yolks, one at a time (6), mixing well with a wooden spoon.

Butter an 8-cup ring mold, sprinkle with bread crumbs, then tap out the excess (7). Pour the mixture into the mold (8), smoothing the top with a spoon (9). Put it in a preheated 350° oven and bake for about 1 hour, or until a skewer inserted in the center comes out clean. If the top becomes too brown during cooking, cover with a sheet of buttered aluminum foil.

Dice the bacon and brown in a skillet with just a bit of butter (if you use a non-stick pan, you can avoid having to use butter).

Delicately unmold the timbale onto a serving dish and garnish with the bacon. Serve hot.

This makes an excellent first course for a hearty meal. If you wish to use it as a proper *entremet*, complete it with a *financière* sauce made with chicken giblets.

1 Chop the onion finely and sauté till it is translucent.

2 Add the diced ham and then, a few minutes later...

3 ...the peas, previously cooked in salted water till just tender.

4 Add a little salt and cook for a few minutes, stirring with a wooden spoon.

5 Make a thick béchamel sauce and add it to the peas and ham.

6 Add the egg yolks, one at a time, mixing well.

7 Butter a ring mold, sprinkle with bread crumbs, and tap out excess.

8 Pour the filling in, trying not to fill the mold quite to the top.

9 Smooth the surface with a spoon and bake in a hot oven for 1 hour.

Timbale with peas and ham

Carrot timbale

- **Yield: 4-6 servings**
- **Time needed: 1½ hours**
- **Difficulty: ****

Ingredients: 2 lb carrots, 5 tbsp butter, 4 tbsp bread crumbs, 1 tbsp sugar, 2 eggs, beaten, 6 tbsp grated Parmesan cheese, 4 slices bread, 4 slices Swiss cheese, salt, pepper.

Peel and wash the carrots and cut into slices. Place them in a pan, add a little salt, cover with cold water, and bring to a boil. Cook for about 10 minutes, then drain. Melt 4 tbsp of the butter in a skillet, add the carrots (1), and sprinkle with the sugar (2), salt, and pepper. Cook till they have lost some of their moisture, then force through a food mill or sieve (3) or purée in a blender. Add the bread crumbs (4), the Parmesan (5), and the beaten eggs (6). Mix everything together well (7). Butter an 8-cup ring mold, and pour in the mixture (8). Smooth the surface and place in a 350° oven for 40-45 minutes.

Meanwhile, cut the crusts off the bread. Cut each slice in two diagonally and spread with a little butter (9). Cover the triangles with the cheese slices (10) and when you take the timbale out of the oven, put the bread in for a few minutes. Unmold the timbale onto a serving plate and arrange the toast around it. Serve at once.

1 Melt the butter in a skillet and add the boiled carrots.

2 Sprinkle sugar over the carrots and cook over a low flame till tender.

3 Force the carrots through a food mill or sieve.

4 Add the bread crumbs to the carrot purée, mixing well.

5 Then add the grated cheese, stirring again to blend well.

6 Beat the eggs and add them to the carrot mixture.

7 Blend until the mixture is smooth.

8 Butter a ring mold and pour in the carrots.

9 Cut the bread slices in half diagonally and spread with butter.

10 Cover each slice with cheese slices of the same size.

Carrot timbale

Mixed vegetables timbale

■ **Yield: 4 servings**
■ **Time needed: 2 hours**
■ **Difficulty: ***

Ingredients: ½ cup flour, 5 tbsp butter, ¾ cup grated Parmesan cheese, 4 oz ham, 4 eggs, separated, 2 large leeks, 2 small heads endive, 2 heads escarole, 1 ¾ cups hot milk, 1 tbsp heavy cream, salt.

Chop the white part of the leeks, the endive, and the escarole, and boil in salted water until tender. Drain well and let cool. Melt 3 tablespoons butter in a saucepan, stir in 5 tablespoons flour, and add the hot milk. Add salt and let the sauce cook for a few minutes, stirring constantly. Squeeze the excess moisture out of the vegetables and sauté them in remaining butter for a few minutes. Add salt and remove from heat. Chop finely. Add vegetables with ½ cup of the cheese and egg yolks to the béchamel sauce and mix well. Beat the egg whites till stiff and gently fold them into the vegetable mixture. Butter and flour a 2-quart mold. Add the mixture and cover with a sheet of aluminum foil. Place in a pot on top of the stove, add hot water to halfway up the sides of the mold, cover the pot, and steam for 1 hour, taking care that the water just simmers. Then place the timbale in a 350° oven for 10-20 minutes or until it is firm.

Put the cream, the rest of the cheese, and the chopped ham in a blender and purée, then heat it gently in a double boiler. Unmold the timbale onto a plate, pour the hot sauce over it, and serve immediately.

Green bean timbale

■ **Yield: 4 servings**
■ **Time needed: 2 hours**
■ **Difficulty: ***

Ingredients: 1½ lb green beans, ¾ cup shredded Gruyère, ½ cup grated Parmesan cheese, ⅓ cup flour, 1 carrot, 5 tbsp. butter, 4 eggs, separated, 1 ¾ cups milk, salt, pepper.

Trim the green beans, wash, and boil with the sliced carrot in salted water until tender. Drain well. Set the carrot slices and a few beans aside. Force the remaining beans through a food mill or purée in a food processor

or blender. Then cook in 2 tablespoons of butter.

Melt remaining butter, stir in flour, and add the hot milk, stirring constantly. Let the béchamel sauce simmer a few minutes, then add salt and pepper and remove from the heat. Add the two cheeses to the sauce, then the string bean purée, and, one by one, the egg yolks. Beat the egg whites till stiff and fold them in gently. Arrange the reserved sliced carrot and string beans on the bottom of a buttered 2-quart ring mold, then fill with the mixture and place in an oven-proof pan one-third filled with boiling water. Cook in a 350° oven for about 45 minutes, or until firm. When done, remove from the oven and let rest a few minutes. Unmold onto a plate. This timbale goes well with poultry or other white meat.

Asparagus timbale

■ **Yield: 4 servings**
■ **Time needed: 2 hours**
■ **Difficulty: ***

Ingredients: 2 lb asparagus, ½ cup grated Parmesan cheese, ½ cup shredded Gruyère, 5 tbsp butter, 5 tbsp flour, 4 eggs, separated, 2 cups milk, salt, pepper.

Trim the asparagus, cutting off any woody parts. Boil or steam until tender, then cut into small pieces and cook in 2 tablespoons butter with a little salt and pepper.

Melt 3 tablespoons butter, add the flour, and cook for a moment before adding the hot milk, stirring constantly. Let the sauce boil a few minutes, then season with salt and pepper and remove from heat. Pass the asparagus through a food mill or purée in a blender or food processor, then add it to the béchamel along with the cheeses and, one at a time, the egg yolks. Finally, beat the egg whites till stiff and gently fold them in.

Butter a 2-quart ring mold. Fill the mold only ¾ full, as the timbale will rise during cooking, and smooth the surface with a spoon. Place in a slightly larger pan filled one-third with water. Cook it in a 350° oven for about 45 minutes or until firm. If the water in the pan begins to boil, add a little cold water.

When the timbale is cooked, let it rest a few minutes and then turn it out onto a serving plate. This goes well with roast pork, calve's liver cooked in white wine, or veal scalloppine.

Croquettes

It is easy to imagine that meatballs and croquettes were invented to use up leftovers, and then gradually were transformed into exceedingly tasty and nutritious preparations. People often confuse these two similar dishes but there is a basic difference. Meatballs are a simple everyday sort of dish, an economical way to prepare ground raw meat or cooked leftovers which are then bound with beaten egg and bread crumbs soaked in milk, or potatoes or rice. After being rolled in flour they are fried and served with a tomato sauce as a main course. Croquettes, on the other hand, originated in France as their name, which means "crisp", suggests. They are not just French in name but in their preparation as well. They are more refined and precise in the amount of ingredients used. Their delicate binders not only serve to hold together the tender vegetables, meats, and fish, but also give this dish its characteristic texture. Originally the ingredients were not as finely minced as they are today but instead were cubed or cut in julienne strips so that the individual flavors stood out. One likes to imagine that the first croquette was made of potatoes and served in honor of the Sun King, who loved the new vegetable. Croquettes are usually cylindrical and about 2 to 3 inches in length. They can also be shaped like discs or lozenges, as is common when they are sweet. In any case, they shouldn't weigh more than 2 or 3 ounces. Their food value is high, though this varies somewhat according to whether they have a meat, fish, cereal, cheese, or vegetable base, making them a complete meal from a dietary standpoint. Croquettes are particularly good for those needing high caloric meals, as well as for children and the elderly since they have the advantage of being made of precooked food which is easy to chew and digest. Croquettes make a good first course, or they may be served as a side dish if made with green vegetables.

Traditionally they are served on a warmed serving plate covered with a folded napkin, and garnished with sprigs of parsley, slices of lemon, and salad greens. They can also be served with a sauce or flavored butter.

The basic ingredients

Croquettes are prepared using a base of meat, fish, vegetables, or cereals to which a binding ingredient is added, such as a béchamel sauce, cream, or beaten egg whites. Sometimes a starch ingredient like potatoes, rice, or bread crumbs soaked in milk, is also added. The binding ingredient should be used in a proportion of one part binder to three parts base, which usually includes egg yolks. The most common croquette is made with potatoes. A thick potato purée is made, egg yolks are added, and if a lighter croquette is desired, beaten egg whites are folded in. These croquettes can be enriched with bits of meat, cheese, or ham. Very delicate croquettes can also be made with vegetables such as spinach, mushrooms, or artichokes; these are bound with eggs and béchamel sauce, and then mixed with other ingredients like cheese to give them more flavor. Leftover meat and fish can be made into very good croquettes. In fact, extra meat or fish is often cooked for the express purpose of making croquettes and is used to make *supplì* and *arancini di riso*. Finally, don't forget that rice croquettes made with ham, peas, or chicken, or croquettes made with cornmeal or other cereals like millet, barley, or oats, can be surprisingly delicious and delicate. Croquettes are all made the same way. First, the basic ingredients are finely minced, then a binding ingredient is added along with the rest of the ingredients, and the croquette paste is left to cool. Sometimes the paste is first spread over a marble slab. Once the mixture is firm, it is rolled out with a rolling pin and shaped into the most appropriate form. Then the croquettes are dipped in flour, beaten eggs, and bread crumbs and fried.

How to fry croquettes

The most suitable method of cooking croquettes is deep-frying. When the oil is hot enough, the moist balls make a crackling sound when they are dropped in. This method also gives the croquettes a golden color without burning or drying them out too much. A classic cast-iron pan, a non-stick pan, or even an electric deep-fryer may be used for frying. A wire basket is also useful, especially one that comes with a fryer as part of a set. This way the croquettes can be dropped into the basket submerged in the hot oil and, when cooked, the basket can be removed so the croquettes can be easily drained. Ordinary liquid cooking oil is the most frequently used frying medium, as it guarantees a crispy exterior. It is best used for larger croquettes. Smaller croquettes which may need an extra bit of flavor can be cooked in butter. Lard is less frequently used, but is good for large quantities of sweet croquettes. Once the croquettes are cooked they should be drained on layers of paper towels and served hot on a napkin-covered plate.

Potato croquettes

1 Boil the potatoes and mash while still hot.

- **Yield: 4 servings**
- **Time needed: 1 1/2 hours**
- **Difficulty: ***

Ingredients: 1 lb baking potatoes, 6 oz mozzarella, 2 oz ham in one slice, 4 tbsp butter, 1/2 cup grated Parmesan cheese, 1/2 cup flour, 2 eggs, 2 egg yolks, nutmeg, bread crumbs, oil for deep-frying, salt.

Wash the potatoes. Boil in salted water until tender, peel, and mash while they are still hot (1). Spoon the potato purée into a pan and add the butter, salt, and a little nutmeg, mixing well. Stir over low heat to dry (2), then remove from the fire. Add the grated Parmesan (3) and, one at a time, the egg yolks, mixing them in well (4).

Cut the ham into small pieces and the mozzarella into small cubes. Flouring your hands from time to time, form the potato mixture into balls, ovals, little cylinders, or pear shapes (5). Make a small hole in the top (6) and poke in some ham (7) and cheese, then close the top again (8), covering the filling completely so that it doesn't seep out during cooking.

Roll the croquettes in flour, then in the eggs, beaten with salt (9), and finally in the bread crumbs.

Heat 3 inches oil in a deep pan and when it is hot (380°), fry the croquettes a few at a time (10), moving them around so that they take on a uniform color (11). If you've made the croquettes in a pear shape, the best way to cook them is in a deep-frying basket, which may be lightly shaken to move the croquettes about in the oil and thus promote even cooking. Drain well on paper towels and place on a serving platter covered with a napkin. Serve croquettes hot as an accompaniment to veal or a roast. If you have made them in a pear shape, place a little sprig of parsley in the top of each one to simulate a stem.

2 Put the purée and butter over low heat and stir to dry a little.

3 Remove the potato purée from the heat, add the Parmesan immediately, and finally...

4 ...beat in the egg yolks one at a time.

5 Flour your hands and shape the croquettes into balls, ovals, cylinders, or pear shapes.

6 Poke a floured finger into the center of each one.

7 Fill the center of each with a little chopped ham...

8 ...and mozzarella, and close the tops over the filling.

9 Roll the croquettes first in flour, then in beaten egg.

10 Heat the oil to 380° and fry the croquettes a few at a time.

11 Move the croquettes about in the hot oil so that they brown evenly.

Potato croquettes

Artichoke croquettes

■ Yield: 4 servings
■ Time needed: 1¹/₂ hours
■ Difficulty: *

Ingredients: 5 artichokes, 4 tbsp butter, 2 large onions, 1 tbsp chopped parsley, 2 cups hot milk, 3 eggs, 2 of them separated, ¹/₂ beef bouillon cube, ¹/₃ cup flour, 1¹/₂-2 cups bread crumbs, juice of 1 lemon, nutmeg, salt, pepper, oil for deep-frying.

Trim artichokes, removing all outer leaves and choke, so that only the bottom remains. Place them in water and lemon juice as trimmed, then boil in salted water till tender, drain, and cut into small cubes. Slice onions and sauté in butter. Add ¹/₃ cup flour (1) and hot milk (2). Add salt, pepper, and nutmeg, and cook for 30 minutes. Force sauce through a food mill or purée in a blender or food processor. Beat 2 egg yolks and add to sauce with bouillon cube, dissolved in 1 tbsp boiling water. Simmer until sauce is very thick. Add artichokes and parsley, and mix well (3). Turn mixture out onto a floured surface and shape into small balls (4). Dip croquettes in remaining egg and the two egg whites beaten with a little salt, then roll in bread crumbs (5) and fry in oil (6).

1 Slice the onions, sauté in butter, and add flour, mixing well.

2 When the onion is soft, add the milk.

3 After adding the egg yolks, add the cooked artichokes.

4 Turn the mixture onto a floured surface and make little balls.

5 Dip the croquettes first in beaten egg, then roll in bread crumbs.

6 Heat the oil and fry the croquettes a few at a time until they are golden.

Artichoke croquettes

Mushroom croquettes

- **Yield: 4 servings**
- **Time needed: 1½ hours**
- **Difficulty: ***

Ingredients: **7 oz fresh or 1 oz dried cèpe mushrooms, 1 large onion, 3 tbsp flour, ½ cup grated Parmesan cheese, 7 tbsp butter,** **6 eggs, 2 of them separated, 1 cup hot milk, parsley, 2 tbsp oil, salt, pepper.**

Chop onions and sauté in 1 tbsp butter and 2 tbsp oil. Slice mushrooms and add to onions (1). (If you are using dried mushrooms, first soak for 30 minutes in tepid water, then drain.) Let them cook a little. Sprinkle with chopped parsley and mix in 3 tbsp flour (2). Add hot milk (3), salt, pepper, and finally cheese. Cook until the mixture has thickened. Cook 3 eggs for 7-8 minutes in boiling water. Peel and chop them and add to mushrooms (4), together with 2 raw egg yolks. Mix together and let cool completely. Then, a spoonful at a time, shape the mixture with floured hands into small round croquettes (5). Dip them into remaining egg and two egg whites, beaten with a pinch of salt (6), and fry in the remaining butter.

1 After sautéeing the onions, add the fresh or dried sliced mushrooms.

2 Sprinkle flour over the cooked mushrooms and stir rapidly to mix well.

3 Cook the flour a little and then add hot milk.

4 Cook 3 of the eggs for 7-8 minutes and add them to the mushrooms.

5 With floured hands, form the mixture into small balls.

6 Dip the croquettes in the remaining beaten egg and egg whites.

Mushroom croquettes

Spinach croquettes

■ **Yield: 4 servings**
■ **Time needed: 1 hour 15 minutes**
■ **Difficulty: ***

Ingredients: 3 lb fresh or frozen spinach, 5 1/2 tbsp butter, 3 tbsp flour, 1/2 cup grated Parmesan cheese, 2 egg yolks, 1 egg, 1 cup milk, 1 1/2-2 cups bread crumbs, 1 clove garlic, nutmeg, oil for deep-frying, salt, pepper.

Trim the spinach and rinse well under running water. Drain and place in a pot. Cook until wilted, adding only a pinch of salt. Drain, let cool, and squeeze out excess moisture. Chop finely or purée using a food mill, blender or food processor. Crush the garlic and sauté in 3 1/2 tablespoons of the butter. When it has browned, remove it and add the spinach. Stir with a wooden spoon for a few minutes and remove from heat.

Prepare a thick béchamel sauce. Melt 2 tablespoons of the butter in a pan, add 3 tablespoons flour, and mix well to get rid of the lumps. Add the hot milk, stirring constantly. Let the sauce boil a few minutes, then add salt, pepper, and nutmeg. Remove from the fire and add the Parmesan and spinach. Pour the mixture into a greased plate (or a marble board), smoothing it out with a spatula so it is of uniform thickness. Let it cool completely, then with floured hands, form it into small cylinders. Dip croquettes into eggs beaten with a pinch of salt, then into bread crumbs, and fry them a few at a time in hot oil. Serve as an accompaniment to a veal or pork roast.

Potato and mushroom croquettes

■ **Yield: 4 servings**
■ **Time needed: 1 hour 15 minutes**
■ **Difficulty: ***

Ingredients: 14 oz fresh cèpe or other mushrooms, 3 1/2 tbsp butter, 2-3 ripe tomatoes, 3 large baking potatoes, 3 eggs, 3 tbsp grated Parmesan cheese, handful chopped parsley, 1 small onion, 1 clove garlic, flour, bread crumbs, oil, salt, pepper.

Trim the mushrooms, cutting off the dried or woody part of the stems. Wipe clean with a damp towel and slice finely. Sauté the chopped onion in a skillet with a little butter. Add the mushrooms and let cook a few minutes, stirring occasionally. Add salt and pepper. Peel and chop the tomatoes and add to the mushrooms. Cook the sauce until all liquid has evaporated.

Boil the potatoes in their skins, then peel, mash, and put into a bowl. Add the Parmesan, chopped parsley, garlic, and two egg yolks. Finally, add the mushrooms and mix everything together well. With floured hands, form the mixture into egg shapes. Dip them into the remaining egg, beaten with a pinch of salt, then roll them in bread crumbs. Fry in hot oil. When they are golden, drain them on paper towels. Lightly salt and serve hot as an accompaniment to stewed or roasted meats.

Pasta croquettes

■ **Yield: 4 servings**
■ **Time needed: 1 hour**
■ **Difficulty: ***

Ingredients: 6 oz leftover buttered spaghetti, 4 oz chopped cooked chicken or other meat, 1/2 cup grated Parmesan, 1 oz dried mushrooms, about 2/3 cup flour, 3 tbsp butter, 2 eggs, 1 egg yolk, 1 1/2-2 cups bread crumbs, 1 cup milk, oil for deep-frying, salt, pepper.

Soak the mushrooms in tepid water for 30 minutes.

Make a thick béchamel. Melt 2 tablespoons of the butter in a pan, add 3 tablespoons of the flour, and mix well to eliminate lumps. Add hot milk, stirring constantly till smooth. Add salt and pepper and simmer for a few minutes.

Melt the rest of the butter in a pan. Squeeze and chop the mushrooms and add to the butter along with salt and pepper. Cook briefly. Add the chopped meat and cook a little longer, mixing well. Stir this mixture into the béchamel sauce. Add the Parmesan, the chopped spaghetti, and an egg yolk. Spread the mixture out on a buttered slab and let cool completely, then cut into squares. Dip croquettes in the remaining flour, then into the eggs, beaten, and finally into the bread crumbs. Fry in hot oil till golden, then drain on paper towels. Serve while hot as a hearty first course.

Pasta croquettes

PRESERVING FRUITS AND VEGETABLES

Preserving
Fruit

Preserving is a means of capturing the flavor and colors of the harvest season. Small quantities can be put up when produce is plentiful, using different methods and procedures, bringing a savings of money as well as time and energy.

The technique of preserving began in the countryside, with thrifty farmers who never wasted anything. It rapidly caught on with cooks everywhere and soon became part of the household routine.

Eventually the food industry realized the potential of preserving, and today the market is flooded with fruits and vegetables of every kind from every corner of the earth.

They are preserved and marketed in such different ways that we are often at a loss as to how to choose among them.

Raw or partially cooked vegetables can be preserved in oil or vinegar or under salt. Nutritive values remain almost unchanged because the preserving methods alter the food very little.

The same thing is true of dried or frozen food. In fact, the flavor and nutritive value of some foods, such as mushrooms and legumes, are increased proportionally when dried.

Tomatoes can be preserved in many different ways to retain a high amount of vitamin C. Fruit preserves, on the other hand, have a high sugar content (and thus many calories), but have little nutritive value.

Marmalades and preserves are made by cooking fruit with sugar, then leaving it whole or puréeing it. Jellies can be made from fruit juices while canned fruits are cooked with sugar and left whole or cut into sections. Candied fruit has so much sugar added that it becomes hard.

In some instances dried fruit loses many of its vitamins when it loses water, but the other nutritive qualities remain unaltered.

The food industry has conserved fruits and vegetables by freeze-drying them in airtight packages.

Dehydrated foods keep their original nutritive value and flavor far better than other industrial methods of preserving food such as purées. In purées, the fruits or vegetables are reduced to minute particles but there are also substances added to improve the flavor and conserve the food longer.

Industrial preserving cannot match homemade preserves, made from recipes which are often handed down from one generation to the next. They hold no special secrets because everyone knows what they are made of—wholesome ingredients, patience, and a love of good things to eat.

Jams and marmalades

Many people are frightened at the very idea of making marmalades or jams in their own kitchens — and this is wrong because they are not at all difficult to make and are nearly foolproof. First of all, let's define our terms. Preserves are made with fruit left whole or cut into sections. Marmalades have pieces of fruit or peel. Jam is made by cooking the fruit till it is a thick purée or by straining it after cooking, before you add sugar. Jelly is made using only the fruit juices. All these preparations have a common denominator of fruit and sugar; at times pectin is also added.

The fruit you choose should all be equally ripe. Keep in mind that delicate fruits like strawberries, blackberries, etc., should not be too ripe, while firm fruits like cherries, apricots, etc., should be at their peak. The fruits should be washed and completely dried, because any excess water increases the cooking time. Preserves and marmalades should consist of 65% sugar, which preserves the fruit. In any case, each recipe tells how much sugar to add depending on the quantity and type of fruit and its natural sweetness. Pectin, a natural substance found in the peel and seeds of certain fruits, such as apples and quince, becomes a jelly under heat. If, during preparation, marmalade is too thin, it may need pectin. We advise adding one apple for every two pounds of fruit. The acid content in preserves and marmalades stops bacteria from developing and the sugar from crystallizing. Usually the fruit already contains enough acid, but if not, the recipe will call for adding additional acid, such as vinegar or lemon juice.

An important phase in making marmalades and jams is the actual cooking. First, the fruit is cooked over high heat to evaporate the excess water. Then the froth that

forms is removed and finally the fruit is cooked over low heat to blend it with the sugar. The actual cooking time depends on the type and quantity of the fruit. The marmalade is ready when it has thickened and is clear. To see if it is done, pour a spoonful into a saucer and turn one edge up slightly. If the marmalade runs down the side of the saucer very slowly, it is thick enough.

Once it is ready, marmalade should be poured into airtight jars. These should be heated first in a kettle of boiling water, then placed on a folded cloth instead of directly on a cold surface so they do not break. When the jars are filled, leave about 1/2 inch empty at the top and seal the jars airtight so they will be self-sterilized. Cold marmalade can be poured directly into jars and a round piece of waxed paper, which has first been dipped in alcohol or vinegar, placed directly on the fruit. The small amount of moisture which adheres to the paper is enough to keep mold from developing. When the jars are filled they should be placed in a cool, dry, dark place. The outside of the jars should be clean and well-labeled. In either the hot or cold canning process, the gaskets of the jars must be perfectly clean. Certain kinds of marmalades must be sterilized thoroughly after sealing them in airtight jars by boiling the jars in a sterilizer or large pot.

One word of caution. From time to time, check jars you have put away for mold. A small amount of mold can be removed and the preserves saved by boiling the marmalade again for a short time. However, don't hesitate to throw out any jar with a bad smell which looks suspicious.

Fruit in syrup

Fruit syrups and juices

Preserving fruit in syrup is the most common way of putting up whole fruits or fruit sections. For this kind of preserve, the choice of fruit is of utmost importance. There are a few rules you must follow. Choose the fruit at the peak of its season, when it is at its very best (and prices are low). Select fruit that is unblemished and perfectly ripe. Remember that if it is too ripe, once it is preserved it will be mushy. If a recipe calls for whole fruit, select ones that are of the same size, if possible, so they can absorb the syrup equally. When you are preparing fruit in a syrup, the most important part is, of course, preparing the syrup. Sugar and water in fixed proportions are boiled together. The amount of water the fruit contains naturally will determine how much syrup it absorbs.

Another way to preserve fruits, which is also one of the easiest ways, it with spirits. All you have to do is pay attention to the choice of fruit and to the alcoholic content of the liquor. You will get the best results using a colorless, refined spirit that is distilled from fruit. Special preparations call for using brandy, grappa, rum, or gin. Sugar is nearly always added to fruit preserved in spirits to give the fruit a better taste and temper the strong taste of the alcohol.

These same methods of preserving fruit can produce highly refreshing and nutritious fruit drinks. To make syrups, which are delightful over ice cream or cakes, the fruit is crushed and in some cases left to sit in its own juices. Fermentation will occur, sooner or later, depending on the type of fruit. After the juice is strained through a cloth, squeezing the fruit well to extract as much juice as possible, the liquid is then filtered till it is clear. It is then put over heat together with enough sugar to make a very heavy syrup that will keep for a long time. Finally the syrup is bottled in glass containers that are completely clean and perfectly dry. A few drops of water left in the bottle can cause the syrup to ferment.

Fruit juices come from squeezing the fruit, which should always be very ripe and of high quality. (According to popular folk wisdom, bees sting the best fruit.) Once the juice has been extracted, it must be boiled, often with sugar added, just long enough for the sugar to dissolve. Juices can be preserved without adding sugar, but in this case it must be frozen or pasteurized. (The latter process requires heating sealed containers to a temperature just below boiling, that is, not above 180°.) In any case, fruit juices should be poured into spotlessly clean bottles, as described for syrups. The best fruits for making syrups are rich in pectin, a substance that gives the juice a certain body; some examples of these fruits are raspberries, gooseberries, apples, quince, sour black cherries, blackberries, and strawberries. Besides oranges, the best fruits to use to make juice are lemons and grapefruits, fruit grown in the wild, cherries, apricots, peaches, apples, and pears.

Very thick syrups should be diluted with water when you are ready to use them. They can be made into refreshing summer drinks or poured over vanilla ice cream. When you use the syrup with desserts, it's a good idea to add some of the fresh fruit as well.

Freezing fruit

1 After cutting the fruit in half or in wedges, remove the pits, peel...

Though any fruit can be frozen, freezing is not the best process of preserving food naturally. Sugar must also be added for the fruit to keep its color and flavor. Freezing is, however, a good way to preserve small fruits such as strawberries, raspberries, blackberries, and blueberries, which have only a short season. These fruits, commonly found in the frozen food department of your grocery store, can be successfully frozen at home, although they will lose a bit of their flavor. Simply sprinkle sugar over the fruit before putting it in the freezer. Other larger fruits, like apricots, peaches, and plums, require sugar added as syrup before freezing. To prepare the fruit, select pieces that are unblemished and ripe, wash and scald the fruit briefly in boiling water, then immerse it in cold water. Cut it in half or in sections, remove the pits, and peel (1). Place in jars or plastic containers taking care not to fill them too full (2). Cover them so all the space between the fruit pieces is filled with a sugar syrup containing 1 3/4 pounds (3 1/2 cups) sugar for each quart of water (3).

When you use small fruit, first wash it carefully and let all the water drip off. Carefully spread on a tray or platter, sprinkle confectioners' sugar over it (4), and put in the freezer for about an hour, till it hardens. Then it can be divided up and put into plastic containers or freezing bags (5). Either kind of container should be carefully sealed and as much air eliminated as possible. Once defrosted at room temperature, frozen fruit can be eaten as is, or it may be poured over cakes and ice cream or made into marmalade, fruit compotes, sauces, or drinks. Frozen fruit usually keeps for one year.

Fruit drinks and fruit mixtures can also be frozen. Simply add a few drops of lemon juice to the fruit.

2 ...and place in jars, taking care not to fill too tightly.

3 Cover the fruit with a heavy sugar syrup.

4 Place small fruit on a platter, sprinkle confectioners' sugar over it…

5 …and when it is frozen, divide into plastic freezing bags.

Some useful advice

—Buy fruit when it is at its peak and select fruit that is fresh, unblemished, and fully ripe.

—Clean the fruit well and don't forget to remove the pits and stems after the fruit has been washed. Peaches should be scalded, peeled, and the pits removed. Apples and pears should be washed, peeled, and cut into four quarters. Citrus fruits should be washed and rubbed clean to remove any trace of pesticides.

—Gather the pits and seeds and put them in a plastic bag. When you make preserves, marmalades, or syrups, add the pits and seeds to the mixture during cooking so that the pectin they contain can act as a thickening agent. Discard pits and seeds after cooking.

—When you preserve fruits in alcohol, make a hole in large fruits. If the fruit has a thick peel, pierce it with a needle heated over a flame. This makes it easier for the alcohol to penetrate the fruit and prevents if from bursting open once the alcohol has been absorbed.

—The sugar you use as a sweetener and as a preservative, should always be pure and refined so it will dissolve quickly. It may be added in granular form or as a syrup.

—For the fruit you are going to freeze, use a cold syrup; for preserved fruit use a hot syrup, and for candied fruits and other recipes, use a syrup that is concentrated from prolonged cooking.

—When you preserve fruit that is a bit acidic, it is best to put the fruit in a thick syrup and cook for only a short time. Add lemon juice when cooking fruit that has little acidity, to give it tartness.

—Choose appropriate materials for cooking and preserving: containers that will not react with the acid in the fruits such as unlined copper, earthenware, or stainless steel for cooking the fruit and airtight glass jars for preserving and sterilizing the fruit.

—It is advisable to use pint or half-pint jars that have a wide mouth. To prevent the jars from breaking when you pour in the boiling liquid, put a stainless steel spoon inside to absorb part of the heat.

The necessary equipment

It has always been a long-standing tradition to use copper or earthenware pots when making jams and marmalades, but stainless steel pots will do nicely if they have a heavy bottom, guaranteeing that the fruit will not stick even though it is cooked for a long time. In any case, the pot you use should be wide and shallow to allow as much of the water in the fruit to evaporate as possible (copper pots that are not lined with tin are ideal).

To mix marmalades and strained fruits you will need a wooden spoon or spatula. A skimmer to remove the froth and a special ladle used only for making preserves are both essential. The special ladle is needed when you make marmalades using blackberries, blueberries, or other dark fruits whose juices stain your other utensils.

You will also need various-sized glasses and at least three fine strainers. A food mill, which is easier to use, can be substituted. You will also find on the market filters which are useful when making syrups and juices. Some are made of paper and some are made of canvas, wool, or muslin. If you don't happen to have one of these you can use a clean linen cloth.

Besides different-sized measuring cups it is useful to have a scale to weigh the various ingredients. There is a wide variety of utensils that are helpful to have, but not strictly necessary. Knives of various sizes, with thin, smooth, or serrated blades, and rounded or pointed tips, are basic equipment. An olive pitter, a lemon stripper, a stainless steel grater that doesn't discolor the fruit, a cherry pitter, and a stainless steel ladle with a spout to pour the fruit into jars are also useful. Finally, you'll need a funnel and, of course, jars, if you are going to preserve fruit.

The latter should close with a screw lid or hook and must be airtight.

Lemon preserves

Ingredients: 7 lb very firm lemons with unblemished peels, 7 cups sugar, 1 cup white rum.

Wash the lemons (1), cut them in half horizontally (2), and let them soak in water for two days (3). Then put the lemon halves into a pot, cover with water, and cook them for 30-45 minutes or until soft. Drain, discarding the water (4), and cut fruit into pieces (5).

Pour 2 quarts of water into a pot (6), add the sugar (7), and boil the syrup till the sugar dissolves completely. Add the pieces of lemon (8) and cook them till the mixture thickens. Remove the preserves from the heat. Let cool and add the rum (9). Mix with a wooden spoon.

Pour the preserves into clean, dry canning jars (10), then close airtight. Store in a dark, dry place. This is a pleasantly bitter preserves.

- **Difficulty: ***
- **Use: At breakfast or with roasted game**
- **Store: Up to 1 year**

1 Choose very firm lemons with unblemished peels and wash in cold water.

2 Remove the stems and cut lemons in half with a knife.

3 Soak the lemons in water for a couple of days, covered with a cloth.

4 Cook the lemons in water till the peel softens, then drain.

5 Let cool a little on a cutting board, then cut into large pieces.

6 Pour 2 quarts water into a pot and bring it to a boil.

7 Add the sugar to the boiling water and mix with a wooden spoon.

8 When the sugar has dissolved completely, add the pieces of lemon.

9 Remove the preserves from the heat, let cool, and add the rum, mixing well.

10 Pour the preserves into jars, seal airtight, and store for future use.

Lemon preserve

Orange and lemon marmalade

■ **Difficulty: ***
■ **Use: At breakfast or as pastry filling**
■ **Store: Up to 1 year**

Ingredients: 2¼ lb oranges, 2¼ lb lemons, 7 cups sugar.

Wash thoroughly; then remove the zest of the fruits (the colored part of the peel) (1). Slice away and discard the white pith underneath, which is bitter (2), and cut the zest into strips (3). Put the pulp, cut into pieces, into a pot made of unlined copper or stainless steel, but not of aluminum (4). Add citrus zest (5) and sugar (6). Put over moderate heat and simmer for 20-30 minutes, stirring often with a wooden spoon (7). Periodically remove the foam with a skimmer (8). When the zest and fruit are translucent, remove the marmalade from the fire and pour it, still hot, into clean, dry jars (9). Attach rubber rings to the underside of the lids (10) and quickly seal the jars airtight (11). Store in a cool, dry, dark place.

Orange marmalade

■ **Difficulty: ***
■ **Use: At breakfast or with pork roasts**
■ **Store: Up to 1 year**

Ingredients: 15 oranges, 1 lb apples, 5½ cups sugar.

Remove the zest (the colored part of the peel) of two of the oranges and cut into thin strips; cut away and discard the white pith underneath. Remove and discard all the peel of the remaining oranges. Cut all the oranges into pieces and place in a pot. Peel the apples, saving the peel. Add the whole apples, apple peel, citrus zest, and sugar and cook for 5 minutes. Remove the apples and purée them, then return to the pot and let the marmalade come to a boil. Skim off any froth. Boil till the marmalade gets as thick as honey. Pour, still hot, into jars and close them airtight. Store in a cool, dry, dark place.

1 Before you use the fruit, wash well with a cloth and then remove the zest.

2 Remove and discard the white part of the peel adhering to the pulp.

3 Cut the zest of the lemons and oranges into very thin strips.

4 Turn the pieces of fruit into a pot made of copper or another noncorroding material (not aluminum).

5 Add the strips of orange and lemon zest.

6 Lastly, add the sugar and stir with a wooden spoon.

7 Place the pot over moderate heat and cook, stirring often with a wooden spoon.

8 After it has boiled for a while, remove accumulated foam with a skimmer.

9 When the marmalade is done, pour it into jars while still hot.

10 Attach the rubber rings to the underside of the lids.

11 While the marmalade is still hot, seal the jars airtight.

Orange and lemon marmelade and Orange marmelade

Tomato marmalade

■ **Difficulty:** *
■ **Use: As a cake or pastry filling**
■ **Store: Up to 1 year**

Ingredients: 7 lb green tomatoes, 2 lemons, 8 cups sugar, 1/2 cup brandy.

Wash the tomatoes (1), cut in half, and squeeze to remove seeds. Cut into pieces (2) and place in a pot. Add the sugar (3), the grated peel of one of the lemons (4), and the strained juice of both lemons (5). Mix well to combine ingredients evenly and boil for 5 minutes (6). Stir frequently (7) and skim off the foam.

When the tomatoes have softened, remove from the heat (8) and purée the mixture in a food mill, food processor, or blender. Return mixture to the pot and cook over moderate heat till it becomes a thick, clear marmalade. To be sure it is cooked enough, pour a little of the marmalade onto a plate and tip slightly. The marmalade should slide down the plate very slowly (9).

Remove from the heat, add the liquor, pour into jars while still hot (10), and seal airtight. Store in a dry, dark place.

1 Wash barely ripe or green tomatoes in cold water.

2 Cut them in half and squeeze them so their seeds and juice come out, then cut into pieces.

3 Place the tomato pieces in a pot and add the sugar...

4 ...and the grated zest of a lemon.

5 Squeeze the two lemons, strain the juice, and add it to the tomato pieces.

6 Mix well to combine ingredients evenly.

7 Pour the mixture into a pot with high sides and boil for 5 minutes, stirring continually.

8 When the tomatoes have softened and the sugar dissolved, remove from the heat.

9 Pour a little marmalade onto a plate and tip. If the marmalade runs down slowly, it's done.

10 Remove the marmalade from the heat and pour it into jars while still hot.

Tomato marmelade

Apricot marmalade

■ **Difficulty:** *
■ **Use: At breakfast or as a pastry filling**
■ **Store: Up to 1 year**

Ingredients: 9 lb ripe unblemished apricots, 8 cups sugar, 1 lemon.

Wash the apricots quickly, drain, and remove the pits. Cut half the apricots into pieces and put into the pot you will cook the marmalade in; purée the rest and add to the pot. Add the juice and grated zest of the lemon, then put over moderate heat and let it come to a boil. Boil slowly for a couple of minutes, skimming any foam. Then add sugar and bring to a boil again. Cook slowly, stirring often. When the marmalade is very thick, remove from the heat. Pour into jars and seal.

Cherry marmalade

■ **Difficulty:** *
■ **Use: At breakfast or as a cake or pastry filling**
■ **Store: Up to 1 year**

Ingredients: 11 lb pitted cherries, 14 cups sugar, a few small cherry leaves (optional).

Remove the stems, wash the cherries, and pit them with a cherry pitter. Place cherries in a large pot (an unlined copper pot works well) and add sugar. Mix. Boil slowly and skim off the foam when necessary. Stir marmalade with a wooden spoon continuously so that it doesn't stick. Test for thickness by pouring a spoonful onto a plate. If it doesn't run when you tilt the plate, remove it from the fire. Pour it into previously heated jars while it is still hot. Place a few cherry leaves in each jar. Close the jars airtight and store in a dark place.

Caramel apple marmalade

■ **Difficulty:** *
■ **Use: At breakfast or as a topping for cakes and puddings**
■ **Store: Up to 1 year**

Ingredients: 5 lb apples, 5¹/₂ cups sugar, 1 lemon, ¹/₂ cup brandy.

Wash the apples. Remove the cores and cut them into pieces. Pour lemon juice over them so they don't turn brown. Set aside. In a pot (do not use aluminum), add 1¹/₃ cups of the sugar and ¹/₄ cup water, and place over moderate heat till it slowly comes to a boil (keep the flame low enough so it doesn't touch the sides of the pot; otherwise the sugar on the sides will burn). Swirling the pan by the handle, simmer until the sugar turns a light brown color, then immediately remove it from the fire. Do not cook too long or the sugar may burn. (The sugar continues cooking even after you have removed it from the heat.) Pour caramel over the apples, standing back in case the sugar spatters. Mix quickly to stop the caramel from hardening and then add the remaining sugar. Place the pot over moderate heat and slowly bring to a boil, stirring continuously. When the apples are cooked (they will be rather dry), remove from the heat and put through a food mill or purée in a blender or food processor. Put the purée back into the pot. If it is already very thick, just bring it to a boil, then remove from heat. If it's thin, simmer till it thickens. Remove from the heat, add the brandy, and pour it into jars immediately.

Strawberry preserves

■ **Difficulty:** *
■ **Use: As a cake or pastry filling**
■ **Store: Up to 6 months**

Ingredients: 7 lb strawberries, 7¹/₂ cups sugar, 1 lemon, ¹/₄ cup maraschino.

Choose strawberries that are at the peak of ripeness, whole and unblemished. Wash, hull, dry, and place them in a glass or earthenware bowl. Squeeze the juice of the lemon over them and then add the grated peel. Combine the sugar over low heat with 1¹/₂ cups water and simmer slowly until the sugar has dissolved completely. Raise heat and boil for 3-4 minutes. Remove syrup from the heat and pour it over the strawberries at once. Mix and let the mixture rest for half an hour. Then pour the strawberries together with the syrup into a pot. Place it over the heat and let it come to a boil very slowly. Stir constantly. When the preserves have reached the right thickness, add the maraschino and, while still hot, pour it into jars and seal airtight. Store in a cool, dark place.

Strawberries are a very delicate fruit, and to preserve them you need ones that are firm and absolutely unblemished. If you are lucky enough to grow them in your own garden, pick them in the morning when the dew has dried. Hot-house strawberries are not recommended for preserves.

Dried apples

■ **Difficulty: ***
■ **Use: As a dessert or as a pastry filling**
■ **Store: Up to 6 months**

Ingredients: Ripe, perfectly unblemished apples.

Peel the apples (1) and carefully remove the cores with an apple corer (2) without breaking them. Then cut them horizontally into slices that are about ³⁄₈ inch thick (3).

Heat your oven to about 105°. Place the slices next to each other on an oven tray, making sure they don't overlap (4). Leave them in the oven for about 24 hours, watching that they don't cook. Take them out when they are nearly dry (5) and put them in the sun so they can finish drying. Turn them two or three times a day. Store in a clean wooden box lined with wax paper (6).

When you are ready to use them just soak the dried apples in a warm water overnight, so they can absorb the liquid they lost when they were dried. When they soak make sure they stay completely under water. If necessary, put a weight over them. You can cook them in the water they soaked in and eat them, warmed up, for dessert.

1 Choose ripe, absolutely unblemished apples and peel them.

2 Remove the cores with an apple corer carefully so they don't break.

3 Cut them immediately into even slices about ³⁄₈ inch thick.

4 Place the slices on an oven tray next to each other and put them into a 105° oven.

5 Remove them from the oven when they are nearly dry.

6 Place them in a wooden box lined with paper when they are completely dry.

Dried apples

Grapes in grappa

- **Difficulty: ***
- **Use: As a dessert or as a cake topping**
- **Store: Up to 1 year**

Ingredients: 4½ lb absolutely unblemished thick-skinned green grapes, 1¾ cups sugar, peel of ½ **lemon, 1 stick cinnamon, 2-inch piece vanilla bean (optional), top-quality grappa, brandy, or other strong liquor.**

Use scissors to cut the grapes from the bunch, leaving a tiny stem at least $\frac{1}{16}$ inch long on each grape (1). Wash the grapes quickly in cold water, then drain well and dry (2). Spread them out on a counter, away from the sun, and let dry completely.

Place the grapes in jars and cover them with sugar (3). In each jar, put a small piece of cinnamon, a few strips of lemon peel (only the yellow zest, not the white pith underneath, which is bitter) and, if you want, a piece of vanilla bean. Cover the grapes with good grappa, brandy, or other strong liquor (4).

Seal the jars airtight and store in a cool dark place. They should be ready to eat in about 1 month.

1 Cut the grapes off the bunch with a pair of scissors, leaving a $\frac{1}{16}$-inch stem.

2 Wash the grapes quickly in cold water, drain, and dry well.

3 Place the grapes in jars and pour in the sugar.

4 After adding cinnamon and lemon peel for flavor, cover the grapes with grappa.

Grapes in grappa

Orange liqueur

- **Difficulty: ***
- **Use: As an after-dinner drink or dessert**
- **Store: 1 year or more**

Ingredients: 1 1/2 lb sweet ripe oranges, 1 3/4 cups sugar, 3 cloves, 3-4 cups vodka, 1 cinnamon stick, 1 lemon.

Clean the oranges well with a cloth (1). Prick them in four or five different places with a big needle or a fork (2). Place them in a large jar with a wide mouth (3). Cover with sugar (4) and add cloves, lemon peel, and pieces of cinnamon stick for flavor (5). Cover completely with vodka (6) and seal, placing a piece of waxed paper just under the lid (7). Shake the jar sideways to dissolve the sugar (8). Store in a cool dry place for about 6 months. Shake it about once a week.

When six months are up, remove the oranges from the jar and pour the liquid through a funnel, lined with filter paper, into a bottle (9). Let the liqueur rest for a few weeks before using it. The oranges can be eaten as a dessert; cut into wedges and sprinkle with sugar (10).

1 Choose oranges that are ripe and not too large; clean well.

2 Prick them in 4 or 5 places with a large needle or a fork.

3 Place them whole in a large jar with a wide mouth.

4 Cover with sugar and add some strips of lemon peel...

5 ...cloves, and 2 or 3 pieces of cinnamon stick.

6 Pour vodka over the oranges once they have been sugared.

7 Close the jars airtight, putting a piece of wax paper under the cover.

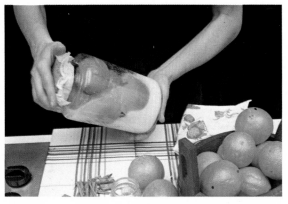

8 Before storing, shake oranges sideways to help dissolve the sugar.

9 After about 6 months, remove the oranges from the jar and filter the liquid into a bottle.

10 Serve the oranges cut into wedges and sprinkled with sugar.

Orange liqueur

Strawberry sauce

■ **Difficulty: ***
■ **Use: As a topping for ice cream and fruits**
■ **Store: Up to 6 months**

Ingredients: 2¼ lb perfectly ripe unblemished strawberries, 8 cups sugar, 1 lemon, 3 cups vodka, 3 cups water.

Trim the stems from the strawberries, but do not wash unless essential (1), and pour them into a large very clean glass or earthenware bowl. Add the sugar (2), the grated zest of the lemon (3), and the lemon juice (4). Mix everything, then cover with a cheesecloth, tying the cheesecloth with string (5). Let the strawberries stand in a cool airy place for about 2 days, stirring up at least twice a day with a wooden spoon (6). When the 2 days are up, add the alcohol (7). Stir up and strain through a fine-meshed drum sieve lined with cheesecloth (8), pressing down hard on the strawberries with the back of the spoon to force some of the pulp through the sieve.

Pour the mixture (which should be almost as thick as heavy cream) into bottles with a wide mouth (10) or into small jars, and seal airtight.

Store in a cool place.

1 Trim the strawberries, removing the stems, and place in a bowl.

2 Add the sugar and mix carefully with a wooden spoon.

3 For flavor, add the grated zest of the lemon.

4 Add the strained juice of the lemon, and mix everything very carefully.

5 Cover the bowl with cheesecloth and tie with string.

6 Let the strawberries stand in a cool place, stirring up at least twice a day.

7 Once the standing period is over, add the alcohol and mix carefully.

8 Strain the mixture through a fine-meshed drum lined with cheesecloth.

9 Press hard on the strawberries to force some of the pulp through the sieve.

10 Pour the mixture, which should be very thick, into bottles with large mouths or small jars.

Strawberry sauce

Blueberry syrup

■ Difficulty: *
■ Use: For refreshing drinks and Italian ices
■ Store: Up to 6 months

Ingredients: 4¹/₂ lb blueberries, 8 cups sugar, juice of 1 lemon and some strips of lemon peel.

Force the blueberries through a fine-meshed strainer (1). Add the sugar (2), some strips of lemon peel (3), and the lemon juice, strained (4). Pour the purée into a glass bowl (5) and let stand for a few hours. Then pour the syrup into an unlined copper or stainless steel pot and let it boil for 2 minutes (6), stirring frequently and skimming off the foam with a skimmer (7). Remove from the heat, remove the lemon peel, let the syrup cool, and pour it into a glass bowl (8). Let cool completely, then pour into a bottle (9). Seal airtight and store in a cool dark place.

This syrup can also be poured over fruit or ice cream and used in cocktails.

Blueberry liqueur

■ Difficulty: *
■ Use: For drinks and Italian ices
■ Store: Up to 6 months

Ingredients: 1 lb blueberries, 2 cups sugar, 1 lemon, 2 oz vodka, 2 oz water, 4 oz sweet sauterne.

In a 4 cup container, place the fruit, sugar, zest from the lemon, liquor, water, and wine. Cover the container and leave it for one month in a sunny place, stirring it often to dissolve the sugar completely. Then store it in a cool, dry, dark place for another four months. This makes an alcoholic liqueur. With water or seltzer added, it becomes a refreshing summer drink. It can also be made into an Italian ice.

1 Force the blueberries through a fine-meshed strainer using the back of a wooden spoon.

2 Add the sugar to the puréed blueberries and...

3 ...add a few strips of lemon zest.

4 Add lemon juice...

5 ...pour the purée into a glass bowl, and let it stand for a few hours.

6 Then pour the syrup into a copper or stainless steel pot and boil for 2 minutes.

7 While it boils, stir the syrup often and remove the foam with a skimmer.

8 Remove the syrup from the heat and let it cool in a bowl.

9 When it has cooled completely, pour it into a very clean, dry bottle.

Blueberry syrup

Raspberry syrup

■ Difficulty: *
■ Use: For drinks and Italian ices
■ Store: Up to 6 months

Ingredients: 4¹/₂ lb ripe unblemished raspberries, 10¹/₂ cups sugar, juice of 2 lemons.

Squeeze the raspberries with your hands to make a coarse purée and put in a glass or ceramic bowl. Let ferment for two or three days or slightly longer, if the temperature is colder than 65°. While it is fermenting, stir it every now and then with a wooden spoon. When the fermentation is over, strain the raspberry sauce through a fine-meshed sieve, forcing the pulp through as well. Add the sugar to the sauce and then the strained lemon juice. Pour into a stainless steel pot and bring slowly to a boil. Simmer for several minutes, stirring and skimming off the foam. Remove from the heat, pour into a glass or ceramic bowl, and let cool completely. When it is cold, pour it into bottles and store in a cool place.

Black cherry and currant jelly

■ Difficulty: *
■ Use: As a pastry filling
■ Store: Up to 6 months

Ingredients: 4¹/₂ lb ripe unblemished pitted black cherries, 1 lb currants, 4¹/₂ lb sugar, 1 lemon, 1 quart water.

Wash the black cherries and put them in a non-aluminum pot. Add the currants, the water, and the lemon peel, cut into thin strips. Put the pot over the heat and boil slowly for 10 minutes. Skim the foam and stir every now and then with a wooden spoon. Remove from the heat and strain through a fine sieve, pressing down on the fruit with the back of a spoon. Return purée to the pot, add the sugar and lemon juice, and bring to a boil. Cook, skimming the foam, until the jelly thickens and turns a deep blood red. Pour into jars and immediately seal airtight. Store in a cool, dark place.

Grape jelly

■ Difficulty: *
■ Use: As a pastry filling
■ Store: Up to 6 month

Ingredients: 7 lb green grapes, 3¹/₂ cups sugar for every quart fruit juice, 2 cups water.

Wash the grapes very carefully, then remove from the stems and put in a stainless steel or earthenware pot. Add the water and cook over low heat till the grapes burst. Strain through a fine-meshed sieve lined with cheesecloth, catching the juice in a bowl. Measure it, add 3¹/₂ cups sugar per quart of juice, and then boil till a drop of jelly holds its shape on a tipped plate without running. At this point turn the heat off, let cool, then pour into jars that have been rinsed with boiling water and dried. Let stand for 24 hours, covered with cheesecloth, then seal jars airtight. Refrigerate the jars after opening.

Grapefruit jelly

■ Difficulty: *
■ Use: As a pastry filling
■ Store: Up to 6 months

Ingredients: 4-5 juicy grapefruits, 3-4 baking apples, 5¹/₂ cups sugar, 2 cups water.

Peel 4 of the grapefruits, cut into pieces, and put the pulp and juice in a bowl. You should have about 1 pound fruit and juice; if less, add another grapefruit. Peel 3 of the apples and cut them up. Weigh, and if less than a pound, add a fourth apple. Combine grapefruit and apples in a pot with water. Bring to a boil and let cook slowly till the apples have practically dissolved (these naturally thicken the jelly). When the fruit is cooked, force is through a fine-meshed strainer or food mill. (To make a clear jelly, you can simply strain out the juice, discarding the solids, but in this case you will have a lot of waste.)

You will now have about 1 quart fruit and juice. Add the sugar and boil slowly for 10 to 25 minutes. When the jelly is thick enough to coat a spoon (watch it carefully because it thickens quickly), remove if from the heat and pour into jars and seal airtight.

Plums in brandy

■ Difficulty: *
■ Use: As a cake topping or in a fruit cocktail
■ Store: Up to 1 year

Ingredients: About 5 lb small firm unblemished plums, ¹/₂ cup sugar, about 1 quart brandy or other strong liquor, 1 vanilla bean, strips of lemon peel, 3 tsp tea leaves, 1 tsp chopped fresh mint, 2 cups water.

Begin by making a rather strong infusion of tea and mint. Bring the water to a boil, add the mint and the tea, remove from the heat, cover, and let steep for 3 minutes. When the infusion has cooled some, add the washed and dried plums and let stand for half a day so they absorb the flavor. Stir carefully 2 or 3 times. Remove the plums from the infusion and prick with a needle in 5 or 6 places. Place the plums in an earthenware or in a ceramic jar, add a chopped vanilla bean and a few strips of lemon peel, sprinkle with the sugar, and cover with the liquor.

Cover the jars and store in a cool, dry, dark place. Allow to mature for 20 days before eating.

Apricots in Marsala

■ **Difficulty: ***
■ **Use: As a cake decoration or an after-dinner drink**
■ **Store: Up to 1 year**

Ingredients: 7 lb firm unblemished apricots, 2²/₃ cups sugar, 2 cups water, 2 cups dry Marsala, 1 lemon, 3 cloves, pinch cinnamon.

Bring the water to a boil with the sugar and simmer just until the sugar dissolves and the syrup goes from cloudy to clear. Remove the syrup from the heat and add the Marsala, the peel (in strips) and the juice of the lemon, the cinnamon, and cloves. Let cool.

In the meantime, wash the apricots quickly in cold water and let dry in the open air. Cut the apricots in half with a paring knife, remove the pits, and place them in jars.

When the Marsala syrup has cooled, pour it over the apricots, leaving the top quarter of the apricots uncovered. This way the liquid will stay a few inches below the rim of the jar. Seal the jars airtight. Wrap in cheesecloth or newspaper, place in a single layer in a high-sided pot (or in a sterilizer), cover completely with water, and boil slowly for 10 minutes.

This sterilization process, though brief, is very important to conserve the fruit perfectly. Let the jars cool in the water, then drain and wipe dry. Store in a cool, dark place.

The syrup will become a delicious after-dinner drink, and the apricots can be used to top cakes and pastries.

Soused black cherries

■ **Difficulty: ***
■ **Use: As a pastry filling or an after-dinner drink**
■ **Store: Up to 1 year**

Ingredients: 5 lb unblemished perfectly ripe black cherries, 1 cup sugar, ¹/₂ cinnamon stick, 3 cloves, 1 tsp almond extract, about 1 quart vodka.

Cut the stems off the cherries about ¹/₈ inch from the base. Wash rapidly (do not let them soak) or just wipe clean with a cloth. Dry carefully. Place the cherries in clean dry jars that seal airtight. Add the sugar, cinnamon, cloves, almond extract, and just enough vodka to cover the cherries. Cover the jars and store them in a dry, dark place.

You should wait about 3 months before eating the cherries so they will have time to absorb the alcohol and blend their juice with the preserving liquid. The syrup is a delicious after-dinner drink, while the cherries can be used to top pastries, ice cream, fruit compotes, and puddings. They can also be dipped in chocolate.

Soused peaches

■ **Difficulty: ***
■ **Use: With fruit cocktails and desserts**
■ **Store: Up to 1 year**

Ingredients: 5 lb ripe firm unblemished peaches, 5 cups sugar, about 1 quart vodka.

Wash the peaches well and peel. Peeling can be done easily if the peaches are placed in boiling water for a few seconds and then put under cold water. Cut peaches in half and remove the pits, sprinkling with lemon juice right away so they don't turn brown. Arrange in layers in perfectly dry jars, covering each layer with sugar. Then cover completely with vodka, leaving about ¹/₈ inch on the top between the fruit and the cover. If you want, add ¹/₂ teaspoon almond extract and 3 or 4 cloves to each jar for extra flavoring. Seal the jars airtight and store in a dry, dark place. Wait three months before eating the fruit.

Preserving Vegetables

If you have a garden it is well worth your while to learn how to preserve vegetables when they are plentiful, so that you can eat different kinds the year round. Even if you don't have a garden it is still worth while to preserve the basic vegetables you use every day, such as tomatoes, spinach, and peas. Buy them at peak season when they are plentiful and cheap.

There are many different ways to preserve vegetables, such as canning, freezing, marinating in oil, pickling, and drying. The vegetables you are going to preserve should be freshly picked (ideally, you should pick them early in the morning before the sun comes up), unblemished, and at the peak of their ripeness. Preserved right away, they don't lose as many of their vitamins. Different vegetables require different treatment. Potatoes, for example, can only be frozen, while produce like tomatoes and peppers can be preserved in several ways. Tomatoes can be made into various sauces, while peppers can be marinated in oil with other ingredients and used as part of an antipasto or as a side dish, straight from the jar. Herbs such as parsley and basil can be marinated in oil, pickled, or frozen.

Preserving in oil

One of the basic ways to preserve vegetables is in oil. The vegetables that lend themselves best to this method are artichokes, eggplants, zucchini, peppers, and mushrooms, but even green beans, celery hearts, dried tomatoes, and certain herbs like parsley and basil can be preserved in oil without any problems.

Green beans, sun-dried tomatoes, and even such herbs as basil and parsley can also be preserved in oil.

The most suitable vegetables for preserving in oil are those with a firm flesh that will hold their shape during pre-cooking in water or vinegar and water and aromatic herbs, and then later when they are placed in the oil they are to be preserved in.

First, wash and dry them. Some must then be blanched in a sort of court bouillon made with wine or water and a little vinegar, flavored with peppercorns, cloves, bay leaves, and other spices. Other vegetables are dried and then spread out on a clean cloth overnight. The next day they can be carefully placed in jars, closely packed in layers. Between layers you can add spices and herbs.

Whether or not these vegetables come out well depends in large part on the kind of oil you use. It should be pure olive oil, but it should never have such a strong flavor that it overpowers the flavor of the vegetables. Other oils don't work as well, but if you want to use them, use peanut oil, never a blend of various unspecified vegetable oils.

Fill the jars with oil and let them sit for a few hours till the vegetables absorb part of the oil, then add a little more oil till the vegetables are covered, leaving a bit of space at the top. Seal the jars airtight and label them. The jars should be stored in an airy dark place for at least 3 months before opening.

Marinated vegetables make a delicious appetizer, hors d'oeuvre, or antipasto. They can be served with cold meats or added to rice or pasta dishes and they are ideal with cold sandwiches. They are often used as a tasty addition to many typical local dishes in southern Italy.

Preserving in vinegar

Besides having jars of vegetables marinated in oil, it's always a good idea to have some vegetables marinated in vinegar to serve with sandwiches and cold meats. The vegetables that are most often preserved in vinegar are capers, cucumbers, cauliflower, and small onions. But there are also good recipes for preserving beets, artichokes, carrots, green beans, olives, peppers, and even leeks, celery, and zucchini in vinegar.

Various ingredients add a savory touch to mixed vegetables preserved in vinegar, such as walnuts, skinned hazelnuts, and green almonds.

Vinegar is a good preserving solution because it stops the growth of bacteria that cause fermentation. A simple white distilled vinegar is usually used: in fact, red vinegar has a stronger flavor and can give the vegetables an unattractive purple tint. As all vingears are strong, it's not a good idea to use a flavored vinegar. It is better to add your own flavors using peppercorns, juniper berries, bay leaves, cloves, and thyme leaves. Furthermore, the vinegar should not be less than 5% acid and it can be made even stronger by boiling. On the other hand, a preserving liquid that is too strong could damage the taste of the vegetables, so it is advisable to dilute a very strong vinegar with water or, better yet, dry white wine. When choosing vegetables to be pickled, look for freshness and top quality. Then clean, cook so they are slightly underdone, and thoroughly dry them before putting them into jars in layers. If they are not completely dry, the water they were cooked in will mix with the vinegar and lower the acidity, thereby lessening its preserving strength. All produce that is going to be preserved should be entirely covered with vinegar, which can be poured in hot or cold, according to the recipe. The vinegar should come up to the neck of the jar so that only a very small air space is left beneath the lid. The jars and covers should be made of materials that won't be corroded by acid and the vegetables should always be removed with wooden utensils, rather than metal or plastic ones. The jars should be stored in a cool, dry place.

Natural preservation

All vegetables can be preserved naturally in a brine solution if the jars they are preserved in are sterilized in boiling water.

Just after you buy the vegetables, they should be trimmed, washed, and then blanched. The blanching time is of utmost importance: if they are cooked even a minute too long, the vegetables can lose their firmness and become mushy. All the vegetables, once they are blanched, should be dried completely and cooled. Then they are placed in jars (1) and completely covered with lightly salted boiling water (2). Lastly, clean rubber rings are attached to the underside of each cover (3) and sealed airtight.

Sterilization — Now the jars must be sterilized in boiling water, which kills all the bacteria. The jars should be wrapped in cloth (4) and placed side by side in a pot

1 After blanching the vegetables, place them in clean jars.

2 Then cover them with lightly salted boiling water.

3 Attach clean rubber rings to the undersides of the covers.

4 Wrap the jars in cloth.

5 Then place them side by side in a large pot or sterilizer.

6 Cover the jars with water and cover the pot or sterilizer.

large enough to hold them or, better, in a sterilizer (5). (This sequence of pictures show an old-fashioned sterilizer; a more modern one is pictured on pages 363-364.) Pour in enough water to cover the jars completely, and cover the pot or sterilizer (6). Place over heat and slowly bring to a boil, boiling about 30 minutes.

The exact sterilization time depends on the vegetable you are preparing and the recipe you are using. Additionally, large jars will require longer times; if the food has been thoroughly precooked, it will need less time. Once the sterilization has been completed, let the jars cool in the water bath and remove the cloth they were wrapped in. At this point you should test the seal. If the cover resists being opened, sterilization has taken place. If the cover is loose, it is wise to put the jars

back into the pot, add more water if necessary, and boil again for at least another 10 minutes.

Note: If you wish to keep the vegetables for more than four months, it is better to sterilize the jars for another 15 minutes and to repeat the process once a day for at least three days.

Salicylic acid — It is also possible to preserve vegetables using salicylic acid, which has anti-fermentation properties. It should be added in the proportion of ¼ teaspoon for every 2½ pounds of produce to be canned. This substance, however, changes the taste of the food slightly and can be harmful to people with kidney problems, so, except for tomato sauce, sterilization is nearly always used instead.

Freezing vegetables

Freezing is, without a doubt, the quickest and safest way to preserve vegetables, and the best way to retain their vitamins. In fact, it has been proved that when food is frozen and thawed correctly, there is negligible loss of vitamins and minerals.

General guidelines — After the vegetables have been trimmed, washed and, if necessary, cut into pieces, put them into a large pot of boiling water for 2 to 3 minutes. Then drain and immediately put them in ice water to prevent wilting and color and flavor loss. Drain them again, and spread in a single layer on a tray or a large plate; put the tray into the freezer for about an hour. When the vegetables are frozen, put them into plastic bags, squeeze out all the air inside the bags, and seal each one.

If you freeze spinach or other leafy vegetables that be-

1 After cooking the tomatoes for 10 minutes, pour into an ice cube tray.

2 Fill only three-quarters full and insert metal or plastic divider.

3 Once the purée has hardened, take out the cubes.

4 Fold them one by one in tin foil or put them into plastic bags.

come soft and lose their shape when they are cooked, we recommend freezing them in small covered plastic containers. This way they will keep for 6 to 8 months. When you're ready to use them, drop the still frozen vegetables into boiling salted water and cook them.

Some vegetables are used so often in cooking that it's convenient to have a good supply of them ready in the freezer. Tomatoes, as well as parsley and other herbs, can be frozen successfully, though once thawed they become limp and should only be added to stews and sauces.

Tomatoes — If you want to freeze tomatoes in large sections, put them in boiling water for a minute, then into cold water. Peel, cut in half, squeeze out the seeds, and put them in a plastic container with a cover and freeze.

If you want to purée the tomatoes before freezing so that they are ready to be made into sauce, peel, remove the seeds, cut into pieces, and cook for 10 minutes without adding anything else. Let the purée cool and pour into ice cube trays (1). Insert the ice cube divider (2) and put into the freezer to harden. When frozen, remove the cubes (3) and wrap each one in tin foil or put into freezer bags (4).

Parsley — Wash, dry, and chop the parsley. Place tablespoonsful of parsley on pieces of aluminum foil (5) and wrap up each portion (6), or else mix the parsley with salt and put in a glass jar (7). You can even freeze whole parsley, wrapping small bunches in individual pieces of aluminum foil (8).

5 Trim, wash, and chop the parsley, then put tablespoonsful on pieces of aluminum foil.

6 Wrap up each portion of parsley and freeze.

7 Alternatively, you can mix the parsley with salt and put it in a glass jar.

8 You can even freeze whole parsley sprigs, wrapping them in foil.

Some useful advice

The necessary equipment

—Choose vegetables that are completely unblemished and freshly picked.

—When you blanch them use a wire basket so they can be quickly immersed in water and then removed and drained completely.

—Any preserving liquid, whether it's brine, oil, or vinegar, must cover the vegetables completely. It should be poured in a little at a time after each layer is added.

—If you are preserving vegetables in oil or vinegar, use clean jars with screw covers. If you are going to can vegetables in brine and then sterilize them, it's imperative to have heat-proof glass jars that have covers with hooks and rubber rings or else two-piece lids that guarantee they are airtight.

—All the jars should be spotlessly clean, boiled, and dried. The rubber rings should never have been used before and they too should be boiled.

—For the sterilization you need boiling water that is over 212°, so salt the boiling water heavily to raise the boiling point.

—When you write out the labels, besides specifying what's inside and the quantity of the contents, also write the date the food was preserved and how long it will keep.

—Store the jars in a dark, cool, dry place to prevent fermentation and mold.

— Every time you remove some of the vegetables kept in oil or vinegar, refill the jars to the brim again with more oil or vinegar.

—To flavor homemade oils and vinegars, marinate the appropriate herbs in them.

—You can finely chop different herbs, then let them dry and store them in a glass bottle with a cork cover.

The jars and bottles in which you preserve food are extremely important. A cardinal rule is to use airtight jars with new rubber rings for each new sterilization. Keep in mind that when you sterilize at 212°, the rubber stretches and eventually won't do its job. The are airtight jars on the market to preserve vegetables, sauces, or marmalades that come with special screw-on covers. These let the air inside escape when they are boiled, creating a vacuum. Part of the cover is porous and when it is heated, the pores expand. As it cools, the pores contract, creating an airtight environment. You can be sure this happens by watching to see that the center of the cover goes down. The only inconvenient thing about these jars is that the covers can only be used once, and then they must be replaced with new ones.

To sterilize the jars you should ideally have a special boiler made of aluminum or stainless steel with a footed rack that holds the jars and keeps them slightly elevated from the bottom of the pot. This pot can come with an outside thermometer so you have a continual reading of the water temperature.

There is also a pressure-canning boiler on the market which allows you to cut the sterilizing time in half and gives surer results. If you don't have either type of special boiler, you can use a normal pot, but a cooking thermometer is still indispensable for controlling the temperature.

There are also many kitchen utensils used to trim and prepare the vegetables. These include the common paring knife with a short pointed blade, a swivel-bladed vegetable peeler, and a serrated knife.

For cooking the vegetables, ladles and wooden spoons are handy.

Brine-packed artichokes

■ **Difficulty:** ***
■ **Use: As a side dish with meats or as an antipasto**
■ **Store: Up to 3 months**

**Ingredients: 5 lb medium artichokes, juice
of 2 lemons, bay leaves, peppercorns, kosher salt.**

Trim the artichokes by removing the tough outer leaves and keeping the tender white hearts and a small piece of the stem, which you should peel with a knife (1). Cut off the thorny tips (2), and as each artichoke is cut, drop it in warm water acidulated with lemon juice. When all the artichokes are ready, place them in a jar, pushing them down to pack tightly (3). Put some peppercorns and a bay leaf between the artichokes in each jar (4). Boil enough water to cover the artichokes (about 1 quart), add a handful of kosher salt (5), stir until all the salt has dissolved, then pour the water over the artichokes (6).

Seal the jars airtight and sterilize in a pressure-canner. Place the perforated rack in the bottom of the pot, with the raised or footed part down (7). Pour in 1½ quarts of water (8) and place the jars on the rack (9). If the jars are small you can make two layers using a second rack to hold the top layer.

Put on the cover making sure that the handle is on the right side, and push down slightly on the sides of the cover (10). Turn the handle to the other side and seal the cover airtight (11). Set the steam valve to 240° (12), then put over the heat (13). Bring to a boil and let boil for 10 minutes (some steam always escapes from the valve). Turn the heat off without releasing the valve. When the pressure indicator shows the pressure has gone down sufficiently, release the handle and open the cover (14). Let the jars cool completely, then take them out of the pot (15). Store in a cool, dry place.

Before you eat the artichokes, wash them in lots of cold water. Then dress them with oil and lemon or with a parsley vinaigrette or slice them and cook them in oil and parsley. Serve as a side dish or appetizer.

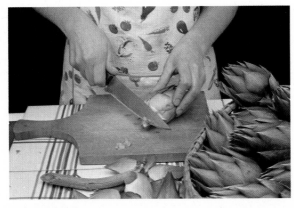

1 With a pointed knife remove most of the artichoke stem.

2 After you have removed all the outer leaves of the artichokes, cut off the thorny tips.

3 After all the artichokes are cleaned, place them in jars, pushing down to fill the empty spaces.

4 Place a few peppercorns and a bay leaf between the artichokes in each jar.

5 Add a handful of kosher salt to boiling water.

6 Pour the boiling water over the artichokes and close the jars airtight before sterilizing.

7 Put the perforated rack into the pressure-canner that will hold the jars.

8 Pour in 1½ quarts for proper sterilization.

9 Place the jars on the rack (make two layers if they are small, using a second rack).

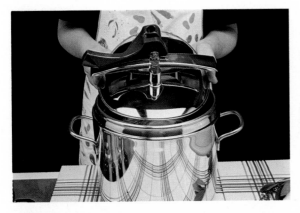

10 Put the cover on, pushing down on its sides so it will go on easily.

11 Turn the handle to the other side so the pot closes airtight.

12 Before you put the pot over heat, set the steam valve to 240°.

13 Place the pot over the heat, bring to a boil, and boil for 10 minutes.

14 Turn off heat and when the pressure has gone down sufficiently, remove the cover.

15 Let the jars cool completely in the water, then remove from pot.

Brine-packed artichokes

Marinated cauliflower

■ **Difficulty: ***
■ **Use: As an antipasto or in a salad**
■ **Store: Up to 1 year**

Ingredients: 7-9 lb perfect cauliflower, 1 tsp tarragon, 2-3 bay leaves, 1-inch piece cinnamon, peel from 1 lemon, 1 ½ quarts white wine vinegar, 1 cup white wine, 10 peppercorns, 1-1 ½ quarts olive oil, salt.

Remove the leaves from the cauliflower (1). Remove the base (2) and break up the flowerets so that they are all more or less the same size (3). Soak cauliflower in heavily salted cold water (4). In the meantime, boil the vinegar and the white wine, adding half the peppercorns, cinnamon, lemon peel, bay leaves (5), and salt. Add the cauliflower (6) and boil for 5 minutes. Drain well (7), let cool, and dry (8). Then place cauliflower in jars (9), add remaining peppercorns (10), cover with olive oil (11), and add some tarragon for flavor (12). Let the cauliflower absorb as much oil as it will, then add more fresh oil to cover before you seal the jars.

1 Wash the cauliflower well under running water and remove all the greenish leaves.

2 Remove the stem with a knife.

3 Remove the flowerets and cut them all the same size.

4 As you remove the flowerets, put them into a bowl of heavily salted water.

5 Boil the vinegar with the wine, peppercorns, cinnamon stick, lemon peel, and bay leaves.

6 Add the cauliflower and boil for about 5 minutes.

7 After the cauliflower has boiled, drain and let cool.

8 Lastly, dry the flowerets carefully so as not to break them.

9 Pack the flowerets tightly in clean dry jars with airtight covers.

10 To add flavor, sprinkle on some white or black peppercorns.

11 Cover with top-quality olive oil and let the cauliflower absorb the oil.

12 Before you cover the jars, add more oil as needed and fresh or dried tarragon.

Marinated cauliflower

Marinated peppers with anchovies

- ■ **Difficulty:** *
- ■ **Use: As an antipasto or cold dish**
- ■ **Store: Up to 6 months**

Ingredients: 10 perfect meaty peppers, 10 oz anchovy fillets, drained, 4 oz capers, drained, 4-5 garlic cloves, bunch parsley, bunch basil, olive oil, white wine, 1 quart white wine vinegar, salt.

Wash the peppers well, dry them, and take out the seeds and whitish ribs (1). Cut them into strips about ¾ inch wide (2).

Put a pot over the heat. Add vinegar and a pinch of salt. When the vinegar comes to a boil, drop the strips of pepper in, a handful at a time (3), being careful to maintain the vinegar at a boil. Boil the peppers for a-bout 10 minutes, then remove with a skimmer (4) and put them on a cloth to dry and cool.

Clean and dry an airtight jar. When the peppers are dry, place a layer in the jar (5) and add a few pieces of garlic (6), a handful of capers (7), some anchovy fillets, some basil leaves (8), and parsley. Continue doing this, layer by layer, till you use up all the ingredients. Fill the jar up to 1 inch from the top. Pour in enough olive oil to cover the peppers completely (9). Cover the jars and wait at least one day so the oil has a chance to penetrate the peppers. Then open the jars. If the oil has been ab-sorbed to below the peppers, add more oil so that the peppers are completely covered. Seal airtight and store in a dark, cool place.

Let at least one month pass before you eat these pep-pers. Then the full flavor wil! have developed.

One word of advice. When you prepare these peppers or any other vegetable preserved in oil, don't skimp on the quality of the oil or you will be disappointed with the results. The oil in which the peppers were preserved can always be reused.

1 After you have washed and dried the peppers, take out the seeds and the white ribs.

2 Use a sharp knife and cut each pepper in 1-inch strips.

3 Bring 1 quart vinegar to boil and add the pepper strips a few at a time.

4 Cook them for about 10 minutes, then remove with a skimmer.

5 When the peppers are dry, put a layer into clean jars.

6 Add slivers of garlic to taste...

7 ...a handful of capers, and some anchovy fillets.

8 For flavor, add fresh basil and parsley.

9 When the jar is filled, pour in olive oil to cover the peppers completely.

Marinated peppers with anchovies

Marinated mushrooms

■ **Difficulty:** *
■ **Use: As an antipasto or in salads or cold dishes**
■ **Store: Up to 6 months**

Ingredients: 5 lb very fresh mushrooms, juice of 1 lemon, 1 tbsp flour, 2 bay leaves, 3-4 cloves, 2 sprigs tarragon, 3 cinnamon sticks, 2 quarts white wine vinegar, 1-2 cups olive oil, peppercorns, salt.

Cut off the dried part of the mushroom stems (1). Clean mushrooms with a damp cloth and place in water combined with half the lemon juice and the flour. Bring 3 cups water to a boil, adding salt and the remaining lemon juice. Drain the mushrooms and add to the pot (2), stir, and let boil over high heat for 3-4 minutes. In another pot combine vinegar (3), cinnamon, cloves, bay leaves, and a pinch of salt and bring to a boil. Drain the mushrooms, dry with a cloth (4), and place them in the jars. Pour in the vinegar through a fine strainer (5). Add some peppercorns and tarragon and pour a bit of oil over the top (6). Seal airtight and store in a dry dark place.

1 Using a pointed paring knife, cut off the dried part of the stems.

2 Put the mushrooms into boiling water to which salt and lemon juice have been added.

3 Pour vinegar into a pot and add the cinnamon, cloves, and bay leaves.

4 Drain the mushrooms, place them on a cloth, and dry well.

5 Boil the vinegar for a few minutes and pour it over the mushrooms through a fine strainer.

6 Before you seal the jars add some peppercorns, a pinch of tarragon, and a bit of oil.

Marinated mushrooms

Sweet-and-sour onions

■ **Difficulty: ***
■ **Use: As an antipasto or a side dish**
■ **Store: Up to 6 months (when sterilized)**

Ingredients: 5 lb small white onions, $^1\!/_2$ cup raisins, 1$^1\!/_2$ cups peeled, seeded, juiced, chopped tomatoes, 1 tbsp sugar, 1 lemon, 2 cloves, 1 stick cinnamon, 1 bay leaf, $^3\!/_4$ cup cider vinegar, $^3\!/_4$ cup dry white wine, salt, pepper.

Peel the onions (1). Put them in a heat-proof dish and add the raisins (2), bay leaf, cinnamon, cloves, and a little grated lemon zest (3). Add the juice of the whole lemon (4), the vinegar (5), wine, sugar (6), tomato (7), and a pinch each of salt and pepper.

Put the dish over the heat and bring to a boil, stirring constantly (8). At this point cover the dish and continue cooking it in the oven or on the burner. When the onions are tender, taste them and add more seasoning if they need it. While they are still hot, put them into clean jars (9), cover with the sauce (10), and seal the jars immediately. If you want to keep them a longer time, process them for 10 minutes in a hot-water bath; otherwise keep them in the refrigerator for up to a week.

1 Peel the onions.

2 Put onions in a heat-proof dish, add the raisins, bay leaf, cinnamon, and cloves...

3 ...flavor with a little grated lemon zest (that is, only the yellow part of the peel)...

4 ...and add the juice from the whole lemon, taking care to keep seeds out.

5 Pour about ¾ cup vinegar over the onions and the same amount of white wine...

6 ...sprinkle on a tablespoon of sugar...

7 ...and add the tomato, either fresh or canned.

8 Put the dish over the heat and bring it to a boil, stirring with a wooden spoon.

9 Place the onions in clean dry jars while they are still hot, packing them tightly.

10 Lastly, cover the onions completely with their sauce.

Sweet-and-sour onions

Marinated onions

■ **Difficulty:** *
■ **Use: As an antipasto or a side dish**
■ **Store: Up to 6 months**

Ingredients: 5 lb small white onions, 5-6 cloves, 1 stick cinnamon, 2 bay leaves, 2 tbsp sugar, 1 cup white wine, 1 quart white wine vinegar, 1-1½ quarts olive oil, peppercorns, salt.

We strongly recommend using only small, well-cooked onions, because others may spoil even though they are in oil.

Peel the onions, taking care not to break them. Put them in a large pot, add the vinegar, white wine, cloves, cinnamon, sugar, bay leaves, and a pinch of salt and bring to a boil.

Let boil slowly for 10 minutes, then drain the onions on a cloth and let stand for a few hours until they are completely dry.

Place them in jars, packing them lightly. Add some peppercorns and cover completely with oil. Seal the jars airtight and store in a dry, dark place.

Pearl onions in vinegar

■ **Difficulty:** *
■ **Use: As an antipasto or a side dish**
■ **Store: Up to 6 months**

Ingredients: 5 lb pearl onions, ½ cup sugar, handful whole fresh basil leaves, 3 bay leaves, about 1 quart white wine vinegar, salt, peppercorns.

Put the onions, unpeeled, in a pot of boiling water to which salt and a few tablespoons of vinegar have been added. Drain after 3 minutes. Peel the onions carefully, taking care not to break them. Place them on a cloth to dry. Then place them in jars, pushing down slightly so you don't leave any empty spaces.

In another pot, pour in the rest of the vinegar, then add the sugar, basil, bay leaves, and a pinch of salt. Put over heat and bring to a boil, then pour this over the onions through a strainer, eliminating the herbs. The onions should be completely covered; add more boiling vinegar if needed. Put some peppercorns and fresh basil leaves in each jar, then seal the jars airtight and store in a cool, dry, dark place.

Small cucumber pickles

■ **Difficulty:** *
■ **Use: As an antipasto or a garnish**
■ **Store: Up to 6 months**

Ingredients: 7 lb small farm-type cucumbers, 3 bay leaves, 1 tsp tarragon, 5-6 cloves, whole fresh basil leaves, about 2 quarts white wine vinegar, 1 tsp peppercorns, 1 cup kosher salt.

Wash and dry the cucumbers. Then put them in a big plastic or ceramic bowl, add 1 cup kosher salt, and let stand for a few hours to draw out some of their juice. Then drain them and put them back into the same bowl, rinsed to remove the salt. Meanwhile put the vinegar over the heat and add the peppercorns, bay leaves, cloves, tarragon, and basil. Bring to a boil, then pour it over the cucumbers. Let marinate for a day. Then pour the vinegar solution into the pot again and bring back to a boil. Taste and add some salt if needed. Pour solution, still boiling hot, over the cucumbers and let marinate for another day. Remove the cloves and add more vinegar if needed to cover the cucumbers. The third day, turn the cucumbers and the vinegar into the pot and boil till the cucumbers are half tender.

Let the cucumbers cool, then place in jars. Strain the vinegar solution over them. Seal the jars airtight and store in a cool, dry, dark place.

Mixed vegetables in salt

■ **Difficulty:** *
■ **Use: In vegetable soups or as a side dish**
■ **Store: Up to 6 months**

Ingredients: 5 lb mixed vegetables (celery, carrots, leeks, zucchini, cabbage, etc.), 1 cup kosher salt.

Trim and wash all the vegetables well. Let them dry completely and cut them into pieces. Put them in a bowl, add salt, and mix. Place the mixture in a clean jar or jars, pushing down with your hands and then weighting the vegetables with a plastic or wooden disk. Cover the jar with clean cheesecloth, then seal airtight and store in a cool, dark place.

If using the vegetables in a soup, let them stand in water for a day, changing the water two or three times. If you add them to a dish that does not contain salt, you may omit the soaking. You can also serve these vegetables buttered, or use as a base for sauces.

Subject Index

FISH

Cooking Fish   9

The necessary equipment   11
Cleaning fish   13
How to fillet porgy or other round fish   14
How to fillet sole or other flat fish   16
How to fillet trout   18
Freezing fish   19
Conserving fish in salt   20
Ways of cooking fish   22
Marinating fish   24

Fish Soups and Stews   25

Baking and Frying   37

Crustaceans   71

Preparation and cooking   73
Lobster: cooking and presentation   74
The necessary equipment   76
Freezing   77
Useful hints   77

Mollusks   95

Preparation and cooking   97
Freezing   98

VEGETABLES

Hot Stuffed Vegetables   133

How to stuff vegetables   135
Cooking stuffed vegetables   136
The necessary equipment   136

Cold Stuffed Vegetables   175

Some useful advice   177

Salads   195

How to make salads   197

Salad dressings   198
The necessary equipment   199

Decorative Garnishes   221

The necessary equipment   222

Sformati and Tortini   257

The basic ingredients   259
Serving sformati   260
The necessary equipment   260

Soufflés and Timbales   283

Preparation and cooking   285
How to serve soufflés and timbales   286
The necessary equipment   286

Croquettes   303

The basic ingredients   305
How to fry croquettes   306

PRESERVES

Preserving Fruit   319

Jams and marmalades   321
Fruit in syrup   323
Fruit syrups and juices   323
Freezing fruit   324
Some useful advice   326
The necessary equipment   326

Preserving Vegetables   353

Preserving in oil   355
Preserving in vinegar   355
Natural preservation   356
Freezing vegetables   358
Some useful advice   360
The necessary equipment   360

Recipe Index

FISH

Fish Soups and Stews

Bouillabaisse	31
Broiled swordfish	36
Cacciucco	27
Catfish with olives	36
Dried cod stew (Baccalà)	32
Dried cod, Vicenza style	34
Fish soup (1)	30
Fish soup (2)	30
Fish soup, Venetian style	31
Fish soup with olives	31
Flounder soup	30
Mullet, Leghorn style	36
Porgy aux fines herbes	36

Baking and Frying

Baked cod	64
Baked hake piquant	64
Baked grouper	47
Baked sheepshead	65
Baked stuffed grouper	44
Bass au gratin with olives	64
Breaded fried whitebait	63
Fillets of sole in anchovy sauce	57
Fillets of sole in cream	57
Fillets of sole in sparkling wine	57
Fish croquettes	60
Fried eels in wine vinegar	51
Fried fillet of perch	67

Fried stuffed sardines	63
Fried whitebait in batter	66
Grilled mullet	39
Grilled sea bass with fennel	47
Grilled trout	67
Hake en brochette	64
Marinated mackerel fillets	65
Mixed fish and vegetable fry	63
Mixed fry	58
Mullet, island style	47
Porgy au gratin	47
Porgy en papillote	42
Porgy with mushrooms	47
Salmon steaks with mushrooms	67
Savory fish rolls	65
Sole Colbert	54
Sole in red wine	57
Stuffed eel	48
Swordfish steaks	65
Trout baked in foil	67
Whitebait in batter	63

Crustaceans

Baked lobster	81
Baked stuffed jumbo shrimp	94
Crab fritters	94
Fried shrimp	94
Grilled lobster	81
Lobster in cream	81
Lobster salad, Sardinian style	81
Lobster soup	78

Mantis shrimp in parsley sauce	88
Shrimp cocktail	82
Shrimp in herbs	94
Shrimp in paprika and brandy	94
Shrimp on the skewer	86
Shrimp with curried rice	90

Mollusks

Broiled mussels	110
Clam soup	106
Fried squid	125
Ligurian style squid	119
Mariscada	103
Octopus stew	116
Oysters on the half-shell	100
Razor clam soup	128
Risotto with squid	128
Shellfish soup	108
Smothered mussels	128
Squid with artichokes	128
Spaghetti with clams	129
Stuffed scallops	112
Stuffed squid	122

VEGETABLES

Hot Stuffed Vegetables

Artichokes, Roman style	144
Artichokes stuffed with meat	144
Artichokes with cheese and olive stuffing	144
Artichokes with red wine	144

Cabbage rolls	165
Celeriac with cheese	162
Eggplant Parmesan	152
Eggplant rolls	149
Fennel with ham au gratin	169
Fried eggplant "sandwiches"	152
Meat-stuffed zucchini	154
Mushrooms on toast	160
Peppers, country style	156
Peppers stuffed with eggplant	152
Pommes Anna	170
Potato pancakes Miriam	172
Potato pancake casserole	172
Potato pancake casserole with ham and cheese	172
Rice-stuffed tomatoes	138
Spicy eggplant rolls	152
Stuffed cabbage	169
Stuffed eggplant au gratin	146
Stuffed fried artichokes	141
Stuffed grape leaves	168
Stuffed onions with tomato sauce	168
Stuffed potatoes	169
Stuffed potatoes in foil	158
Stuffed zucchini blossoms	168
Stuffed zucchini au gratin	168
Tomatoes stuffed with cheese	140
Tomatoes stuffed with mushrooms	140
Tomatoes stuffed with pasta	140

Cold Stuffed Vegetables

Artichokes in a piquant sauce	185

Artichokes with poached eggs — 182
Dressed-up tomatoes — 181
Pepper rolls — 186
Stuffed celery hors d'oeuvre — 185
Stuffed celery stalks — 185
Stuffed onions — 190
Tomato "sandwiches" — 181
Tomatoes stuffed with tuna — 178
Tomatoes with green mayonnaise — 181
Tomatoes with pâté — 181
Tuna-stuffed peppers — 185

Salads
California salad — 220
Capricious salad — 217
Corn salad — 220
Crispy salad — 207
Endive and orange salad — 219
Grapefruit and avocado salad — 218
Grilled radicchio salad with anchovies — 218
Kiwi salad — 217
Lettuce and fennel salad — 218
Midsummer salad — 217
Mixed salad with yogurt dressing — 215
Mushroom and shrimp salad — 217
Pepper and eggplant salad — 220
Russian salad — 200
Salade niçoise — 213
Sliced-egg salad — 218
Spinach salad — 204

Triple delight salad — 220
Vegetables in aspic — 210
Zucchini salad with mint — 202

Decorative Garnishes
A bouquet of leeks — 235
A bouquet of radishes — 229
A cabbage basket — 237
A potato basket — 240
Artichoke flowers — 228
Carrot garnishes — 224
Lemon garnishes — 244
Mushroom flowers — 243
Pickle flowers and fans — 234
Potato garnishes — 238
Tomato flowers and baskets — 231

Sformati and Tortini
Bread and mozzarella pie — 282
Cheese delight — 280
Cheese sformato — 282
Cheese tortino — 276
Golden dome sformato — 268
Ham and onion sformato — 282
Mushroom tortino — 280
Potato tortino — 280
Pumpkin sformato — 265
Spinach and potato casserole — 278
Spinach sformato — 262
Spinach timbales — 282

Swiss chard pie	280	Blueberry liqueur	348
Tricolor sformato	273	Blueberry syrup	348
		Caramel apple marmalade	337
Soufflés and Timbales		Cherry marmalade	337
Aspargus timbale	302	Dried apples	338
Carrot timbale	299	Grape jelly	351
Cheese soufflé	288	Grapes in grappa	340
Green bean timbale	302	Grapefruit jelly	351
Green pea timbale	294	Lemon preserves	328
Mixed vegetable soufflé	293	Orange and lemon marmalade	331
Mixed vegetable timbale	302	Orange liqueur	342
Spinach and carrot soufflé	293	Orange marmalade	331
Timbale with peas and ham	296	Plums in brandy	351
Tomato soufflé	290	Raspberry syrup	351
Toasted almond soufflé	293	Soused black cherries	352
		Soused peaches	352
Croquettes		Strawberry preserves	337
Artichoke croquettes	310	Strawberry sauce	345
Mushroom croquettes	312	Tomato marmalade	334
Pasta croquettes	314		
Potato croquettes	307	**Vegetable preserves**	
Spinach croquettes	314	Brine-packed artichokes	362
Potato and mushroom croquettes	314	Marinated cauliflower	366
		Marinated mushrooms	372
PRESERVES		Marinated onions	377
		Marinated peppers with anchovies	369
		Mixed vegetables in salt	377
Fruit Preserves		Pearl onions in vinegar	377
Apricots in Marsala	352	Small cucumber pickles	377
Apricot marmalade	337	Sweet-and-sour onions	374
Black cherry and currant jelly	351